Critical Essays on Hawthorne's The Scarlet Letter

Critical Essays on Hawthorne's The Scarlet Letter

David B. Kesterson

G. K. Hall & Co. • Boston, Massachusetts

Library of Congress Cataloging-in-Publication Data

Critical essays on Hawthorne's The scarlet
letter / David B. Kesterson [editor].
  p. cm. -- (Critical essays on American literature)
Includes index.
ISBN 0-8161-8883-1
  1. Hawthorne, Nathaniel, 1804–1864. Scarlet Letter.
I. Kesterson, David B., 1938– . II. Series.
PS1868.C75 1988

813'.3--dc19

This publication is printed on permanent/durable acid-free paper
MANUFACTURED IN THE UNITED STATES OF AMERICA

CRITICAL ESSAYS ON AMERICAN LITERATURE

This series seeks to anthologize the most important criticism on a wide variety of topics and writers in American Literature. Our readers will find in various volumes not only a generous selection of reprinted articles and reviews but original essays, bibliographies, manuscript sections, and other materials brought to public attention for the first time. This volume is a collection of reviews and essays tracing the critical reputation of *The Scarlet Letter*. The book contains both a sizable gathering of early reviews and a broad selection of more modern scholarship, including essays that present a New Critical, Psychological, Historical, Biographical, Feminist, Structuralist, Post Modernist, and Semiologist interpretation. Among noted early reviewers are Evert A. Duyckinck, George Ripley, Edwin Percy Whipple, and Orestes Brownson. The historic reactions of William Dean Howells and Henry James are also included. Among the authors of reprinted articles are John Gerber, Roy Male, Frederick C. Crews, Hyatt Waggoner, Terence Martin, Nina Baym, and Millicent Bell. There are also four original essays commissioned specifically for publication in this volume, new studies by Rita K. Gollin, Thomas Woodson, James M. Mellard, and Richard D. Rust. We are confident that this book will make a permanent and significant contribution to American literary study.

JAMES NAGEL, GENERAL EDITOR

Northeastern University

To my wife, Cheryl

CONTENTS

INTRODUCTION

Nathaniel Hawthorne had been serving as Surveyor of Customs in Salem, Massachusetts, since the autumn of 1846 when he was suddenly relieved of his position on 8 June 1849. The Whig party had risen to power with Zachary Taylor's recent election to the presidency, and Hawthorne—an ardent Democrat—fell victim to the new regime, being, in his own words, "decapitated" by the opposition.

Rarely has a firing proven more beneficial to an individual, his legacy, and his posterity. Although Hawthorne chafed sorely over the incident and made a concerted effort to fight his eviction—hoping to regain the office or at least put his "executioners" in their place—he was able now to settle down to the business of writing his book, something he had simply not been able to do while gainfully employed. As he complained in "The Custom-House" introductory to *The Scarlet Letter*, "So little adapted is the atmosphere of a Custom-House to the delicate harvest of fancy and sensibility, that, had I remained there through ten Presidencies yet to come, I doubt whether the tale of 'The Scarlet Letter' would ever have been brought before the public eye. My imagination was a tarnished mirror. It would not reflect, or only with miserable dimness, the figures with which I did my best to people it."[1]

In his upstairs study at the Mall Street house in Salem, he began writing *The Scarlet Letter* by September 1849, after experiencing a devastating summer of suffering not only the sting of removal from office, but enduring the agonizing, lingering illness and, finally, death of his mother on 31 July. Once at work on his novel, Hawthorne wrote so quickly that "The Custom-House" and all but the last three chapters of the novel were in the publisher's hands by 15 January 1850. Hawthorne had originally intended for his book to include *The Scarlet Letter* and several related tales. That idea was dropped, however, apparently when he and publisher James T. Fields agreed that the novel proper, along with the introductory sketch, was sufficient length for a volume.

Just how long Hawthorne had had the story of Hester Prynne and her scarlet letter in mind is unclear. The idea possibly dated as far back as 1837, when he wrote the story "Endicott and the Red Cross," in which,

1

among sinners being publicly punished, is "a young woman, with no mean share of beauty, whose doom it was to wear the letter A on the breast of her gown, in the eyes of all the world and her own children."[2] However long the incubation period actually was, his work was finished on 3 February 1850. On that night he read the conclusion to his wife, Sophia, the ending sending her to bed with a "grievous headache," a reaction which Hawthorne interpreted as a mark of the book's "triumphant success."[3]

The Scarlet Letter was published on Saturday, 16 March 1850, by Ticknor and Company with copies available in Boston that day. The first edition of 2,500 copies sold out in three days. On 22 April a second edition of 2,500 copies was released, followed by a third edition of 1,000 published in September. Before the second edition was printed, Hawthorne was asked by his publisher if he wished to answer the critics who found "The Custom-House" too caustic, combative, and personal. In the "Preface To The Second Edition," Hawthorne recognized the furor created by his "sketch of official life," but saw it as harmless, and chose to "republish his introductory sketch without the change of a word."[4]

In Hawthorne's native Salem, Caleb Foote was the first to review the book, writing in the *Salem Gazette* three days after publication, "It is indeed a wonderful book, and we venture to predict that no one will put it down before he reaches the last page of it, unless it is forcibly taken out of his hands."[5] On 21 March the editor of the *Salem Register*, John Chapman, praised the novel in general: "It is marked by all the exquisiteness of Hawthorne's genius, but with less of that dreamy indistinctness which has sometimes made not a few of his productions unintelligible to an ordinary mind."[6] He blasted the "Custom-House" preface, however, for its "calumnious caricatures" of the Salem Custom-House officers, a common reaction of Boston and also New York reviewers.[7]

On the same day as Chapman's review, just five days after publication of the novel, an anonymous reviewer in the *Boston Post* attested to the book's instant popularity ("hundreds of our readers must already be conversant with the book")[8] and praised its virtues: "The merits of the book lie in its vigorous conception of scenes, its vivid master-strokes of character, and its thickly-scattered gems of thought and expression."[9] Ultimately, *The Scarlet Letter* "is a prose poem, and must be regarded as such, and judged by poetical standards only."[10]

Evert A. Duyckinck, writing in the 30 March issue of *Literary World*, was the first to call Hawthorne's novel a "psychological romance": "It is a tale of remorse, a study of character in which the human heart is anatomized, carefully, elaborately, and with striking poetic and dramatic power."[11] Duyckinck also recognized the darker, more puritanical, "less companionable" Hawthorne in *The Scarlet Letter* as opposed to the sunnier nature exhibited in *Twice-Told Tales* (1837, 1842). "The spirit of his old Puritan ancestors, to whom he refers in the preface, lives in Nathaniel Hawthorne."[12]

George Ripley's review of 1 April in the *New York Daily Tribune*, although consisting mainly of quotations from the novel, paraphrases of passages, and character sketches of the principals, does comment cogently on Hawthorne's use of the shadowy, legendary past, contrasting his gothicism with Poe's: it is a dark, tragic view of life, pregnant "with a wonderful insight and skill, to which the intellect of Poe was a stranger."[13] The "elements of terror" in the book, however, are so "blended with such sweet gushes of natural feeling, such solemn and tender relations of the deepest secrets of the heart, that the painful impression is greatly mitigated, and the final influence of his most startling creation is a serene sense of refreshment, without its stupor and bewilderment occasioned by a drugged cup of intoxication."[14] Ripley takes the sharp tone of "The Custom-House" in stride by saying that Hawthorne's "querulous tone in which he alludes to his removal from the Custom House, may be forgiven to the sensitiveness of a poet, especially as this is so rare a quality in Uncle Sam's officeholders."[15]

Edwin Percy Whipple, in his *Graham's Magazine* review of May 1850, extolled the novel as emblematic and worthy of "the fine and deep genius" which resides in the author.[16] This is the book for which both the *Twice-Told Tales* and *Mosses from an Old Manse* (1846) were preparatory, he writes, a culmination that evinces "a true artist's certainty of touch and expression in the exhibition of characters and events, and a keen-sighted and far-sighted vision into the essence and purpose of spiritual laws."[17] If the book has a flaw, it is in the "almost morbid intensity with which the characters are realized, and the consequent lack of sufficient geniality in the delineation."[18] In the controversial "Custom-House" portraits, on the contrary, Whipple finds a "vital spirit of humor," which shows "how rich and exhaustless a fountain of mirth Hawthorne has at his command."[19]

Holden's *Dollar Magazine* published two anonymous reviews of *The Scarlet Letter* in May and June of 1850.[20] The earlier one, though praising the novel in general, attacks "The Custom-House" for being incongruous with the novel proper and concludes that it ought to be omitted in future editions (a not uncommon view of many early critics). The second response, identified as by one Rev. Henry Giles, is a long article that offers one of the most probing early analyses of the book, one that dwells on the moral instruction of its pages. Again, Hawthorne's "genius" is extolled.[21]

English critic Henry Chorley, writing briefly on the novel in the *Athenaeum* in June 1850, admits to the "powerful" nature of the book and to finding Hawthorne "fascinating," but considers the story "painful" in its events and character portrayals and wonders if it is a subject suitable for literature. He concedes, however, that "if Sin and Sorrow in their most fearful forms are to be presented in any work of art, they have rarely been treated with a loftier severity, purity, and sympathy than in Mr. Hawthorne's *Scarlet Letter.*"[22]

A most interesting, largely praiseful review by Anne Abbott appeared in the *North American Review* in July of 1850. After beginning with a lengthy comment on Hawthorne's removal from the Salem Custom House, a propitious act for the literary world since it "has brought him back to our admiring and . . . congenial society,"[23] Abbott discusses what she believes to be the ethereal, dreamlike nature of the book. Readers feel an "enchantment" in Hawthorne's style and presentation and are admonished not to lay the book down before finishing it or they will surrender "the magic power of the style" and lose "half the weird beauty."[24] The four major characters themselves are like phantoms, with only Dimmesdale showing some "power" and distinctness as a character. The magical spell and the fine writing of the book are marred only by its "revolting" subject; indeed the beautiful writing cannot relieve the "ugliness of pollution and vice" any more than the "rose tree" can the "gloom of the prison."[25] In contrast, Abbott finds "The Custom-House" a pleasingly "naughty" chapter that proves "more piquant than anything in the book."[26]

The Transcendental-oriented *Massachusetts Quarterly Review* for September 1850 carried a lengthy, highly enthusiastic, at times didactic review by George B. Loring. Loring sees *The Scarlet Letter* depicting a "strange and shifting picture of the mature heart of man."[27] Only in this book has Hawthorne "presented so clear and perfect image of himself, as a speculative philosopher, an ethical thinker, a living man."[28] Loring analyzes Dimmesdale and Hester at substantial length, commenting on the depths and complexities of their natures as so admirably drawn by Hawthorne. Indeed, Loring's is the most thorough and penetrating, if at times overly laudatory, view of Hester and Dimmesdale found among the contemporary reviews. He is wholly captivated by what Hawthorne was doing with theme and characterization in the novel.

The following month brought the recently Catholicized Orestes Brownson's largely negative reaction in *Brownson's Quarterly Review*. Brownson is as skeptical as Loring was positive. While finding Hawthorne "a man of true genius and a highly cultivated mind" and *The Scarlet Letter* a work "of rare, . . . fearful power," Brownson faults the novel on moralistic grounds — it is a story, simply, "that should not have been told. It is a story of crime, of an adulteress and her accomplice," and though crimes were real in the world of the Puritans, "they are not fit subjects for popular literature, and moral health is not promoted by leading the imagination to dwell on them."[29] Hawthorne errs, moreover, in not making the suffering of Hester and Dimmesdale "excite the horror of the readers for their crimes." In short, as a glimpse of Puritan times the book is meritorious if viewed "from the position of a moderate transcendentalist and liberal of the modern school," but the overall picture is unjust, and

Brownson would "commend where the author condemns, and condemn where he commends."[30]

Finally, among the early reviewers, Arthur Cleveland Coxe in the Episcopal publication *Church Review* for January 1851 joins hands with Brownson in condemning Hawthorne's novel on moralistic grounds. In fact, the aim of Coxe's review is to save Hawthorne from committing further literary crimes: America needs no further imitators of George Sand and Eugene Sue.[31] While lauding Hawthorne for what he does with the history of the Puritan era, Coxe is "astonished at the kind of incident which he has selected for romance."[32] He shudders over the hero and heroine "wallowing in their filth"[33] and not being duly sorrowful or repentant. Hester extolls wholly improper feminist principles, and Hawthorne himself is in danger — if not "stopped short" — of developing a whole career "in such brothelry." Rather, Coxe hopes, Hawthorne's future career "may redeem this misstep, and prove a blessing to this country,"[34] for what the country needs is writers who teach their readers "to love truth and follow virtue."[35]

The contemporary reviews, thus, ran the gamut from the likes of Whipple's and Duyckinck's commendations to scurrilous attacks by some of the Christian moralists in the school of Brownson and Coxe. As Bertha Faust has pointed out, however, the success of *The Scarlet Letter* very quickly elevated Hawthorne to literary stardom, negative reviews like those of Brownson and Coxe having "little effect on the reputation of the book."[36] Even Hawthorne's "enemies" recognized his genius and, as did Coxe and Brownson in equating him with Washington Irving, considered him, without exception, a distinguished man of letters.[37]

If *The Scarlet Letter* caused a sensation among its contemporary reviewers, its popularity was sustained during the rest of the nineteenth century and invited critical commentary from many quarters. The most significant piece of criticism before 1900 was Henry James, Jr.'s discussion of the novel in his 1879 study, *Nathaniel Hawthorne*.

An interesting link between James's criticism and that of the early reviewers just discussed is his mention of "dimly" remembering, as a child, "the sensation the book produced, and the little shudder with which people alluded to it, as if a peculiar horror were mixed with its attractions."[38] Approaching *The Scarlet Letter* with only a momentary stop at "The Custom-House," which he calls "one of the most perfect of Hawthorne's compositions, and one of the most gracefully and humorously autobiographic,"[39] James pronounces the book not only Hawthorne's masterpiece, but considers it "the finest piece of imaginative writing yet put forth in the country."[40] Having finally produced a novel that "belonged to literature, and to the forefront of it," America could at last send a novel to Europe "as exquisite in quality as anything that had been received, and the best of it was that the thing was absolutely American." James calls the book "beautiful, admirable, extraordinary," feeling that it contains "an indefinable purity and lightness of conception."[41]

There are faults in Hawthorne's novel, James asserts, though they be "of the slenderest and most venial kind."[42] The main problems are its lack of reality and abundance of the fanciful and a "certain superficial symbolism."[43] To prove his point James engages in a substantial comparison of Hawthorne's novel with John Gibson Lockhart's *Adam Blair*, a far more "realistic" account of a Calvinistic minister who is lover to a married woman and who confesses his sin publicly and then retires to a farm. Whereas Lockhart's novel is not nearly the artistic equal of *The Scarlet Letter*, it has a clarity of vision and expression of strong feeling that are lacking in Hawthorne's more impressionistic, almost coldly classical work. And the symbolism of *The Scarlet Letter* does bother James: "It is overdone at times, and becomes mechanical; it ceases to be impressive, and grazes triviality."[44] In concluding, however, James again insists that the flaws are minor — "they are light flaws and inequalities of surface," not blights on the book's "essence." *The Scarlet Letter*, finally, "has the beauty and harmony of all original and complete conceptions."[45]

Seven years after James's book appeared, Julian Hawthorne, in an *Atlantic* article, took up the cause of his father's modernity and his new breed of fiction, the psychological, represented by *The Scarlet Letter*; and he disagreed with James's objection to Hawthorne's symbolism. The symbolism, indeed, is at the very heart and meaning of Hawthorne's novel; it "uplifts the theme from the material to the spiritual level. . . . It transmutes the prose into poetry."[46] Symbolism "serves as a formula for the conveyance of ideas otherwise too subtle for words, as well as to enhance the gloomy picturesqueness of the moral scenery."[47] Julian answers, moreover, the prudish charges of early reviewers over the "unsuitable" nature of the story of *The Scarlet Letter* by saying that a writer "who works with deep insight and truthful purpose can never be guilty of a lack of decency. Indecency is a creation, not of God or of nature, but of the indecent."[48] Besides, Hawthorne was far more interested in portraying the effects of the misdeeds on his characters' minds and lives than in the illicit passion itself. "It is with the subjective consequences of a sinner's act that our understanding of him begins."[49]

In a somewhat unusual view of the characters in *The Scarlet Letter*, Julian singles out Pearl as the "true creation of the book." "Every touch upon her portrait is a touch of genius, and her very conception is an inspiration."[50] He draws a parallel between Pearl and Beatrice of "Rappaccini's Daughter," arguing that both girls were "poisoned" in a sense by the actions of parents.

While Julian Hawthorne focused on Pearl, William Dean Howells fittingly launched twentieth-century criticism of *The Scarlet Letter* by viewing "Hawthorne's Hester Prynne" as "chief" among the characters of the novel. After analyzing two major scenes involving Hester — the opening scaffold scene and the forest "interview" with Dimmesdale — he posits that "in all fiction one could hardly find a character more boldly, more simply, more quietly imagined."[51] Actually, Howells makes the point that all the characters in *The Scarlet Letter* except Pearl are of a "robust" "verity."[52] He praises almost without qualification Hawthorne's artistry in *The Scarlet Letter*, from its form, atmosphere, and substance to its modern tone; indeed, despite his preference for *The Blithedale Romance* because of its realism, he sees *The Scarlet Letter* as "the modernest and maturest" of Hawthorne's novels.[53] In comparing Hawthorne with his contemporary English counterpart, Dickens, Howells discerns a more refined, aesthetically pleasing form of fiction in Hawthorne than in Dickens. Hawthorne's characters, moreover, are less "types" than Dickens's: "In their mystical world, withdrawn afar from us in the past, or apart from us in anomalous conditions, the characters of Hawthorne speak and act for themselves; . . . in times, terms, and places analogous to those in which actual men have their being, the types of Dickens are always speaking for him, in fulfillment of a mechanical conception and rigid limitation of their function in the drama."[54]

The debate over which character in *The Scarlet Letter* is Hawthorne's fullest, most successful creation has never ceased, albeit Hester has enjoyed the edge in recent years. Theodore Munger, in his 1904 *Atlantic* article "Notes on *The Scarlet Letter*," swung the emphasis back to Pearl. Hester's child, he believes, is "the one consummate flower of Hawthorne's genius — unsurpassed by himself and absolutely original."[55] The novel itself is "the most consummate work in literature yet produced in this country"; it reaches "perfection" in its art and contains "corresponding subtlety and correctness of thought," boasting a style that "both fascinates and commands."[56] Above all, the novel succeeds because of the "sleuthhound thoroughness with which sin is traced up and down and into every corner of its heart and life, and even into nature, where it transforms all things."[57] If there are flaws in the book, they are slight — "perhaps too much symbolism" and "parable." These can be overlooked, however, in view of the novel's overall attainment of greatness. Munger reminds his readers that in the fifty years of burgeoning American literature since *The Scarlet Letter*'s publication in 1850, nothing has appeared that is "worthy to stand by the side of this short story of sin and shame and remorse." He alludes, moreover, to the novel's popularity in England, saying it is "read more widely there than here, and is held in steadier estimate than we accord, who read as gregariously as sheep crop the grass."[58]

Munger's theme of *The Scarlet Letter*'s consummate greatness and uniqueness generally prevailed through the first fifty years of twentieth-century criticism, with detractors being the rare exception. One such exception was Lucy L. Cable, writing on "Old Salem and 'The Scarlet Letter,' " in 1907. As "immortal" a creation and "triumphant success" as it was in its day, the novel, in Cable's opinion, would not prove so if written in modern times. Jamesian in her taste, she judges that "the new generation has new needs. . . . we demand a more vivid, a more realistic touch than the keenly imaginative Hawthorne ever gave to his characters or even to their environs."[59] Still, *The Scarlet Letter*, in her view, "remains to us an integral part of our hereditary literature and of the immortal literature of the whole world."[60]

Two years after Cable's article, William Cary Brownell published his subsequently well-known reaction to the novel in *American Prose Masters*. After labeling *The Scarlet Letter* an "original work in a field where originality is the next thing to a miracle,"[61] Brownell stresses the novel's psychological dimensions. It is neither a story about adultery or illicit love, he avers, but rather "a story of concealment. Its psychology is that of the concealment of sin amid circumstances that make a sin of concealment itself."[62] In fact, the sin involved "might . . . be almost any other. And this constitutes no small part of the book's formal originality." Devoid of passion and sensuality — at times too coldly and rigidly so — the novel is the "Puritan 'Faust' " and our "chief prose masterpiece," one difficult to "overpraise."[63]

Two articles in *Bookman* by Llewellyn Jones (1924) and Julian Hawthorne (1931) dwell, respectively, on the Freudian psychology of the novel and, once again, the importance of Pearl as a character. Jones lauds Hawthorne as psychologist, especially "when dealing with the soul that harbors a sin"[64] and sees a display of Freudian psychology in "the devotion of Roger Chillingworth to his slow and subtle and satisfying mode of revenge. Its motive power he tells us was something like the motive power of love."[65] Of Hawthorne's Pearl, however, Jones has little praise: artistically she is "almost a hopeless loss. About all she does is to skip and prance and bedevil her mother. . . ."[66] Julian Hawthorne, on the other hand, some forty-five years after his earlier treatment of the novel, is still of the firm belief that Pearl is a "unique" conception who "takes precedence over the other characters," the main reason being that this "child of his imagination" was modeled on Hawthorne's daughter Una, who was "constantly in his sight and thought during the composition of the story."[67] Julian's treatment of Pearl here, however, is more probing and provocative than that found in his earlier essay.

A condescending and somewhat chauvinistic view of both Hawthorne and *The Scarlet Letter* is sounded by English critic Pelham Edgar in 1933. Edgar charges that Hawthorne differs from his English precursors only in his uses of symbolism and "external commentary," and his symbolism is too extreme. Singling out Hawthorne's tone as his differentiating quality, Edgar complains that Hawthorne was more "temperamentally depressed" than any writer before him: "none had ever carried the cult of joylessness to such curious and, strange to say, such exquisite conclusions."[68] If *The Scarlet Letter* is "artistically the most satisfying of his longer stories,"[69] it is overwrought in its symbolism, and the rest of the novel is "sufficiently conventional."[70] Hawthorne's power resides in the "peculiar cast of his mentality, and the fascination with which certain moral problems attracted and repelled him."[71] But the book lacks "sun and circulation" and depicts a "narrow segment" of life only.[72]

Back on this side of the Atlantic, Frederic I. Carpenter in 1944 voiced his own reservations about the novel in "Scarlet A Minus," an essay that has become the classic negative response. Carpenter grants *The Scarlet Letter* its appeal down through the years, but feels that the book's portrayal of sin was appropriate mainly for the middle nineteenth century. In modern times it is less pertinent. Other books, such as *Anna Karenina*, have focused on sin "with a richer humanity and a greater realism."[73] Carpenter assesses the novel as a classic "of a minor order," one that seems "ambiguous" in its logic and "moralistic" in its conclusion. Indeed, it is Hawthorne's "moralistic, subjective criticism of Hester Prynne" that constitutes the major flaw of the work.[74] The central problem is Hawthorne's seeming confusion "between the romantic and the transcendental moralities. While the characters of the novel objectively act out the tragic conflict between the traditional morality and the transcendental dream, Hawthorne subjectively damns the transcendental for being romantically immoral."[75] If the greatness of the novel finally resides in the character of Hester, then Hawthorne as author does her a major disservice by condemning her in a morality construct of his own, rather than removing himself from her dilemma with proper artistic distance.

John C. Gerber's "Form and Content in *The Scarlet Letter*" (1944) topped off the criticism of the first half of the twentieth century, serving inadvertently as a kind of corrective to Carpenter's and Edgar's views. To this day Gerber's essay is one of the most significant analytical pieces written on the novel.

Gerber's main point is that form and content are so intricately and effectively interwoven in the novel that their union bespeaks "a work of rather astonishing sophistication."[76] Contending that form is four-layered (community, Chillingworth, Hester, and Dimmesdale) and content is trifold (sin, isolation, and reunion—the three concerns which "dominate the thoughts and actions of the characters"),[77] Gerber shows how these two aspects of the novel mesh. He dwells particularly on the subject of isolation, which he believes is the chief "study" of the novel.

There were other important statements on *The Scarlet Letter* in the first half of the twentieth century, of course. D. H. Lawrence's provocative, if controversial, treatment in *Studies in Classic American Literature* (1923)[78] and F. O. Matthiessen's chapter in *American Renaissance* (1941)[79] are among the most notable examples. But Gerber's essay on form and content, coming at mid-century, seems more than any of the others in or near its time to set the stage for many of the critical trends that were to develop after 1950.

By paying specific attention to form and content in *The Scarlet*

Letter, Gerber anticipated the New Critical approach of the 1950s, the critical "school" that truly held sway in Hawthorne studies throughout the decade and shows its influence to this day. The major New Critical names of the fifties in Hawthorne studies were Richard Harter Fogle, Hyatt H. Waggoner, and Roy R. Male. Fogle's *Hawthorne's Fiction: The Light and the Dark* (1952) closely examined Hawthorne's central images and symbols in an effort to show an overall pattern of "light" (clarity of design) and "dark" (tragic complexity in Hawthorne's fiction). In his chapter on *The Scarlet Letter* Fogle dwells on four "states of being" in the novel — one subhuman (nature), two human (the heart versus the head), and one superhuman or heavenly ("the sphere of absolute insight, justice, and mercy"),[80] with an examination of the "intensity" of the book. Waggoner's *Hawthorne: A Critical Study* (1955) also looks closely at image patterns and symbolism, especially color imagery and nature, heart, name, and shape symbolism. Waggoner concludes that the aggregate tone of the book "suggests that Hawthorne's vision of death was a good deal stronger and more constant than his vision of life."[81] Roy Male's perception of Hawthorne's "tragic vision," in his book by that title, is that mankind "must become fully involved with time yet retain his unique ability to stand aside from its fleeting onrush and contemplate the eternal."[82] Like Fogle and Waggoner, Male examines the text very closely, identifying the central metaphor of *The Scarlet Letter* as the "tongue of flame." He interprets the metaphor as suggesting "the ability to address 'the whole human brotherhood in the heart's native language.' " The image represents "intuitive communication, the expression of 'the highest truths through the humblest medium of familiar words and images.' "[83]

The 1960s brought revised editions of Waggoner's *Hawthorne: A Critical Study* (1963) and Fogle's *Hawthorne's Fiction: The Light and the Dark* (1964), Terence Martin's balanced, insightful chapter on *The Scarlet Letter* in his 1965 study *Nathaniel Hawthorne* (revised 1983),[84] and Millicent Bell's important treatment of Hawthorne's aesthetics, *Hawthorne's View of the Artist* (1962).[85] But the book that attracted the most attention in the sixties was Frederick C. Crews's *The Sins of the Fathers: Hawthorne's Psychological Themes* (1966), a Freudian view of Hawthorne's works. In his chapter on *The Scarlet Letter* entitled "The Ruined Wall," Crews puts Dimmesdale under the microscope, examining his psychological makeup and dilemma. Dimmesdale's "psychological damage was done," says Crews, when his higher self — the conscience or ascetic side — "violently expelled and denied the sensual impulse, once gratified."[86] The "libidinal impulse," now bearing guilt with it, is the "potential invader of the citadel." The metaphor of the besieged citadel shows that Dimmesdale is not a "free moral agent," but rather "a victim of feelings he can neither understand nor control."[87] If the "chain of compulsion" that controls Dimmesdale is ultimately "relaxed" when he makes public confession, for Hester the "drama on the scaffold can never be completely over."[88] She returns to Boston from overseas "to resume, or rather to begin, her state of penitence," but it is not a theological penitence. The final tragedy of the novel lies in the "inner world of frustrated desires" on the part of the major characters. Hester, Dimmesdale, and Chillingworth "have been ruled by feelings only half perceived, much less understood and regulated by consciousness. . . ." Hawthorne leaves us with "a tale of passion through which we glimpse the ruined wall — the terrible certainty that, as Freud put it, the ego is not master in its own house."[89] Crews's study was not the first psychological view of Hawthorne and *The Scarlet Letter*, of course, but certainly the most significant up to its time and perhaps still so. It has spawned a host of further psychological studies — Freudian, Jungian, Lacanian (see James Mellard's new essay in this volume), and others that have probed nearly every possible hidden meaning in Hawthorne's book.

In 1953, C. C. Walcutt classified five types of readings of *The Scarlet Letter*: orthodox Christian, a variant thereof (*Felix Culpa*), Romantic, Transcendentalist, and Relativist (psychological).[90] He explained reasons for the varying interpretations of the book and in so doing touched on the critical contributions to criticism on *The Scarlet Letter* of some dozen scholars — among them Austin Warren, Newton Arvin, Lloyd Morris, Mark Van Doren, and George Woodberry. Though written now over thirty years ago, and certainly limited in its recognition of possible readings of the book, Walcutt's article stands in anticipation of the expansion of critical approaches throughout the four decades since 1950. Indeed, from 1960 on, attention to *The Scarlet Letter* has increased to the point that a veritable outpouring of articles, book chapters, and collections of essays has occurred.

During the seventies and eighties, while critical focus on *The Scarlet Letter* has continued to produce source studies and structuralist / formalist approaches and further New Critical treatments, the most significant critical directions have been the historical, the biographical, the psychological, the feminist, and the deconstructionist / reader response strains.

The historical approach, of course, has a firmly entrenched place in *Scarlet Letter* criticism. Its importance — along with limitless possibilities of the historical perspective — was reaffirmed in the Hawthorne Centennial Year — 1964 — by Charles Feidelson, Jr., in his essay on *The Scarlet Letter* in *Hawthorne Centennial Essays*. Working from the premise that *The Scarlet Letter* is "distinctively historical, and historical in a rather complex way,"[91] Feidelson shows that the novel is about the Puritan past but also very much about Hawthorne's world too. The book, thus, is "most profoundly historical because it is not only *about* but also *written out of* a felt historical situation."[92] A reading by David Levin in 1967 concludes that Hawthorne's thorough knowledge of New England history helped make *The Scarlet Letter* his greatest book.[93] More recently, Michael Colacurcio has looked perceptively into newer dimensions of Hawthorne and history, contributing such important articles as "Footsteps of Ann Hutchinson: The Context of *The Scarlet Letter*" (1972),[94] and " 'The Woman's Own Choice': Sex, Metaphor, and the Puritan 'Sources' of *The Scarlet Letter*" (1985)[95] in what constitutes a meaningful blend of revisionist and conventional historical views. Colacurcio's studies effectively link the Puritan past with Hawthorne's times.

Biographical studies of *The Scarlet Letter*, often with a focus on "The Custom-House," have increased in a decade that has witnessed to date the publication of two important biographies of Hawthorne by Arlin Turner[96] and James R. Mellow[97] and the first four volumes of Hawthorne's letters,[98] to name only a few of many biographically related publications. Thus, it should not be surprising that two of the essays written expressly for this volume, Rita K. Gollin's " 'Again a Literary Man': Vocation and *The Scarlet Letter*" and Thomas Woodson's "Hawthorne, Upham, and *The Scarlet Letter*," are biographical at base. Even Richard D. Rust's new essay, " 'Take Shame' and 'Be True': Hawthorne and His Characters in *The Scarlet Letter*" has biographical underpinnings, though it is to a large extent psychological also. Gollin, drawing from the newly published letters, shows how *The Scarlet Letter* reflects Hawthorne's self-vindication of his career choice of authorship and his disparagement and rejection of the professions of medicine, the ministry, and the law. Woodson's treatment of the Hawthorne-Upham relationship and how it informed the "Custom-House" essay and the novel itself is the most comprehensive picture of that subject to date and is likewise based on evidence found in Hawthorne's letters. Rust feels that by writing *The Scarlet Letter* Hawthorne shows not only "the good and bad traits of the Puritans . . . exemplified by his ancestors," but worked through and rid himself of "his feelings of revenge toward those who expelled him from office" while also asserting "his self-identity and his identity as a creative artist of value. . . ."

The psychological interest in *The Scarlet Letter* that William Cary Brownell took early in the twentieth century has continued to be a central focus of many scholars. Both the "Custom-House" preface and the novel proper have been probed for the psychological themes pertinent to the characters or to Hawthorne himself. Already discussed are Crews and Rust, but there are several other recent examples. In *Nathaniel Hawthorne and the Truth of Dreams* (1979), Rita Gollin explores the two daydreams in *The Scarlet Letter* (Hester's while on the scaffold with Pearl, and Dimmesdale's in his study prior to the confession scene) to show how they are crucial to the development of the novel's major concern — "the causes and . . . the effects of sin on the two sinners. The reveries are deliberately initiated acts of introspection that implicitly explain their public behavior."[99] Gloria C. Erlich, in *Family Themes and Hawthorne's Fiction: The Tenacious Web* (1984), draws on Hawthorne's lack of a father in his youth for her premise that "maternal presence and paternal absence are the positive and negative poles that generate" *The Scarlet Letter*.[100] Pearl's search and need for a father are not unlike Nathaniel's own. In "The Custom-House," Hawthorne—in giving "filial obedience" to Surveyor Pue—"ignores his own father and bypasses his forefathers and guardian, to create the ghostly father he needs."[101]

If Frederick Crews has offered the most formative psychological study of Dimmesdale (at least in the Freudian sense), James Mellard limns a different psychological construct for Pearl and Hester in his essay written for this volume, "Pearl and Hester: A Lacanian Reading." Believing that *The Scarlet Letter* readily illustrates the principles of Jacques Lacan because (1) its "dominate symbol is precisely Lacan's: the letter, and (2) it focuses on four characters whose experiences exemplify its major psychoanalytic issues as Lacan conceives them," Mellard explores and analyzes the mother-daughter pair in the novel because they are the "normal," as opposed to the "neurotic or psychotic" characters. Mellard's argument is an attempt in part to show wherein the Freudian reading of *The Scarlet Letter*, as best seen in Crews, is necessarily a limited one, whereas the Lacanian is clearly more comprehensive and balanced.

As mentioned above, since the publication of *The Scarlet Letter* there has been a debate over whether Hester or Dimmesdale is the leading character. Dimmesdale took the early lead; then Hester gained ground with Howells's 1901 essay, only to fall behind again in the New Criticism of the mid-twentieth century. Darrell Abel's "Hawthorne's Hester" (1952) was representative of the criticism of the fifties. Abel scoffs at the idea of Hester's being a heroine who represents an admirable "romantic individualism," demonstrates what he views as the "inadequacy of such a philosophy," and shows that besides breaking heavenly and earthly laws, Hester "failed to secure even the natural satisfaction she sought."[102] Recent feminist criticism, however, has risen to Hester's defense and given her her due as heroine and protagonist. In "The Significance of Plot in Hawthorne's Romances" (1981), Nina Baym accosts Abel for his short-sighted view of Hester's position in the novel, pointing out that of the twenty-four chapters, "thirteen are 'about' Hester, three are 'about' Hester and Dimmesdale both, and eight are 'about' Dimmesdale."[103] Further, it is Hester, not Dimmesdale, who is mentioned in the "Custom-House" sketch, and it is her scarlet letter that is discussed as the source of the story. Baym concludes that the New Critical view of Hester as a secondary figure can spring only from "its strong sense of appropriate male / female roles and its consequent conviction that it would be improper for a woman character to be the protagonist in what might well be the greatest American book."[104] In this article, as well as in several other important contributions, Baym reestablishes Hester as Hawthorne's major character, even presenting her in *The Shape of Hawthorne's Career* (1970)[105] as a symbol of Hawthorne's own rebellious feelings at the time he wrote the novel when, like Hester, he had been ousted from his society (because of the political firing). Baym has recently commented that the feminist viewpoint "allows one to see how Hawthorne was concerned, in developing Hester, with the question of the status of women in society, as well as the different commitments men and women tend to make to romantic love."[106] Baym herself has become the leading feminist critic of Hawthorne and *The Scarlet Letter*, having advanced some of the most provocative and cogent analyses in Hawthorne criticism over the last ten years.

With its ambiguity of meaning and its very crux being a letter which is also ambiguous in meaning, *The Scarlet Letter* has played readily into the hands of the deconstructionists, semiologists, and reader response theorists. These critics question not only the meaning of the novel to the contemporary reader, but also to Hawthorne himself, who, according to their approach, may have struggled with the question of textual construct. There is no better example of this school of criticism than Millicent Bell's "The Obliquity of Signs: *The Scarlet Letter*." Bell views Hawthorne's novel as an "essay in semiology" whose main theme is the "indeterminacy of signs."[107] Pointing to a loss of confidence in the meaning of signs in an age of Jacques Derrida, Bell conjectures that Hawthorne himself "may have been at the threshold of our condition, though he was still formally committed to other views."[108] Indeed, in *The Scarlet Letter* "he gives play to all of his mingled feelings—his tenderness for the poetry of a lost faith in essences, his ironic detachment and disbelief, and his fear of such disbelief in himself or others."[109] It just could be, Bell continues, that Hawthorne, despite his attempts to believe in "ultimate revelation," might have suspected that "no ultimate meanings exist."[110]

Whether or not the deconstructionists and semiologists should have the last word, it is true—and clearly evident from all the points of view catalogued in this introduction—that *The Scarlet Letter* is a novel of many meanings. The very "elusiveness of the the text," as Nina Baym has put it, is "the essential reason for its fascination throughout the years."[111] Rich in its critical tradition, the novel continues to be compelling to readers because, again to quote Baym, it "creates a world that we each enter in our own way, indeed, that each of us may enter in different ways at different points in our lives."[112]

DAVID B. KESTERSON

University of North Texas

Notes

1. *The Centenary Edition of the Works of Nathaniel Hawthorne*, ed. William Charvat et al., vol. 1 (Columbus: Ohio State University Press, 1962), 34.

2. Ibid., vol. 9, 435.

3. Letter to Horatio Bridge, 4 February 1850, *Works of Nathaniel Hawthorne*, vol. 16, 311.

4. See C. E. Frazer Clark, Jr., "Posthumous Papers of a Decapitated Surveyor: *The Scarlet Letter* in the Salem Press," *Studies in the Novel* 2 (Winter 1970):403.

5. Ibid., 401.

6. Ibid., 402.

7. Ibid.

8. Benjamin Lease, " 'The Whole Is a Prose Poem': An Early Review of *The Scarlet Letter*," *American Literature* 44 (March 1972):128.

9. Ibid., 129–30.

10. Ibid., 130.

11. Review of *The Scarlet Letter* 6 (30 March 1850):323.

12. Ibid., 324.

13. Review of *The Scarlet Letter* 9 (1 April 1850):2. Rpt. in *Littel's Living Age* 25 (4 May 1850):203–7.

14. Ibid., 2.

15. Ibid.

16. Review of *The Scarlet Letter* 36 (May 1850):345.

17. Ibid., 345.

18. Ibid., 346.

19. Ibid., 345.

20. See Daniel R. Barnes, "Two Reviews of *The Scarlet Letter* in the *Dollar Magazine*," *American Literature* 44 (January 1973):648–52.

21. Ibid., 652.

22. Henry Chorley, review of *The Scarlet Letter*, *Athenaeum*, no. 1180 (15 June 1850):634.

23. Anne Abbott, review of *The Scarlet Letter*, *North American Review* 71 (July 1850):136.

24. Ibid., 139.

25. Ibid., 147.

26. Ibid., 139.

27. George B. Loring, review of *The Scarlet Letter*, *Massachusetts Quarterly Review* 3 (September 1850):484.

28. Ibid., 485.

29. Orestes Brownson, review of *The Scarlet Letter*, *Brownson's Quarterly Review* 4, no. 4 (October 1850):529.

30. Ibid., 532.

31. Arthur Cleveland Coxe, "The Writings of Nathaniel Hawthorne," *Church Review* 3 (January 1851):489–511. Rpt. as "*The Scarlet Letter* by Nathaniel Hawthorne" in Albert Mordell, ed., *Notorious Literary Attacks* (New York: Boni and Liveright, 1926), 122–37. Citations are to the reprinting; here, 122–23.

32. Ibid., 127.

33. Ibid., 134.

34. Ibid., 136.

35. Ibid., 137.

36. Bertha Faust, *Hawthorne's Contemporaneous Reputation: A Study of Literary Opinion in America and England, 1828–1864* (Philadelphia: University of Pennsylvania Press, 1939), 85.

37. Ibid., 85.

38. Henry James, *Nathaniel Hawthorne* (New York: Harper & Brothers, 1879), 107.

39. Ibid., 103.

40. Ibid., 108.

41. Ibid.

42. Ibid., 116.

43. Ibid.

44. Ibid., 113.

45. Ibid., 116.

46. Julian Hawthorne, "Problems of *The Scarlet Letter*," *Atlantic* 57 (April 1886):71–85. Rpt. in Kenneth W. Cameron, ed., *Hawthorne Among His Contemporaries* (Hartford: Transcendental Books, 1968), 282–89. Citations are to the reprinting; here, 282.

47. J. Hawthorne, "Problems," 282.

48. Ibid., 283.

49. Ibid.

50. Ibid., 284.

51. William Dean Howells, "Hawthorne's Hester Prynne," *Heroines of Fiction*, vol. 1 (New York and London: Harper and Brothers, 1901), 174.

52. Ibid., 165.

53. Ibid., 167.

54. Ibid., 162.

55. Theodore Munger, "Notes on *The Scarlet Letter*," *Atlantic* 93 (April 1904):527.

56. Ibid., 525.

57. Ibid., 531.

58. Ibid., 525.

59. Lucy C. Cable, "Old Salem and 'The Scarlet Letter,' " *Bookman* 26 (December 1907):403.

60. Ibid., 403.

61. William Cary Brownell, *American Prose Masters* (New York: Scribner, 1909), 80; Rpt. Howard M. Jones, ed. (Cambridge: Belknap Press of Harvard University Press, 1967).

62. Ibid., 81.

63. Ibid., 84.

64. Llewellyn Jones, "Mr. Hawthorne's *Scarlet Letter*," *Bookman* 57 (January 1924):624.

65. Ibid., 625.

66. Ibid., 623.

67. Julian Hawthorne, "The Making of *The Scarlet Letter*," *Bookman* 74 (December 1931):407.

68. Pelham Edgar, "Nathaniel Hawthorne and *The Scarlet Letter*," *The Art of the Novel: From 1700 to the Present Time* (New York: Macmillan Co., 1933), 125.

69. Ibid., 126.

70. Ibid., 127.

71. Ibid.

72. Ibid., 128.

73. Frederic I. Carpenter, "Scarlet A Minus," *College English* 5 (January 1944):173.

74. Ibid., 177.

75. Ibid., 177–78.

76. John C. Gerber, "Form and Content in *The Scarlet Letter*," *New England Quarterly* 17 (March 1944):25.

77. Ibid., 26.

78. D. H. Lawrence, *Studies in Classic American Literature* (New York: Thomas Seltzer, 1923. rpt. New York: Doubleday / Anchor, 1953, 92–110.

79. F. O. Matthiessen, *American Renaissance* (New York: Oxford University Press, 1941), 275–82.

80. Richard Harter Fogle, *Hawthorne's Fiction: The Light and the Dark* (Norman: University of Oklahoma Press, 1952; rpt. 1964), 137.

81. Hyatt H. Waggoner, *Hawthorne: A Critical Study* (Cambridge: Harvard University Press, 1955; rpt. and rev. 1963), 149.

82. Roy Male, *Hawthorne's Tragic Vision* (Austin: University of Texas Press, 1957), 177.

83. Ibid., 101.

84. Terence Martin, *Nathaniel Hawthorne* (New York: Twayne Publishers, 1984).

85. Millicent Bell, *Hawthorne's View of the Artist* (Albany: State University of New York Press, 1962).

86. Frederick C. Crews, *The Sins of the Fathers: Hawthorne's Psychological Themes* (New York: Oxford University Press, 1966), 138.

87. Ibid., 139–40.

88. Ibid., 152.

89. Ibid., 153.

90. C. C. Walcutt, "*The Scarlet Letter* and Its Modern Critics," *Nineteenth-Century Fiction* 7 (March 1953):251–64.

91. Charles Feidelson, Jr., *Hawthorne Centennial Essays*, ed. Roy Harvey Pearce (Columbus: Ohio State University Press, 1964), 31.

92. Ibid., 32.

93. David Levin, *In Defense of Historical Literature* (New York: Hill & Wang, 1967), 98–117.

94. Michael J. Colacurcio, "Footsteps of Ann Hutchinson: The Context of *The Scarlet Letter*" *ELH* 39, no. 3 (September 1972):459–94.

95. *New Essays on The Scarlet Letter*, ed. Michael J. Colacurcio (Cambridge, London, New York: Cambridge University Press, 1985), 101–35.

96. Arlin Turner, *Nathaniel Hawthorne: A Biography* (Oxford and New York: Oxford University Press, 1980).

97. James R. Mellow, *Nathaniel Hawthorne in His Times* (Boston: Houghton Mifflin Co., 1980).

98. *Centenary Edition of the Works of Nathaniel Hawthorne, The Letters*, ed. Thomas Woodson, et al., vols. 15, 16, 17, 18 (Ohio State University Press, 1984, 1985, 1987).

99. Rita K. Gollin, *Nathaniel Hawthorne and the Truth of Dreams* (Baton Rouge: Louisiana State University Press, 1979), 141.

100. Gloria C. Erlich, *Family Themes and Hawthorne's Fiction: The Tenacious Web* (New Brunswick: Rutgers University Press, 1984), 27.

101. Ibid., 26.

102. Darrell Abel, "Hawthorne's Hester," *College English* 13 (March 1952):303.

103. Nina Baym, "The Significance of Plot in Hawthorne's Romances," *Ruined Eden of the Present: Hawthorne, Melville, and Poe: Critical Essays in Honor of Darrel Abel*, ed. G. R. Thompson and Virgil L. Lokke (West Lafayette: Purdue University Press, 1981), 51.

104. Ibid., 51–52.

105. Nina Baym, *The Shape of Hawthorne's Career* (Ithaca: Cornell University Press, 1976). Chapter 4 is on *The Scarlet Letter*.

106. Nina Baym, *The Scarlet Letter: A Reading* (Boston: Twayne Publishers, 1986), xxix.

107. Millicent Bell, "The Obliquity of Signs: *The Scarlet Letter*," *Massachusetts Review* 23, no. 1 (Spring 1982):9.

108. Ibid., 12.

109. Ibid., 13.

110. Ibid., 26.

111. Baym, *The Scarlet Letter: A Reading*, xxix.

112. Ibid.

Reviews

Posthumous Papers of a Decapitated Surveyor: *The Scarlet Letter* in the Salem Press
C. E. Frazer Clark, Jr.*

Hawthorne's cordial relations with the Salem press took a turn in June of 1849 when the news broke that Mr. Surveyor Hawthorne was to be cast out of office. Hawthorne's head was put on the political block to the delight of his political enemies and the dismay of his friends. Such a political decapitation was accepted practice in the application of the spoils system to a local patronage office. What was surprising was the enormity of the furor Hawthorne's axing generated and the way in which it cut across party lines. Hawthorne fought the dismissal as a matter of economic necessity (the loss of the job put him in desperate straits), and he lined up strong support in the Whig camp as well as among his Democratic friends, all to no avail.

The Whig paper in Salem, the *Salem Register*, treated the news of Hawthorne's dismissal casually and with a tongue-in-cheek sympathy in the beginning. As the hue and cry developed over Hawthorne's discharge as "one of the most heartless acts of this heartless administration," the *Register* retaliated with passionate attacks on "Mr. Surveyor Hawthorne."[1] Support for the effort to reinstate Hawthorne appeared in the *Salem Gazette*, where Foote reprinted a defense written by George Hillard, prominent Whig friend, and matched it with Hawthorne's own defense, as front page copy.[2]

Hawthorne's political guillotining was a political issue too good for the local and national press to pass up—the story was picked up throughout New England. "Hawthorne removed! Can it be possible? If every other Democratic incumbent of office had been swept by the board, we should still have looked to see an exception made in the case of the gentle Elia of our American literature. . . ."[3]

The New England press seized upon the removal of Hawthorne as a politically opportune way to attack the newly elected Taylor administration.[4] The active role the press played in publicizing the Hawthorne issue is clear. What is less clearly perceived is that no furor of such national

*Reprinted in part from *Studies in the Novel* 2 (Winter 1970):395–419, by permission of the journal.

19

proportions would have been possible if Hawthorne's stature as a figure of national importance in American literature had not already been established with the reading public, thanks in large part to the working press. Hawthorne's dismissal was news because Hawthorne was newsworthy.

Painful as the agonies of decapitation were to Hawthorne, the act worked to his benefit in two ways. "The real human being, all this time, with his head safely on his shoulders, had brought himself to the comfortable conclusion, that every thing was for the best; and, making an investment in ink, paper, and steel-pens, had opened his long-disused writing-desk, and was again a literary man."[5] In addition to providing an incentive to write, the exposure in print proved to be a profitable experience in further bringing Hawthorne's name before the public and served as an effective pre-sales campaign for *The Scarlet Letter*. Ticknor, Reed, and Fields could never have drummed up a public relations campaign so happily calculated to ensure the immediate success of a book as the press coverage of Hawthorne's execution proved to be. It is tempting to think that the exploitable possibilities of Hawthorne's prominence occurred to the canny James T. Fields and prompted his timely visit to inquire about the possibility that Hawthorne might have something ready for publication.

The Scarlet Letter was published on Saturday, March 16, 1850, with copies available in Boston on that day. Henry Whipple, Hawthorne's friendliest Salem bookseller, had expected copies in Salem the day before, and had an advertisement standing ready for insertion in the Friday, March 15, *Salem Gazette*. The advertisement was held for insertion in the following Tuesday issue of the *Gazette*, by which time stock was on hand. Salem first learned that *The Scarlet Letter* was out with the Monday morning *Register* for March 18, announcing that copies were for sale by W. & S. B. Ives and Henry Whipple. Ives advertised the new book as by the "author of Thrice [*sic*] Told Tales." (Hawthorne might have agreed, but the confusion could also have stemmed from a recollection of Hawthorne's impressively sized separate printing of *The Gentle Boy: A Thrice Told Tale* (1839), copies of which Ives handled.)

For the next two weeks, copies of *The Scarlet Letter* were advertised in the Salem press as available from one end to the other of the Essex Street booksellers' row. Whipple, Ives, Brooks, Perley, Putnam, and Creamer all advertised and sold the title. Of a total of eighteen advertisements located, Ives had three single title insertions, Brooks one single title insertion, Perley three group listings, Putnam three single title insertions, Creamer six group listings, and Whipple two single title insertions, scattered through the *Gazette, Register, Observer*, and *Courier*.[6] The majority of the single title advertisements feature Hawthorne's name, playing local reputation first. By the end of the first week, with time for a reaction to the reviews, D. R. Brooks picked up the book and advertised its controversial aspect, listing the work with the header "The Salem Custom House," and "Hawthorne's last work—'The Scarlet Letter,' " following.

Caleb Foote first reviewed Hawthorne's new book for Salem readers. Foote's review continued the *Gazette*'s cordiality to Hawthorne: "It is indeed a wonderful book, and we venture to predict that no one will put it down before he reaches the last page of it, unless it is forcibly taken out of his hands."[7] It is noteworthy that Foote, privy to the secret, reveals in his review a clue to the authorship of some of Hawthorne's early anonymous work: "In all his earlier writings, the interest of the story has been completely subordinated to the charm of fancy, and the unequalled power of language which has made a Carrier's Address or a Peter Parley's Universal History, as bewitching as a romance."

While Foote was involved in the action to remove Hawthorne from the Custom-House post, he had kept the *Gazette* largely out of the fray, bending it, actually, to support his friend's cause. Besides his respect for author Hawthorne, he may have remembered Hawthorne's willingness to help him financially in years past.[8] The incendiary nature of Hawthorne's sketch of the Custom-House must have been perfectly clear to Foote, but he chose to avoid the risks of renewed controversy and made no mention of "The Custom-House" section in his review of *The Scarlet Letter*.

The *Salem Register* reacted to the publication of *The Scarlet Letter* in the Thursday morning, March 21, issue with a long review, presumably written by editor John Chapman. The *Register* well remembered Mr. Surveyor Hawthorne and was not chary of rising to renewed political battle. Before it picked up the bloodied ax, and notwithstanding its bias, the *Register* gave the author his literary due: "So far as the Scarlet Letter is concerned, it will more than meet the public expectation, and increase the enviable reputation which the author long ago acquired."[9] (Even by *Register* standards, Hawthorne was never "the obscurest man of letters in America.") "It is marked by all the exquisiteness of Hawthorne's genius, but with less of that dreamy indistinctness which has sometimes made not a few of his productions unintelligible to an ordinary mind."

Having dispensed with an impressive appreciation of Hawthorne's authorial powers in regard to *The Scarlet Letter*, Chapman then turns another kind of attention to the "Ex-Surveyor's" remarks about the Salem Custom-House and its officers. "We were almost induced to throw down the book in disgust, without venturing on the Scarlet Letter, so atrocious, so heartless, so undisguised, so utterly inexcusable seemed his calumnious caricatures of inoffensive men, who could not possibly have given occasion for such wanton insults. . . . The *'Posthumous Papers of a Decapitated Surveyor'* amply vindicate the justice of this application of the political guillotine."[10] In the following issue, Monday morning, March 25, the *Register* continued its attack on "The 'Scarlet Letter' Prefix," by cataloguing excerpts from the Boston and New York papers, also incensed by

Hawthorne's Custom-House sketch.[11] Thus satisfied in its position, the *Register* ceased fire.

The initial demand for *The Scarlet Letter* was great enough to signal the need for a new edition almost immediately, and Hawthorne was asked if he cared to make any alterations in the book, which had really been put to bed in haste (Fields had lost no time once he saw what Hawthorne had written).[12] This provided Hawthorne an opportunity to answer his critics, which he did by preparing a "Preface To The Second Edition," which he dated March 30, 1850 — the Saturday of the second week of reviews and advertisements in the Salem press. In his "Preface," Hawthorne acknowledges that "his sketch of official life, introductory to *The Scarlet Letter*, has created an unprecedented excitement in the respectable community immediately around him. It could hardly have been more violent, indeed, had he burned down the Custom-House, and quenched its last smoking ember in the blood of a certain venerable personage, against whom he is supposed to cherish a peculiar malevolence."[13] While Hawthorne had some opportunity to know what the papers outside Salem were saying — he had access to the same papers the *Register* did — it was still too soon after publication for outside reaction to have the kind of impact on him as did the accusations of his townspeople (both in and out of print). It was this attack, particularly what was printed in the *Register*, to which he addressed his "Preface." Hawthorne felt absolutely no compunction to modify what he had written, and he announced in his "Preface" that he would "republish his introductory sketch without the change of a word." This announcement ended things, as far as Hawthorne was concerned, although neither he nor the outraged Salemites ever forgot the matter. Hawthorne had already decided to leave Salem, as he had announced in his "Posthumous Papers," before *The Scarlet Letter* was published. He was confirmed in his resolve by the not unexpected reception afforded his book.

In many respects, Hawthorne was a victim of the distinction he felt had long eluded him. If he had not in fact achieved a measure of the fame he sought, he would not have been designated a worthy candidate for the "political guillotine" and the wake that followed — one in which, as he tells us, "the press had taken up my affair, and kept me, for a week or two, careering through the public prints, in my decapitated state, like Irving's Headless Horseman; ghastly and grim, and longing to be buried, as a politically dead man ought."[14]

The Salem press was inescapably involved in the elevation and decapitation, and, ultimately, in the successful reincarnation manifest in *The Scarlet Letter*. As to the people, if the bitterness generated by what Hawthorne felt was a grievous political and public betrayal had destroyed his affection for the dried-out soil of his ancestral home, he could take satisfaction in the fact that he had amply demonstrated that the pen was indeed mightier than the stencil. . . .

Notes

1. Attacks on Hawthorne in the *Salem Register* for 1849 are printed in the issues for June 11, 14, 18, 21, and 25, all on p. 2, col. 1.

2. *Salem Gazette*, 23 June 1849, p. 1, cols. 3–5.

3. *Albany Atlas*, 17 June 1849.

4. For a comprehensive analysis of the political aspects of Hawthorne's removal, see Paul Cortissoz, "The Political Life of Nathaniel Hawthorne" (Ph.D. diss., New York University, 1955).

5. *The Scarlet Letter* (Boston, 1850), p. 51.

6. See appendix 2.

7. *The Salem Gazette*, 19 March 1850, p. 2, col. 2. See appendix 3.

8. Hawthorne wrote to Caleb Foote on January 17, 1842, regarding a note due Hawthorne in the amount of $500. Letter in the collection of C. E. Frazer Clark, Jr.

9. *Salem Register*, 21 March 1850, p. 2, cols. 1–2. See appendix 4.

10. *Ibid.*

11. *Ibid.*, 25 March 1850, p. 2, col. 2. See appendix 3.

12. For a discussion of the publication of *The Scarlet Letter*, see William Charvat, "Introduction to *The Scarlet Letter*," in *The Scarlet Letter*, Volume I of The Centenary Edition of the Works of Nathaniel Hawthorne (Columbus, Ohio: The Ohio State University Press, 1962), pp. xv–xxviii.

13. *Ibid.*, p. 1.

14. *Ibid.*, pp. 42–43.

[A "Psychological Romance"]   Evert A. Duyckinck*

Mr. Hawthorne introduces his new story to the public, the longest of all that he has yet published, and most worthy in this way to be called a romance, with one of those pleasant personal descriptions which are the most charming of his compositions, and of which we had so happy an example in the preface to his last collection, the *Mosses from an Old Manse*. In these narratives everything seems to fall happily into its place. The style is simple and flowing, the observation accurate and acute; persons and things are represented in their minutest shades, and difficult traits of character presented with an instinct which art might be proud to imitate. They are, in fine, little cabinet pictures exquisitely painted. The readers of the *Twice Told Tales* will know the pictures to which we allude. They have not, we are sure, forgotten "Little Annie's Ramble," or the "Sights from a Steeple." This is the Hawthorne of the present day in the sunshine. There is another Hawthorne less companionable, of sterner Puritan aspect, with the shadow of the past over him, a reviver of witchcrafts and of those dark agencies of evil which lurk in the human

*Reprinted in part from *Literary World* 6 (30 March 1850):323–25.

soul, and which even now represent the old gloomy historic era in the microcosm and eternity of the individual; and this Hawthorne is called to mind by such tales as "The Minister's Black Veil" or "The Old Maid in the Winding Sheet," and reappears in *The Scarlet Letter*, a romance. Romantic in sooth! Such romance as you may read in the intensest sermons of old Puritan divines, or in the mouldy pages of that Marrow of Divinity, the ascetic Jeremy Taylor.

The Scarlet Letter is a psychological romance. The hardiest Mrs. Malaprop would never venture to call it a novel. It is a tale of remorse, a study of character in which the human heart is anatomized, carefully, elaborately, and with striking poetic and dramatic power. Its incidents are simply these. A woman in the early days of Boston becomes the subject of the discipline of the court of those times, and is condemned to stand in the pillory and wear henceforth, in token of her shame, the scarlet letter A attached to her bosom. She carries her child with her to the pillory. Its other parent is unknown. At this opening scene her husband from whom she had been separated in Europe, preceding him by ship across the Atlantic, reappears from the forest, whither he had been thrown by shipwreck on his arrival. He was a man of a cold intellectual temperament, and devotes his life thereafter to search for his wife's guilty partner and a fiendish revenge. The young clergyman of the town, a man of a devout sensibility and warmth of heart, is the victim, as this Mephistophilean old physician fixes himself by his side to watch over him and protect his health, an object of great solicitude to his parishioners, and, in reality, to detect his suspected secret and gloat over his tortures. This slow, cool, devilish purpose, like the concoction of some sublimated hell broth, is perfected gradually and inevitably. The wayward, elfish child, a concentration of guilt and passion, binds the interests of the parties together, but throws little sunshine over the scene. These are all the characters, with some casual introductions of the grim personages and manners of the period, unless we add the scarlet letter, which, in Hawthorne's hands, skilled to these allegorical, typical semblances, becomes vitalized as the rest. It is the hero of the volume. The denouement is the death of the clergyman on a day of public festivity, after a public confession in the arms of the pilloried, branded woman. But few as are these main incidents thus briefly told, the action of the story, or its passion, is "long, obscure, and infinite." It is a drama in which thoughts are acts. The material has been thoroughly fused in the writer's mind, and springs forth an entire, perfect creation. We know of no American tales except some of the early ones of Mr. Dana, which approach it in conscientious completeness. Nothing is slurred over, superfluous, or defective. The story is grouped in scenes simply arranged, but with artistic power, yet without any of those painful impressions which the use of the words, as it is the fashion to use them, "grouping" and "artistic" excite, suggesting artifice and effort at the expense of nature and ease.

Mr. Hawthorne has, in fine, shown extraordinary power in this volume, great feeling and discrimination, a subtle knowledge of character in its secret springs and outer manifestations. He blends, too, a delicate fancy with this metaphysical insight. We would instance the chapter towards the close, entitled "The Minister in a Maze," where the effects of a diabolic temptation are curiously depicted, or "The Minister's Vigil," the night scene in the pillory. The atmosphere of the piece also is perfect. It has the mystic element, the weird forest influences of the old Puritan discipline and era. Yet there is no affrightment which belongs purely to history, which has not its echo even in the unlike and perversely commonplace custom-house of Salem. Then for the moral. Though severe, it is wholesome, and is a sounder bit of Puritan divinity than we have been of late accustomed to hear from the degenerate successors of Cotton Mather. We hardly know another writer who has lived so much among the new school who would have handled this delicate subject without an infusion of George Sand. The spirit of his old Puritan ancestors, to whom he refers in the preface, lives in Nathaniel Hawthorne.

[The Gothic, the Supernatural, the Imagination]

George Ripley*

The weird and ghostly legends of the Puritanic history present a singularly congenial field for the exercise of Mr. Hawthorne's peculiar genius. From this fruitful source he has derived the materials for his most remarkable creations. He never appears so much in his element as when threading out some dim, shadowy tradition of the twilight age of New England, peering into the faded records of our dark-visaged forefathers for the lingering traces of the preternatural, and weaving into his gorgeous web of enchantment the slender filaments which he has drawn from the distaff of some muttering witch on Gallows-Hill. He derives the same terrible excitement from these legendary horrors, as was drawn by Edgar Poe from the depths of his own dark and perilous imagination, and brings before us pictures of deathlike, but strangely fascinating agony, which are described with the same minuteness of finish — the same slow and fatal accumulation of details — the same exquisite coolness of coloring, while everything creeps forward with irresistible certainty to a soul-harrowing climax — which made the last-named writer such a consummate master of the horrible and infernal in fictitious composition. Hawthorne's tragedies, however, are always *motived* with a wonderful insight and skill, to which the intellect of Poe was a stranger. In the most terrific scenes with which

*Reprinted in part from *Littel's Living Age* 25 (4 May 1850): 203–7. Originally published in *New York Daily Tribune* 9 (1 April 1850):2.

he delights to scare the imagination, Hawthorne does not wander into the region of the improbable; you scarcely know that you are in the presence of the supernatural, until your breathing becomes too thick for this world; it is the supernatural relieved, softened, made tolerable, and almost attractive, by a strong admixture of the human; you are tempted onward by the mild, unearthly light, which seems to shine upon you like a healthful star; you are blinded by no lurid glare; you acquiesce in the necessity of the wizard journey; instead of being provoked to anger by a superfluous introduction to the company of the devil and his angels.

The elements of terror, which Mr. Hawthorne employs with such masterly effect, both in the original conception of his characters and the scenes of mystery and dread in which they are made to act, are blended with such sweet gushes of natural feeling, such solemn and tender relations of the deepest secrets of the heart, that the painful impression is greatly mitigated, and the final influence of his most startling creation is a serene sense of refreshment, without the stupor and bewilderment occasioned by a drugged cup of intoxication.

The "Scarlet Letter," in our opinion, is the greatest production of the author, beautifully displaying the traits we have briefly hinted at, and sustained with a more vigorous reach of imagination, a more subtle instinct of humanity, and a more imposing splendor of portraiture, than any of his most successful previous works. . . .

We have not intended to forestall our readers with a description of the plot, which it will be perceived abounds in elements of tragic interest, but to present them with some specimens of a genuine native romance, which none will be content without reading for themselves. The moral of the story—for it has a moral for all wise enough to detect it—is shadowed forth rather than expressed in a few brief sentences near the close of the volume.

But there was a more real life for Hester Prynne here, in New England, than in that unknown region where Pearl had found a home. Here had been her sin; here her sorrow; and here was yet to be her penitence. She had returned, therefore, and resumed—of her own free will, for not the sternest magistrate of that iron period would have imposed it—resumed the symbol of which we have related so dark a tale. Never afterwards did it quit her bosom. But, in the lapse of the toilsome, thoughtful, and self-devoted years that made up Hester's life, the scarlet letter ceased to be a stigma which attracted the world's scorn and bitterness, and became a type of something to be sorrowed over, and looked upon with awe, yet with reverence too. And as Hester Prynne had no selfish ends, nor lived in any measure for her own profit and enjoyment, people brought all their sorrows and perplexities, and besought her counsel as one who had herself gone through a mighty trouble. Women, more especially—in the continually recurring trials of wounded, wasted, wronged, misplaced, or erring and sinful passion—or with the

dreary burden of a heart unyielded, because unvalued and unsought—
came into Hester's cottage, demanding why they were so wretched, and
what the remedy! Hester comforted and counselled them, as best she
might. She assured them, too, of her firm belief, that, at some brighter
period, when the world should have grown ripe for it, in Heaven's own
time, a new truth would be revealed, in order to establish the whole
relation between man and woman on a surer ground of mutual happiness.
Earlier in life Hester had vainly imagined that she herself might be the
destined prophetess, but had long since recognized the impossibility that
any mission of divine and mysterious truth should be confided to a woman
stained with sin, bowed down with shame, or even burdened with a life-
long sorrow. The angel and apostle of the coming relation must be a
woman, indeed, but lofty, pure and beautiful; and wise, moreover, not
through dusky grief, but the ethereal medium of joy; and showing how
sacred love should make us happy, by the truest test of a life successful to
such an end!

The introduction, presenting a record of savory reminiscences of the
Salem Custom House, a frank display of autobiographical confessions, and
a piquant daguerreotype of his ancient colleagues in office, while surveyor
of that port, is written with Mr. Hawthorne's unrivalled force of graphic
delineation, and will furnish an agreeable amusement to those who are so
far from the scene of action as to feel no wound in their personal relations,
by the occasional too sharp touches of the caustic acid, of which the
"gentle author" keeps some phials on his shelf for convenience and use.
The querulous tone in which he alludes to his removal from the Custom
House, may be forgiven to the sensitiveness of a poet, especially as this is so
rare a quality in Uncle Sam's office-holders.

[A True Artist's Certainty of Touch and Expression]   Edwin Percy Whipple*

In this beautiful and touching romance Hawthorne has produced
something really worthy of the fine and deep genius which lies within
him. The "Twice Told Tales," and "Mosses from an Old Manse," are
composed simply of sketches and stories, and although such sketches and
stories as few living men could write, they are rather indications of the
possibilities of his mind than realizations of its native power, penetration,
and creativeness. In "The Scarlet Letter" we have a complete work,
evincing a true artist's certainty of touch and expression in the exhibition
of characters and events, and a keen-sighted and far-sighted vision into the

*Reprinted from *Graham's Magazine* 36 (May 1850):345–46.

essence and purpose of spiritual laws. There is a profound philosophy underlying the story which will escape many of the readers whose attention is engrossed by the narrative.

The book is prefaced by some fifty pages of autobiographical matter, relating to the author, his native city of Salem, and the Custom House, from which he was ousted by the Whigs. These pages, instinct with the vital spirit of humor, show how rich and exhaustless a fountain of mirth Hawthorne has at his command. The whole representation has the dreamy yet distinct remoteness of the purely comic ideal. The view of Salem streets; the picture of the old Custom House at the head of Derby's wharf, with its torpid officers on a summer's afternoon, their chairs all tipped against the wall, chatting about old stories, "while the frozen witticisms of past generations were thawed out, and came bubbling with laughter from their lips"—the delineation of the old Inspector, whose "reminiscences of good cheer, however ancient the date of the actual banquet, seemed to bring the savor of pig or turkey under one's very nostrils," and on whose palate there were flavors "which had lingered there not less than sixty or seventy years, and were still apparently as fresh as that of the mutton-chop which he had just devoured for his breakfast," and the grand view of the stout Collector, in his aged heroism, with the honors of Chippewa and Fort Erie on his brow, are all encircled with that visionary atmosphere which proves the humorist to be a poet, and indicates that his pictures are drawn from the images which observation has left on his imagination. The whole introduction, indeed, is worthy of a place among the essays of Addison and Charles Lamb.

With regard to "The Scarlet Letter," the readers of Hawthorne might have expected an exquisitely written story, expansive in sentiment, and suggestive in characterization, but they will hardly be prepared for a novel of so much tragic interest and tragic power, so deep in thought and so condensed in style, as is here presented to them. It evinces equal genius in the region of great passions and elusive emotions, and bears on every page the evidence of a mind thoroughly alive, watching patiently the movements of morbid hearts when stirred by strange experiences, and piercing, by its imaginative power, directly through all the externals to the core of things. The fault of the book, if fault it have, is the almost morbid intensity with which the characters are realized, and the consequent lack of sufficient geniality in the delineation. A portion of the pain of the author's own heart is communicated to the reader, and although there is great pleasure received while reading the volume, the general impression left by it is not satisfying to the artistic sense. Beauty bends to power throughout the work, and therefore the power displayed is not always beautiful. There is a strange fascination to a man of contemplative genius in the psychological details of a strange crime like that which forms the plot of the Scarlet Letter, and he is therefore apt to become, like Hawthorne, too painfully anatomical in his exhibition of them.

If there be, however, a comparative lack of relief to the painful emotions which the novel excites, owing to the intensity with which the author concentrates attention on the working of dark passions, it must be confessed that the moral purpose of the book is made more definite by this very deficiency. The most abandoned libertine could not read the volume without being thrilled into something like virtuous resolution, and the roué would find that the deep-seeing eye of the novelist had mastered the whole philosophy of that guilt of which practical roués are but childish disciples. To another class of readers, those who have theories of seduction and adultery modeled after the French school of novelists, and whom libertinism is of the brain, the volume may afford matter for very instructive and edifying contemplation; for, in truth, Hawthorne, in The Scarlet Letter, has utterly undermined the whole philosophy on which the French novels rest, by seeing farther and deeper into the essence both of conventional and moral laws; and he has given the results of his insight, not in disquisitions and criticisms, but in representations more powerful even than those of Sue, Dumas, or George Sand. He has made his guilty parties end, not as his own fancy or his own benevolent sympathies might dictate, but as the spiritual laws, lying back of all persons, dictated to him. In this respect there is hardly a novel in English literature more purely objective.

As everybody will read "The Scarlet Letter," it would be impertinent to give a synopsis of the plot. The principal characters, Dimmesdale, Chillingworth, Hester, and little Pearl, all indicate a firm grasp of individualities, although from the peculiar method of the story, they are developed more in the way of logical analysis than by events. The descriptive portions of the novel are in a high degree picturesque and vivid, bringing the scenes directly home to the heart and imagination, and indicating a clear vision of the life as well as forms of nature. Little Pearl is perhaps Hawthorne's finest poetical creation, and is the very perfection of ideal impishness.

In common, we trust, with the rest of mankind, we regretted Hawthorne's dismissal from the Custom House, but if that event compels him to exert his genius in the production of such books as the present, we shall be inclined to class the Honorable Secretary of the Treasury among the great philanthropists. In his next work we hope to have a romance equal to The Scarlet Letter in pathos and power, but more relieved by touches of that beautiful and peculiar humor, so serene and so searching, in which he excels almost all living writers.

[A "Powerful but Painful Story"]   Henry Chorley*

This is a most powerful but painful story. Mr. Hawthorne must be well known to our readers as a favourite with the *Athenæum*. We rate him as among the most original and peculiar writers of American fiction. There is in his works a mixture of Puritan reserve and wild imagination, of passion and description, of the allegorical and the real, which some will fail to understand, and which others will positively reject, — but which, to ourselves, is fascinating, and which entitles him to be placed on a level with Brockden Brown and the author of *Rip Van Winkle*. *The Scarlet Letter* will increase his reputation with all who do not shrink from the invention of the tale; but this, as we have said, is more than ordinarily painful. When we have announced that the three characters are a guilty wife, openly punished for her guilt, — her tempter, whom she refuses to unmask, and who during the entire story carries a fair front and an unblemished name among his congregation, — and her husband, who, returning from a long absence at the moment of her sentence, sits himself down betwixt the two in the midst of a small and severe community to work out his slow vengeance on both under the pretext of magnanimous forgiveness, — when we have explained that *The Scarlet Letter* is the badge of Hester Prynne's shame, we ought to add that we recollect no tale dealing with crime so sad and revenge so subtly diabolical, that is at the same time so clear of fever and of prurient excitement. The misery of the woman is as present in every page as the heading which in the title of the romance symbolizes her punishment. Her terrors concerning her strange elvish child present retribution in a form which is new and natural: — her slow and painful purification through repentance is crowned by no perfect happiness, such as awaits the decline of those who have no dark and bitter past to remember. Then, the gradual corrosion of heart of Dimmesdale, the faithless priest, under the insidious care of the husband, (whose relationship to Hester is a secret known only to themselves), is appalling; and his final confession and expiation are merely a relief, not a reconciliation. — We are by no means satisfied that passions and tragedies like these are the legitimate subjects for fiction; we are satisfied that novels such as *Adam Blair* and plays such as *The Stranger* may be justly charged with attracting more persons than they warn by their excitement. But if Sin and Sorrow in their most fearful forms are to be presented in any work of art, they have rarely been treated with a loftier severity, purity, and sympathy than in Mr. Hawthorne's *Scarlet Letter*. The touch of the fantastic befitting a period of society in which ignorant and excitable human creatures conceived each other and themselves to be under the direct "rule and governance" of the Wicked One, is

*Reprinted from *The Athenaeum*, no. 1180 (15 June 1850):634.

most skilfully administered. The supernatural here never becomes grossly palpable: — the thrill is all the deeper for its action being indefinite, and its source vague and distant.

[The Magic Power of Hawthorne's Style]

Anne Abbott*

No one who has taken up the Scarlet Letter will willingly lay it down till he has finished it; and he will do well not to pause, for he cannot resume the story where he left it. He should give himself up to the magic power of the style, without stopping to open wide the eyes of his good sense and judgment, and shake off the spell; or half the weird beauty will disappear like a "dissolving view." To be sure, when he closes the book, he will feel very much like the giddy and bewildered patient who is just awaking from his first experiment of the effects of sulphuric ether. The soul has been floating or flying between earth and heaven, with dim ideas of pain and pleasure strangely mingled, and all things earthly swimming dizzily and dreamily, yet most beautiful, before the half shut eye. That the author himself felt this sort of intoxication as well as the willing subjects of his enchantment, we think, is evident in many pages of the last half of the volume. His imagination has sometimes taken him fairly off his feet, insomuch that he seems almost to doubt if there be any firm ground at all, — if we may so judge from such mistborn ideas as the following.

> But, to all these shadowy beings, so long our near acquaintances, — as well Roger Chillingworth as his companions, — we would fain be merciful. It is a curious subject of observation and inquiry, whether hatred and love be not the same thing at bottom. Each, in its utmost development, supposes a high degree of intimacy and heart-knowledge; each renders one individual dependent for the food of his affections and spiritual life upon another; each leaves the passionate lover, or the no less passionate hater, forlorn and desolate by the withdrawal of his object. Philosophically considered, therefore, the two passions seem essentially the same, except the one happens to be seen in a celestial radiance, and the other in a dusky and lurid glow. In the spiritual world, the old physician and the minister — mutual victims as they have been — may, unawares, have found their earthly stock of hatred and antipathy transmuted into golden love.

Thus devils and angels are alike beautiful, when seen through the magic glass; and they stand side by side in heaven, however the former may be supposed to have come there. As for Roger Chillingworth, he seems to have so little in common with man, he is such a gnome-like

*Reprinted in part from *North American Review* 71 (July 1850):135–48.

phantasm, such an unnatural personification of an abstract idea, that we should be puzzled to assign him a place among angels, men, or devils. He is no more a man than Mr. Dombey, who sinks down a mere *caput mortuum*, as soon as pride, the only animating principle, is withdrawn. These same "shadowy beings" are much like "the changeling the fairies made o' a benweed." Hester at first strongly excites our pity, for she suffers like an immortal being; and our interest in her continues only while we have hope for her soul, that its baptism of tears will reclaim it from the foul stain which has been cast upon it. We see her humble, meek, self-denying, charitable, and heartwrung with anxiety for the moral welfare of her wayward child. But anon her humility catches a new tint, and we find it pride; and so a vague unreality steals by degrees over all her most humanizing traits—we lose our confidence in all—and finally, like Undine, she disappoints us, and shows the dream-land origin and nature, when we were looking to behold a Christian.

There is rather more power, and better keeping, in the character of Dimmesdale. But here again we are cheated into a false regard and interest, partly perhaps by the associations thrown around him without the intention of the author, and possibly contrary to it, by our habitual respect for the sacred order, and by our faith in religion, where it has once been rooted in the heart. We are told repeatedly, that the Christian element yet pervades his character and guides his efforts; but it seems strangely wanting. "High aspirations for the welfare of his race, warm love of souls, pure sentiments, natural piety, strengthened by thought and study, and illuminated by revelation—all of which invaluable gold was little better than rubbish" to Roger Chillingworth, are little better than rubbish at all, for any use to be made of them in the story. Mere suffering, aimless and without effect for purification or blessing to the soul, we do not find in God's moral world. The sting that follows crime is most severe in the purest conscience and the tenderest heart, in mercy, not in vengeance, surely; and we can conceive of any cause constantly exerting itself without its appropriate effects, as soon as of a seven years' agony without penitence. But here every pang is wasted. A most obstinate and unhuman passion, or a most unwearying conscience it must be, neither being worn out, or made worse or better, by such a prolonged application of the scourge. Penitence may indeed be life-long; but as for this, we are to understand that there is no penitence about it. We finally get to be quite of the author's mind, that "the only truth that continued to give Mr. Dimmesdale a real existence on this earth, was the anguish in his inmost soul, and the undissembled expression of it in his aspect. Had he once found power to smile, and wear an aspect of gayety, there had been no such man." He duly exhales at the first gleam of hope, an uncertain and delusive beam, but fatal to his misty existence. From that time he is a fantasy, an opium dream, his faith a vapor, his reverence blasphemy, his charity mockery, his sanctity impurity, his love of souls a ludicrous impulse to teach little boys bad words; and nothing is left to bar the utterance of "a volley of good, round, solid, satisfactory, heaven-defying oaths," (a phrase which seems to smack its lips with a strange *goût!*) but good taste and the mere outward shell, "the buckramed habit of clerical decorum." The only conclusion is, that the shell never possessed any thing real, — never was the Rev. Arthur Dimmesdale, as we have foolishly endeavored to suppose; that he was but a changeling, or an imp in grave apparel, not an erring, and consequently suffering human being, with a heart still upright enough to find the burden of conscious unworthiness and undeserved praise more intolerable than open ignominy and shame, and refraining from relieving his withering conscience from its load of unwilling hypocrisy, if partly from fear, more from the wish to be yet an instrument of good to others, not an example of evil which should weaken their faith in religion. The closing scene, where the satanic phase of the character is again exchanged for the saintly, and the pillory platform is made the stage for a triumphant *coup de théatre*, seems to us more than a failure.

But Little Pearl — gem of the purest water — what shall we say of her? That if perfect truth to childish and human nature can make her a mortal, she is so; and immortal, if the highest creations of genius have any claim to immortality. Let the author throw what light he will upon her, from his magical prism, she retains her perfect and vivid human individuality. When he would have us call her elvish and implike, we persist in seeing only a capricious, roguish, untamed child, such as many a mother has looked upon with awe, and a feeling of helpless incapacity to rule. Every motion, every feature, every word and tiny shout, every naughty scream and wild laugh, come to us as if our very senses were conscious of them. The child is a true child, the only genuine and consistent mortal in the book; and wherever she crosses the dark and gloomy track of the story, she refreshes our spirit with pure truth and radiant beauty, and brings to grateful remembrance the like ministry of gladsome childhood, in some of the saddest scenes of actual life. We feel at once that the author must have a "Little Pearl" of his own, whose portrait, consciously or unconsciously, his pen sketches out. Not that we would deny to Mr. Hawthorne the power to call up any shape, angel or goblin, and present it before his readers in a striking and vivid light. But there is something more than imagination in the picture of "Little Pearl." The heart takes a part in it, and puts in certain inimitable touches of nature here and there, such as fancy never dreamed of, and only a long and loving observation of the ways of childhood could suggest. . . .

We know of no writer who better understands and combines the elements of the picturesque in writing than Mr. Hawthorne. His style may be compared to a sheet of transparent water, reflecting from its surface blue skies, nodding woods, and the smallest spray or flower that peeps over its grassy margin; while in its clear yet mysterious depths we espy rarer and stranger things, which we must dive for, if we would examine.

Whether they might prove gems or pebbles, when taken out of the fluctuating medium through which the sun-gleams reach them, is of no consequence to the effect. Every thing charms the eye and ear, and nothing looks like art and pains-taking. There is a naturalness and a continuous flow of expression in Mr. Hawthorne's books, that makes them delightful to read, especially in this our day, when the fear of triteness drives some writers, (even those who might otherwise avoid that reproach), to adopt an abrupt and dislocated style, administering to our jaded attention frequent thumps and twitches, by means of outlandish idioms and forced inversions, and now and then flinging at our heads an incomprehensible, break-jaw word, which uncivilized missile stuns us to a full stop, and an appeal to authority. No authority can be found, however, which affords any remedy or redress against determined outlaws. After bumping over "rocks and ridges, and gridiron bridges," in one of these prosaic latter-day omnibuses, how pleasant it is to move over flowery turf upon a spirited, but properly trained Pegasus, who occasionally uses his wings, and skims along a little above *terra firma*, but not with an alarming preference for cloudland or rarefied air. One cannot but wonder, by the way, that the master of such a wizard power over language as Mr. Hawthorne manifests should not choose a less revolting subject than this of the Scarlet Letter, to which fine writing seems as inappropriate as fine embroidery. The ugliness of pollution and vice is no more relieved by it than the gloom of the prison is by the rose tree at its door. There are some palliative expressions used, which cannot, even as a matter of taste, be approved.

Regarding the book simply as a picture of the olden time, we have no fault to find with costume or circumstance. All the particulars given us, (and he is not wearisomely anxious to multiply them to show his research), are in good keeping and perspective, all in softened outlines and neutral tint, except the ever fresh and unworn image of childhood, which stands out from the canvas in the gorgeously attired "Little Pearl." He forbears to mention the ghastly gallows-tree, which stood hard by the pillory and whipping-post, at the city gates, and which one would think might have been banished with them from the precincts of Boston, and from the predilections of the community of whose opinions it is the focus. When a people have opened their eyes to the fact, that it is not the best way of discountenancing vice to harden it to exposure and shame, and make it brazen-faced, reckless, and impudent, they might also be convinced, it would seem, that respect for human life would not be promoted by publicly violating it, and making a spectacle, or a newspaper theme, of the mental agony and dying struggles of a human being, and of him least fit, in the common belief, to be thus hurried to his account. "Blood for blood!" We are shocked at the revengeful custom among uncivilized tribes, when it bears the aspect of private revenge, because the executioners must be of the kindred of the slain. How much does the legal retribution in kind, which civilized man exacts, differ in reality from the custom of the savage? The law undertakes to avenge its own dignity, to use a popular phrase; that is, it regards the community as one great family, and constitutes itself the avenger of blood in its behalf. It is not punishment, but retaliation, which does not contemplate the reform of the offender as well as the prevention of crime; and where it wholly loses the remedial element, and cuts off the opportunity for repentance which God's mercy allows, it is worthy of a barbarous, not a Christian, social alliance. What sort of combination for mutual safety is it, too, when no man feels safe, because fortuitous circumstances, ingeniously bound into a chain, may so entangle Truth that she cannot bestir herself to rescue us from the doom which the judgment of twelve fallible men pronounces, and our protector, the law, executes upon us?

But we are losing sight of Mr. Hawthorne's book, and of the old Puritan settlers, as he portrays them with few, but clearly cut and expressive, lines. In these sketchy groupings, Governor Bellingham is the only prominent figure, with the Rev. John Wilson behind him, "his beard, white as a snowdrift, seen over the Governor's shoulder."

> Here, to witness the scene which we are describing, sat Governor Bellingham himself, with four sergeants about his chair, bearing halberds as a guard of honor. He wore a dark feather in his hat, a border of embroidery on his cloak, and a black velvet tunic beneath; a gentleman advanced in years, and with a hard experience written in his wrinkles. He was not ill-fitted to be the head and representative of a community, which owed its origin and progress, and its present state of development, not to the impulses of youth, but to the stern and tempered energies of manhood, and the sombre sagacity of age; accomplishing so much, precisely because it imagined and hoped so little.

With this portrait, we close our remarks on the book, which we should not have criticized at so great length, had we admired it less. We hope to be forgiven, if in any instance our strictures have approached the limits of what may be considered personal. We would not willingly trench upon the right which an individual may claim, in common courtesy, not to have his private qualities or personal features discussed to his face, with everybody looking on. But Mr. Hawthorne's example in the preface, and the condescending familiarity of the attitude he assumes therein, are at once our occasion and our apology.

[An Unfit Subject for Literature]   Orestes Brownson*

Mr. Hawthorne is a writer endowed with a large share of genius, and in the species of literature he cultivates has no rival in this country, unless it be Washington Irving. His *Twice-told Tales*, his *Mosses from an Old Manse*, and other contributions to the periodical press, have made him familiarly known, and endeared him to a large circle of readers. The work before us is the largest and most elaborate of the romances he has as yet published, and no one can read half a dozen pages of it without feeling that none but a man of true genius and a highly cultivated mind could have written it. It is a work of rare, we may say of fearful power, and to the great body of our countrymen who have no well defined religious belief, and no fixed principles of virtue, it will be deeply interesting and highly pleasing.

We have neither the space nor the inclination to attempt an analysis of Mr. Hawthorne's genius, after the manner of the fashionable criticism of the day. Mere literature for its own sake we do not prize, and we are more disposed to analyze an author's work than the author himself. Men are not for us mere psychological phenomena, to be studied, classed, and labelled. They are moral and accountable beings, and we look only to the moral and religious effect of their works. Genius perverted, or employed in perverting others, has no charms for us, and we turn away from it with sorrow and disgust. We are not among those who join in the worship of passion, or even of intellect. God gave us our faculties to be employed in his service, and in that of our fellow-creatures for his sake, and our only legitimate office as critics is to inquire, when a book is sent us for review, if its author in producing it has so employed them.

Mr. Hawthorne, according to the popular standard of morals in this age and this community, can hardly be said to pervert God's gifts, or to exert an immoral influence. Yet his work is far from being unobjectionable. The story is told with great naturalness, ease, grace, and delicacy, but it is a story that should not have been told. It is a story of crime, of an adulteress and her accomplice, a meek and gifted and highly popular Puritan minister in our early colonial days, — a purely imaginary story, though not altogether improbable. Crimes like the one imagined were not unknown even in the golden days of Puritanism, and are perhaps more common among the descendants of the Puritans than it is at all pleasant to believe; but they are not fit subjects for popular literature, and moral health is not promoted by leading the imagination to dwell on them. There is an unsound state of public morals when the novelist is permitted, without a scorching rebuke, to select such crimes, and invest them with all the fascinations of genius, and all the charms of a highly polished style. In

*Reprinted from *Brownson's Quarterly Review* 4, no. 4 (October 1850):528–32.

a moral community such crimes are spoken of as rarely as possible, and when spoken of at all, it is always in terms which render them loathsome, and repel the imagination.

Nor is the conduct of the story better than the story itself. The author makes the guilty parties suffer, and suffer intensely, but he nowhere manages so as to make their sufferings excite the horror of his readers for their crime. The adulteress suffers not from remorse, but from regret, and from the disgrace to which her crime has exposed her, in her being condemned to wear emblazoned on her dress the Scarlet Letter which proclaims to all the deed she has committed. The minister, her accomplice, suffers also, horribly, and feels all his life after the same terrible letter branded on his heart, but not from the fact of the crime itself, but from the consciousness of not being what he seems to the world, from his having permitted the partner in his guilt to be disgraced, to be punished, without his having the manliness to avow his share in the guilt, and to bear his share of the punishment. Neither ever really repents of the criminal deed; nay, neither ever regards it as really criminal, and both seem to hold it to have been laudable, because they *loved* one another, — as if the love itself were not illicit, and highly criminal. No man has the right to love another man's wife, and no married woman has the right to love any man but her husband. Mr. Hawthorne in the present case seeks to excuse Hester Prynne, a married woman, for loving the Puritan minister, on the ground that she had no love for her husband, and it is hard that a woman should not have some one to love; but this only aggravated her guilt, because she was not only forbidden to love the minister, but commanded to love her husband, whom she had vowed to love, honor, cherish, and obey. The modern doctrine that represents the affections as fatal, and wholly withdrawn from voluntary control, and then allows us to plead them in justification of neglect of duty and breach of the most positive precepts of both the natural and the revealed law, cannot be too severely reprobated.

Human nature is frail, and it is necessary for every one who standeth to take heed lest he fall. Compassion for the fallen is a duty which we all owe, in consideration of our own failings, and especially in consideration of the infinite mercy our God has manifested to his erring and sinful children. But however binding may be this duty, we are never to forget that sin is sin, and that it is pardonable only through the great mercy of God, on condition of the sincere repentance of the sinner. But in the present case neither of the guilty parties repents of the sin, neither exclaims with the royal prophet, who had himself fallen into the sin of adultery and murder, *Misere mei Deus, secundum magnam misericordiam; et secundum multitudinem miserationum tuarum, dele iniquitatem meam. Amplius lava me ab iniquitate mea; et a peccato munda me. Quoniam iniquitatem meam cognosco, et peccatum meum contra me est semper.* They hug their illicit love; they cherish their sin; and after the lapse of seven years are ready, and actually agree, to depart into a foreign country, where they may indulge it without disguise and without restraint. Even to the last, even when the minister, driven by his agony, goes so far as to throw off the mask of hypocrisy, and openly confess his crime, he shows no sign of repentance, or that he regarded his deed as criminal.

The Christian who reads *The Scarlet Letter* cannot fail to perceive that the author is wholly ignorant of Christian asceticism, and that the highest principle of action he recognizes is pride. In both the criminals, the long and intense agony they are represented as suffering springs not from remorse, from the consciousness of having offended God, but mainly from the feeling, especially on the part of the minister, that they have failed to maintain the integrity of their character. They have lowered themselves in their own estimation, and cannot longer hold up their heads in society as honest people. It is not their conscience that is wounded, but their pride. *He* cannot bear to think that he wears a disguise, that he cannot be the open, frank, stainless character he had from his youth aspired to be, and *she*, that she is driven from society, lives a solitary outcast, and has nothing to console her but her fidelity to her paramour. There is nothing Christian, nothing really moral, here. The very pride itself is a sin; and pride often a greater sin than that which it restrains us from committing. There are thousands of men and women too proud to commit carnal sins, and to the indomitable pride of our Puritan ancestors we may attribute no small share of their external morality and decorum. It may almost be said, that, if they had less of that external morality and decorum, their case would be less desperate; and often the violation of them, or failure to maintain them, by which their pride receives a shock, and their self-complacency is shaken, becomes the occasion, under the grace of God, of their conversion to truth and holiness. As long as they maintain their self-complacency, are satisfied with themselves, and feel that they have outraged none of the decencies of life, no argument can reach them, no admonition can startle them, no exhortation can move them. Proud of their supposed virtue, free from all self-reproach, they are as placid as a summer morning, pass through life without a cloud to mar their serenity, and die as gently and as sweetly as the infant falling asleep in its mother's arms. We have met with these people, and after laboring in vain to waken them to a sense of their actual condition, till completely discouraged, we have been tempted to say, Would that you might commit some overt act, that should startle you from your sleep, and make you feel how far pride is from being either a virtue, or the safeguard of virtue, — or convince you of your own insufficiency for yourselves, and your absolute need of Divine grace. Mr. Hawthorne seems never to have learned that pride is not only sin, but the root of all sin, and that humility is not only a virtue, but the root of all virtue. No genuine contrition or repentance ever springs from pride, and the sorrow for sin because it mortifies our pride, or lessens us in our own eyes, is nothing but the effect of pride. All true remorse, all genuine repentance, springs from humility, and is sorrow for having offended God, not sorrow for having offended ourselves.

Mr. Hawthorne also mistakes entirely the effect of Christian pardon upon the interior state of the sinner. He seems entirely ignorant of the religion that can restore peace to the sinner, — true, inward peace, we mean. He would persuade us, that Hester had found pardon, and yet he shows us that she had found no inward peace. Something like this is common among popular Protestant writers, who, in speaking of great sinners among Catholics that have made themselves monks or hermits to expiate their sins by devoting themselves to prayer, and mortification, and the duties of religion, represent them as always devoured by remorse, and suffering in their interior agony almost the pains of the damned. An instance of this is the Hermit of Engeddi in Sir Walter Scott's *Talisman*. These men know nothing either of true remorse, or of the effect of Divine pardon. They draw from their imagination, enlightened, or rather darkened, by their own experience. Their speculations are based on the supposition that the sinner's remorse is the effect of wounded pride, and that during life the wound can never be healed. All this is false. The remorse does not spring from wounded pride, and the greatest sinner who really repents, who really does penance, never fails to find interior peace. The mortifications he practises are not prompted by his interior agony, nor designed to bring peace to his soul; they are a discipline to guard against his relapse, and an expiation that his interior peace already found, and his overflowing love to God for his superabounding mercy, lead him to offer to God, in union with that made by his blessed Lord and Master on the cross.

Again, Mr. Hawthorne mistakes the character of confession. He does well to recognize and insist on its necessity; but he is wrong in supposing that its office is simply to disburden the mind by communicating its secrets to another, to restore the sinner to his self-complacency, and to relieve him from the charge of cowardice and hypocrisy. Confession is a duty we owe to God, and a means, not of restoring us to our self-complacency, but of restoring us to the favor of God, and reëstablishing us in his friendship. The work before us is full of mistakes of this sort, in those portions where the author really means to speak like a Christian, and therefore we are obliged to condemn it, where we acquit him of all unchristian intention.

As a picture of the old Puritans, taken from the position of a moderate transcendentalist and liberal of the modern school, the work has its merits; but as little as we sympathize with those stern old Popery-haters, we do not regard the picture as at all just. We should commend where the author condemns, and condemn where he commends. Their treatment of the adulteress was far more Christian than his ridicule of it. But enough of fault-finding, and as we have no praise, except what we have given, to offer, we here close this brief notice.

[A "Compromise of . . . Literary Character"]

Arthur Cleveland Coxe*

As yet our literature, however humble, is undefiled, and as such is a just cause for national pride, nor, much as we long to see it elevated in style, would we thank the Boccaccio who should give it the classic stamp, at the expense of its purity. Of course we cannot expect to see it realize that splendid ideal which a thoughtful Churchman would sketch for it, as equally chaste in morals, lofty in sentiment, uncorrupt in diction, and in all points conformable to truth; but surely we may demand that it shall keep itself from becoming an offence to faith, and a scandal to virtue. Not that we expect the literary pimp to cease from his disgusting trade, but that we hope to keep writers of that class out of the pale of Letters, and to effect the forcible expulsion of any one of a higher class, who, gaining upon our confidence by dealing at first in a sterling article, afterwards debases his credit, by issuing with the same stamp a vile, but marketable, alloy. In a word, we protest against any toleration to a popular and gifted writer, when he perpetuates bad morals. Let this brokerage of lust be put down at the very beginning. Already, among the million, we have imitations enough of George Sand and Eugene Sue; and if as yet there be no reputable name, involved in the manufacture of a Brothel Library, we congratulate the country that we are yet in time to save such a reputation as that of Hawthorne. Let him stop where he has begun, lest we should be forced to select an epitaph from *Hudibras*, for his future memorial:

> Quoth he—for many years he drove
> A kind of broking trade in love,
> Employed in all th' intrigues and trust
> Of feeble, speculative lust;
> Procurer to th' extravaganzy
> And crazy ribaldry of fancy.

It is chiefly, in hopes, to save our author from embarking largely into this business of Fescennine romance, that we enter upon a brief examination of his latest and most ambitious production, *The Scarlet Letter*.

The success which seems to have attended this bold advance of Hawthorne, and the encouragement which has been dealt out by some professed critics,[1] to its worst symptoms of malice prepense, may very naturally lead, if unbalanced by a moderate dissent, to his further compromise of his literary character. We are glad, therefore, that *The Scarlet Letter* is, after all, little more than an experiment, and need not be regarded as a step necessarily fatal. It is an attempt to rise from the composition of petty tales, to the historical novel; and we use the expression *an attempt*, with no disparaging significance, for it is confes-

*Reprinted from *Church Review* 3 (January 1851):489–511.

sedly a trial of strength only just beyond some former efforts, and was designed as part of a series. It may properly be called a novel, because it has all the ground-work, and might have been very easily elaborated into the details, usually included in the term; and we call it *historical*, because its scene-painting is in a great degree true to a period of our Colonial history, which ought to be more fully delineated. We wish Mr. Hawthorne would devote the powers which he only partly discloses in this book, to a large and truthful portraiture of that period, with the patriotic purpose of making us better acquainted with the stern old worthies, and all the *dramatis personæ* of those times, with their yet surviving habits, recollections, and yearnings, derived from maternal England. Here is, in fact, a rich and even yet an unexplored field for historic imagination; and touches are given in *The Scarlet Letter*, to secret springs of romantic thought, which opened unexpected and delightful episodes to our fancy, as we were borne along by the tale. Here a maiden reminiscence, and here a grave ecclesiastical retrospection, clouding the brow of the Puritan colonists, as they still remembered home, in their wilderness of lasting exile! Now a lingering relic of Elizabethan fashion in dress, and now a turn of expression, betraying the deep traces of education under influences renounced and foresworn, but still instinctively prevalent!

Time has just enough mellowed the facts, and genealogical research has made them just enough familiar, for their employment as material for descriptive fiction; and the New England colonies might now be made as picturesquely real to our perception, as the Knickerbocker tales have made the Dutch settlements of the Hudson. This, however, can never be done by the polemical pen of a blind partisan of the Puritans; it demands Irving's humorously insinuating gravity and all his benevolent satire, with a large share of honest sympathy for at least the earnestness of wrong-headed enthusiasm. We are stimulated to this suggestion by the very lifelike and striking manner in which the days of Governor Winthrop are sketched in the book before us, by the beautiful picture the author has given us of the venerable old pastor Wilson, and by the outline portraits he has thrown in, of several of their contemporaries. We like him, all the better for his tenderness of the less exceptionable features of the Puritan character; but we are hardly sure that we like his flings at their failings. If it should provoke a smile to find us sensitive in this matter, our consistency may be very briefly demonstrated. True, we have our own fun with the follies of the Puritans; it is our inseparable privilege as Churchmen, thus to compensate ourselves for many a scar which their frolics have left on our comeliness. But when a degenerate Puritan, whose Socinian conscience is but the skimmed-milk of their creamy fanaticism, allows such a conscience to curdle within him, in dyspeptic acidulation, and then belches forth derision at the sour piety of his forefathers — we snuff at him, with an honest scorn, knowing very well that he likes the Puritans for their worst enormities, and hates them only for their redeeming merits.

The Puritan rebelling against the wholesome discipline of that Ecclesiastical Law, which Hooker has demonstrated, with Newtonian evidence, to be but a moral system of central light with its dependent order and illumination; the Puritan with his rough heel and tough heart, mounted upon altars, and hacking down crosses, and sepulchres, and memorials of the dead; the Puritan with his axe on an Archbishop's neck, or holding up in his hand the bleeding head of a martyred king; the Puritan in all this guilt, has his warmest praise, and his prompt witness that he allows the deeds of his fathers, and is ready to fill up the measure of their iniquity; but the Puritans, with a blessed inconsistency, repeating liturgic doxologies to the triune GOD, or, by the domestic hearth, bowing down with momentary conformity, to invoke the name of Jesus, whom the Church had taught him to adore as an atoning Saviour—these are the Puritans at whom the driveller wags his head, and shoots out his tongue! We would not laugh in that man's company. No—no! we heartily dislike the Puritans, so far as they were Puritan; but even in them we recognize many good old English virtues, which Puritanism could not kill. They were in part our ancestors, and though we would not accept the bequest of their enthusiasm, we are not ashamed of many things to which they clung, with principle quite as characteristic. We see no harm in a reverent joke now and then, at an abstract Puritan, in spite of our duty to our progenitors, and *Hudibras* shall still be our companion, when, at times, the mental bow requires fresh elasticity, and bids us relax its string. There is, after all, something of human kindness, in taking out an old grudge in the comfort of a hearty, side-shaking laugh, and we think we are never freer from bitterness of spirit, than when we contemplate the Banbury zealot hanging his cat on Monday, and reflect that Strafford and Montrose fell victims to the same mania that destroyed poor puss. But there is another view of the same Puritan, which even a Churchman may charitably allow himself to respect, and when precisely that view is chosen by his degenerate offspring for unfilial derision, we own to a sympathy for the grim old Genevan features, at which their seventh reproduction turns up a repugnant nose; for sure we are that the young Ham is gloating over his father's nakedness, with far less of sorrow for the ebriety of a parent, than of satisfaction in the degradation of an orthodox patriarch. Now without assserting that it is so, we are not quite so sure, as we would like to be, that our author is not venting something of this spirit against the Puritans, in his rich delineation of "godly Master Dimmesdale," and the sorely abused confidence of his flock. There is a provoking concealment of the author's motive, from the beginning to the end of the story; we wonder what he would be at; whether he is making fun of all religion, or only giving a fair hint of the essential sensualism of enthusiasm. But, in short, we are astonished at the kind of incident which he has selected for romance. It may be such incidents were too common, to be wholly out of the question, in a history of the times, but it seems to us that good taste might be pardoned for not giving them prominence in fiction. In deference to the assertions of a very acute analyst, who has written ably on the subject of colonization, we are inclined to think, as we have said before, that barbarism was indeed "the first danger" of the pilgrim settlers. Of a period nearly cotemporary with that of Mr. Hawthorne's narrative, an habitual eulogist has recorded that "on going to its Church and court records, we discover mournful evidences of incontinence, even in the respectable families; as if, being cut off from the more refined pleasures of society, their baser passions had burnt away the restraints of delicacy, and their growing coarseness of manners had allowed them finally to seek, in these baser passions, the spring of their enjoyments." We are sorry to be told so, by so unexceptionable a witness.[2] We had supposed, with the Roman satirist, that purity might at least be credited to those primitive days, when a Saturnian simplicity was necessarily revived in primeval forests, by the New England colonists:

> Quippe aliter tunc orbe novo, cœloque recenti
> Vivebant homines:

but a Puritan doctor in divinity publishes the contrary, and a Salemite novelist selects the intrigue of an adulterous minister, as the groundwork of his ideal of those times! We may acknowledge, with reluctance, the historical fidelity of the picture, which retailers of fact and fiction thus concur in framing, but we cannot but wonder that a novelist should select, of all features of the period, that which reflects most discredit upon the cradle of his country, and which is in itself so revolting, and so incapable of receiving decoration from narrative genius.

And this brings inquiry to its point. Why has our author selected such a theme? Why, amid all the suggestive incidents of life in a wilderness; of a retreat from civilization to which, in every individual case, a thousand circumstances must have concurred to reconcile human nature with estrangement from home and country; or amid the historical connections of our history with Jesuit adventure, savage invasion, regicide outlawry, and French aggression, should the taste of Mr. Hawthorne have preferred as the proper material for romance, the nauseous amour of a Puritan pastor, with a frail creature of his charge, whose mind is represented as far more debauched than her body? Is it, in short, because a running undertide of filth has become as requisite to a romance, as death in the fifth act to a tragedy? Is the French era actually begun in our literature? And is the flesh, as well as the world and the devil, to be henceforth dished up in fashionable novels, and discussed at parties, by spinsters and their beaux, with as unconcealed a relish as they give to the vanilla in their ice cream? We would be slow to believe it, and we hope our author would not willingly have it so, yet we honestly believe that *The Scarlet Letter* has already done not a little to degrade our literature, and to encourage social licentiousness: it has started other pens on like enterprises, and has loosed the restraint of many tongues, that have made it an apology for "the evil communications which corrupt good manners." We are painfully tempted to believe that it is a book made for the market, and that the market has made it merchantable, as they do game, by letting everybody understand that the commodity is in high condition, and smells strongly of incipient putrefaction.

We shall entirely mislead our reader if we give him to suppose that *The Scarlet Letter* is coarse in its details, or indecent in its phraseology. This very article of our own, is far less suited to ears polite, than any page of the romance before us; and the reason is, we call things by their right names, while the romance never hints the shocking words that belong to its things, but, like Mephistopheles, insinuates that the arch-fiend himself is a very tolerable sort of person, if nobody would call him Mr. Devil. We have heard of persons who could not bear the reading of some Old Testament Lessons in the service of the Church: such persons would be delighted with our author's story; and damsels who shrink at the reading of the Decalogue, would probably luxuriate in bathing their imagination in the crystal of its delicate sensuality. The language of our author, like patent blacking, "would not soil the whitest linen," and yet the composition itself, would suffice, if well laid on, to Ethiopize the snowiest conscience that ever sat like a swan upon that mirror of heaven, a Christian maiden's imagination. We are not sure we speak quite strong enough, when we say, that we would much rather listen to the coarsest scene of Goldsmith's *Vicar*, read aloud by a sister or daughter, than to hear from such lips, the perfectly chaste language of a scene in *The Scarlet Letter*, in which a married wife and her reverend paramour, with their unfortunate offspring, are introduced as the actors, and in which the whole tendency of the conversation is to suggest a sympathy for their sin, and an anxiety that they may be able to accomplish a successful escape beyond the seas, to some country where their shameful commerce may be perpetuated. Now, in Goldsmith's story there are very coarse words, but we do not remember anything that saps the foundations of the moral sense, or that goes to create unavoidable sympathy with unrepenting sorrow, and deliberate, premeditated sin. The *Vicar of Wakefield* is sometimes coarsely virtuous, but *The Scarlet Letter* is delicately immoral.

There is no better proof of the bad tendency of a work, than some unintentional betrayal on the part of a young female reader, of an instinctive consciousness against it, to which she has done violence, by reading it through. In a beautiful region of New England, where stage-coaches are not yet among things that were, we found ourselves, last summer, one of a travelling party, to which we were entirely a stranger, consisting of young ladies fresh from boarding-school, with the proverbial bread-and-butter look of innocence in their faces, and a nursery thickness about their tongues. Their benevolent uncle sat outside upon the driver's box, and ours was a seat next to a worshipful old dowager, who seemed to bear some matronly relation to the whole coach-load, with the single exception of ourselves. In such a situation it was ours to keep silence, and we soon relapsed into nothingness and a semi-slumberous doze. Meanwhile our young friends were animated and talkative, and as we were approaching the seat of a College, their literature soon began to expose itself. They were evidently familiar with the Milliners' Magazines in general, and even with Graham's and Harper's. They had read James, and they had read Dickens; and at last their criticisms rose to Irving and Walter Scott, whose various merits they discussed with an artless anxiety to settle for ever the question whether the one was not "a charming composer," and the other "a truly beautiful writer." Poor girls! had they imagined how much harmless amusement they were furnishing to their drowsy, dusty, and very unentertaining fellow traveller, they might, quite possibly, have escaped both his praise and his censure! They came at last to Longfellow and Bryant, and rhythmically regaled us with the "muffled drum" of the one, and the somewhat familiar opinion of the other, that

"Truth crushed to earth will rise again."

And so they came to Hawthorne, of whose *Scarlet Letter* we then knew very little, and that little was favourable, as we had seen several high encomiums of its style. We expected a quotation from the *Celestial Railroad*, for we were travelling at a rate which naturally raised the era of railroads in one's estimation, by rule of contrary; but no — the girls went straight to *The Scarlet Letter*. We soon discovered that one Hester Prynne was the heroine, and that she had been made to stand in the pillory, as, indeed, her surname might have led one to anticipate. We discovered that there was a mysterious little child in the question, that she was a sweet little darling, and that her "sweet, pretty little name," was "Pearl." We discovered that mother and child had a meeting, in a wood, with a very fascinating young preacher, and that there was a hateful creature named Chillingworth, who persecuted the said preacher, very perseveringly. Finally, it appeared that Hester Prynne was, in fact, Mrs. Hester Chillingworth, and that the hateful old creature aforesaid had a very natural dislike to the degradation of his spouse, and quite as natural a hatred of the wolf in sheep's clothing who had wrought her ruin. All this leaked out in conversation, little by little, on the hypothesis of our protracted somnolency. There was a very gradual approximation to the point, till one inquired — "didn't you think, from the first, that he was the one?" A modest looking creature, who evidently had not read the story, artlessly inquired — "what one?" — and then there was a titter at the child's simplicity, in the midst of which we ventured to be quite awake, and to discover by the scarlet blush that began to circulate, that the young ladies were not unconscious to themselves that reading *The Scarlet Letter* was a thing to be ashamed of. These school-girls had, in fact, done injury to their young sense of delicacy, by devouring such a dirty story; and after talking about it before folk, inadvertently, they had enough of mother Eve in them, to know that they were ridiculous, and that shame was their best retreat.

Now it would not have been so if they had merely exhibited a familiarity with *The Heart of Mid-Lothian*, and yet there is more mention of the foul sin in its pages, than there is in *The Scarlet Letter*. Where then is the difference? It consists in this—that the holy innocence of Jeanie Deans, and not the shame of Effie, is the burthen of that story, and that neither Effie's fall is made to look like virtue, nor the truly honourable agony of her stern old father, in bewailing his daughter's ruin, made a joke, by the insinuation that it was quite gratuitous. But in Hawthorne's tale, the lady's frailty is philosophized into a natural and necessary result of the Scriptural law of marriage, which, by holding her irrevocably to her vows, as plighted to a dried up old book-worm, in her silly girlhood, is viewed as making her heart an easy victim to the adulterer. The sin of her seducer too, seems to be considered as lying not so much in the deed itself, as in his long concealment of it, and, in fact, the whole moral of the tale is given in the words—"Be true—be true," as if sincerity in sin were virtue, and as if "Be clean—be clean," were not the more fitting conclusion. "The untrue man" is, in short, the hang-dog of the narrative, and the unclean one is made a very interesting sort of a person, and as the two qualities are united in the hero, their composition creates the interest of his character. Shelley himself never imagined a more dissolute conversation than that in which the polluted minister comforts himself with the thought, that the revenge of the injured husband is worse than his own sin in instigating it. "Thou and I never did so, Hester"—he suggests: and she responds—"never, never! What we did had. *a consecration of its own*, we felt it so—we said so to each other!" This is a little too much—it carries the Bay-theory a little too far for our stomach! "Hush, Hester!" is the sickish rejoinder; and fie, Mr. Hawthorne! is the weakest token of our disgust that we can utter. The poor bemired hero and heroine of the story should not have been seen wallowing in their filth, at such a rate as this.

We suppose this sort of sentiment must be charged to the doctrines enforced at "Brook-farm," although "Brook-farm" itself could never have been Mr. Hawthorne's home, had not other influences prepared him for such a Bedlam. At all events, this is no mere slip of the pen; it is the essential morality of the work. If types, and letters, and words can convey an author's idea, he has given us the key to the whole, in a very plain intimation that the Gospel has not set the relations of man and woman where they should be, and that a new Gospel is needed to supersede the seventh commandment, and the bond of Matrimony. Here it is, in full: our readers shall see what the world may expect from Hawthorne, if he is not stopped short, in such brotherly. Look at this conclusion:—

> *Women*—in the continually recurring trials of wounded, wasted,
> wronged, misplaced, or erring and sinful passion, or with the dreary

burden of a heart unyielded, because unvalued and unsought — came to Hester's cottage, demanding why they were so wretched, and what the remedy! Hester comforted and counselled them as best she might. She assured them too *of her firm belief,* that, at some brighter period, when the world should have grown ripe for it, in Heaven's own time, *a new truth would be revealed, in order to establish the whole relation between man and woman on a surer ground of mutual happiness.*

This is intelligible English; but are Americans content that such should be the English of their literature? This is the question on which we have endeavoured to deliver our own earnest convictions, and on which we hope to unite the suffrages of all virtuous persons in sympathy with the abhorrence we so unhesitatingly express. To think of making such speculations the amusement of the daughters of America! The late Convention of females at Boston, to assert the "rights of woman," may show us that there are already some, who think the world is even now *ripe for it*; and safe as we may suppose our own fair relatives to be above such a low contagion, we must remember that to a woman, the very suggestion of a mode of life for her, as preferable to that which the Gospel has made the glorious sphere of her duties and her joys, is an insult and a degradation, to which no one that loves her would allow her to be exposed.

We assure Mr. Hawthorne, in conclusion, that nothing less than an earnest wish that his future career may redeem this misstep, and prove a blessing to his country, has tempted us to enter upon a criticism so little suited to our tastes, as that of his late production. We commend to his attention the remarks of Mr. Alison, on cotemporary popularity, to be found in the review of Bossuet. We would see him, too, rising to a place amongst those immortal authors who have "clothed the lessons of religion in the burning words of genius;" and let him be assured, that, however great his momentary success, there is no lasting reputation for such an one as he is, except as it is founded on real worth, and fidelity to the morals of the Gospel. The time is past, when mere authorship provokes posthumous attention; there are too many who write with ease, and too many who publish books, in our times, for an author to be considered anything extraordinary. Poems perish in newspapers nowadays, which, at one time, would have made, at least, a name for biographical dictionaries; and stories lie dead in the pages of magazines, which would once have secured their author a mention with posterity. Hereafter those only will be thought of, who have embalmed their writings in the hearts and lives of a few, at least, who learned from them to love truth and follow virtue. The age of "mute inglorious Milton," is as dead as the age of chivalry. Everybody can write, and everybody can publish. But still, the wise are few; and it is only the wise, who can attain, in any worthy sense, to shine as the stars for ever.

Notes

1. See a later article in the *Massachusetts Quarterly.*
2. *Barbarism the first Danger*, by H. Bushnell, D.D.

Criticism to 1950

[The Scarlet Letter]   Henry James, Jr.*

The work has the tone of the circumstances in which it was produced. If Hawthorne was in a sombre mood, and if his future was painfully vague, *The Scarlet Letter* contains little enough of gaiety or of hopefulness. It is densely dark, with a single spot of vivid colour in it; and it will probably long remain the most consistently gloomy of English novels of the first order. But I just now called it the author's masterpiece, and I imagine it will continue to be, for other generations than ours, his most substantial title to fame. The subject had probably lain a long time in his mind, as his subjects were apt to do; so that he appears completely to possess it, to know it and feel it. It is simpler and more complete than his other novels; it achieves more perfectly what it attempts, and it has about it that charm, very hard to express, which we find in an artist's work the first time he has touched his highest mark — a sort of straightness and naturalness of execution, an unconsciousness of his public, and freshness of interest in his theme. It was a great success, and he immediately found himself famous. The writer of these lines, who was a child at the time, remembers dimly the sensation the book produced, and the little shudder with which people alluded to it, as if a peculiar horror were mixed with its attractions. He was too young to read it himself; but its title, upon which he fixed his eyes as the book lay upon the table, had a mysterious charm. He had a vague belief, indeed, that the "letter" in question was one of the documents that come by the post, and it was a source of perpetual wonderment to him that it should be of such an unaccustomed hue. Of course it was difficult to explain to a child the significance of poor Hester Prynne's blood-coloured A. But the mystery was at last partly dispelled by his being taken to see a collection of pictures (the annual exhibition of the National Academy), where he encountered a representation of a pale, handsome woman, in a quaint black dress and a white coif, holding between her knees an elfish-looking little girl, fantastically dressed, and crowned with flowers. Embroidered on the woman's breast was a great

*Reprinted in part from *Nathaniel Hawthorne* (New York: Harper and Brothers, 1879), 102–18.

crimson *A*, over which the child's fingers, as she glanced strangely out of the picture, were maliciously playing. I was told that this was Hester Prynne and little Pearl, and that when I grew older I might read their interesting history. But the picture remained vividly imprinted on my mind; I had been vaguely frightened and made uneasy by it; and when, years afterwards, I first read the novel, I seemed to myself to have read it before, and to be familiar with its two strange heroines. I mention this incident simply as an indication of the degree to which the success of *The Scarlet Letter* had made the book what is called an actuality. Hawthorne himself was very modest about it; he wrote to his publisher, when there was a question of his undertaking another novel, that what had given the history of Hester Prynne its "vogue" was simply the introductory chapter. In fact, the publication of *The Scarlet Letter* was in the United States a literary event of the first importance. The book was the finest piece of imaginative writing yet put forth in the country. There was a consciousness of this in the welcome that was given it — a satisfaction in the idea of America having produced a novel that belonged to literature, and to the forefront of it. Something might at last be sent to Europe as exquisite in quality as anything that had been received, and the best of it was that the thing was absolutely American; it belonged to the soil, to the air; it came out of the very heart of New England.

It is beautiful, admirable, extraordinary; it has in the highest degree that merit which I have spoken of as the mark of Hawthorne's best things — an indefinable purity and lightness of conception, a quality which in a work of art affects one in the same way as the absence of grossness does in a human being. His fancy, as I just now said, had evidently brooded over the subject for a long time; the situation to be represented had disclosed itself to him in all its phases. When I say in all its phases, the sentence demands modification; for it is to be remembered that if Hawthorne laid his hand upon the well-worn theme, upon the familiar combination of the wife, the lover, and the husband, it was, after all, but to one period of the history of these three persons that he attached himself. The situation is the situation after the woman's fault has been committed, and the current of expiation and repentance has set in. In spite of the relation between Hester Prynne and Arthur Dimmesdale, no story of love was surely ever less of a "love-story." To Hawthorne's imagination the fact that these two persons had loved each other too well was of an interest comparatively vulgar; what appealed to him was the idea of their moral situation in the long years that were to follow. The story, indeed, is in a secondary degree that of Hester Prynne; she becomes, really, after the first scene, an accessory figure; it is not upon her the *dénoûment* depends. It is upon her guilty lover that the author projects most frequently the cold, thin rays of his fitfully-moving lantern, which makes here and there a little luminous circle, on the edge of which hovers the livid and sinister figure of the injured and retributive husband. The story goes on, for the most part,

between the lover and the husband—the tormented young Puritan minister, who carries the secret of his own lapse from pastoral purity locked up
beneath an exterior that commends itself to the reverence of his flock,
while he sees the softer partner of his guilt standing in the full glare of
exposure and humbling herself to the misery of atonement—between this
more wretched and pitiable culprit, to whom dishonour would come as a
comfort and the pillory as a relief, and the older, keener, wiser man, who,
to obtain satisfaction for the wrong he has suffered, devises the infernally
ingenious plan of conjoining himself with his wronger, living with him,
living upon him; and while he pretends to minister to his hidden ailment
and to sympathise with his pain, revels in his unsuspected knowledge of
these things, and stimulates them by malignant arts. The attitude of Roger
Chillingworth, and the means he takes to compensate himself—these are
the highly original elements in the situation that Hawthorne so ingeniously
treats. None of his works are so impregnated with that after-sense of the
old Puritan consciousness of life to which allusion has so often been made.
If, as M. Montégut says, the qualities of his ancestors *filtered* down
through generations into his composition, *The Scarlet Letter* was, as it
were, the vessel that gathered up the last of the precious drops. And I say
this not because the story happens to be of so-called historical cast, to be
told of the early days of Massachusetts, and of people in steeple-crowned
hats and sad-coloured garments. The historical colouring is rather weak
than otherwise; there is little elaboration of detail, of the modern realism
of research; and the author has made no great point of causing his figures
to speak the English of their period. Nevertheless, the book is full of the
moral presence of the race that invented Hester's penance—diluted and
complicated with other things, but still perfectly recognisable. Puritanism, in a word, is there, not only objectively, as Hawthorne tried to place
it there, but subjectively as well. Not, I mean, in his judgment of his
characters in any harshness of prejudice, or in the obtrusion of a moral
lesson; but in the very quality of his own vision, in the tone of the picture,
in a certain coldness and exclusiveness of treatment.

The faults of the book are, to my sense, a want of reality and an abuse
of the fanciful element—of a certain superficial symbolism. The people
strike me not as characters, but as representatives, very picturesquely
arranged, of a single state of mind; and the interest of the story lies, not in
them, but in the situation, which is insistently kept before us, with little
progression, though with a great deal, as I have said, of a certain stable
variation; and to which they, out of their reality, contribute little that
helps it to live and move. I was made to feel this want of reality, this over-
ingenuity, of *The Scarlet Letter*, by chancing not long since upon a novel
which was read fifty years ago much more than to-day, but which is still
worth reading—the story of *Adam Blair*, by John Gibson Lockhart. This
interesting and powerful little tale has a great deal of analogy with
Hawthorne's novel—quite enough, at least, to suggest a comparison

between them; and the comparison is a very interesting one to make, for it speedily leads us to larger considerations than simple resemblances and divergences of plot. . . .

In *The Scarlet Letter* there is a great deal of symbolism; there is, I think, too much. It is overdone at times, and becomes mechanical; it ceases to be impressive, and grazes triviality. The idea of the mystic *A* which the young minister finds imprinted upon his breast and eating into his flesh, in sympathy with the embroidered badge that Hester is con- demned to wear, appears to me to be a case in point. This suggestion should, I think, have been just made and dropped; to insist upon it and return to it, is to exaggerate the weak side of the subject. Hawthorne returns to it constantly, plays with it, and seems charmed by it; until at last the reader feels tempted to declare that his enjoyment of it is puerile. In the admirable scene, so superbly conceived and beautifully executed, in which Mr. Dimmesdale, in the stillness of the night, in the middle of the sleeping town, feels impelled to go and stand upon the scaffold where his mistress had formerly enacted her dreadful penance, and then, seeing Hester pass along the street, from watching at a sick-bed, with little Pearl at her side, calls them both to come and stand there beside him — in this masterly episode the effect is almost spoiled by the introduction of one of these superficial conceits. What leads up to it is very fine — so fine that I cannot do better than quote it as a specimen of one of the striking pages of the book.

> But before Mr. Dimmesdale had done speaking, a light gleamed far and wide over all the muffled sky. It was doubtless caused by one of those meteors which the nightwatcher may so often observe burning out to waste in the vacant regions of the atmosphere. So powerful was its radiance that it thoroughly illuminated the dense medium of cloud betwixt the sky and earth. The great vault brightened, like the dome of an immense lamp. It showed the familiar scene of the street with the distinctness of mid-day, but also with the awfulness that is always imparted to familiar objects by an unaccustomed light. The wooden houses, with their jutting stories and quaint gable-peaks; the doorsteps and thresholds, with the early grass springing up about them; the garden-plots, black with freshly-turned earth; the wheel-track, little worn, and, even in the market-place, margined with green on either side; — all were visible, but distinct and tantalising manner, estranged from Pearl; as if the child, in her lonely ramble through the forest, had strayed out of the sphere in which she and her mother dwelt together, and was now vainly seeking to return to it.

And Hawthorne devotes a chapter to this idea of the child's having, by putting the brook between Hester and herself, established a kind of spiritual gulf, on the verge of which her little fantastic person innocently mocks at her mother's sense of bereavement. This conception belongs, one would say, quite to the lighter order of a story-teller's devices, and the reader hardly goes with Hawthorne in the large development he gives to it. He hardly goes with him either, I think, in his extreme predilection for a small number of vague ideas which are represented by such terms as "sphere" and "sympathies." Hawthorne makes too liberal a use of these two substantives; it is the solitary defect of his style; and it counts as a defect partly because the words in question are a sort of specialty with certain writers immeasurably inferior to himself.

I had not meant, however, to expatiate upon his defects, which are of the slenderest and most venial kind. *The Scarlet Letter* has the beauty and harmony of all original and complete conceptions, and its weaker spots, whatever they are, are not of its essence; they are mere light flaws and inequalities of surface. One can often return to it; it supports familiarity, and has the inexhaustible charm and mystery of great works of art. It is admirably written. Hawthorne afterwards polished his style to a still higher degree; but in his later productions — it is almost always the case in a writer's later productions — there is a touch of mannerism. In *The Scarlet Letter* there is a high degree of polish, and at the same time a charming freshness; his phrase is less conscious of itself. His biographer very justly calls attention to the fact that his style was excellent from the beginning; that he appeared to have passed through no phase of learning how to write, but was in possession of his means, from the first, of his handling a pen. His early tales, perhaps, were not of a character to subject his faculty of expression to a very severe test; but a man who had not Hawthorne's natural sense of language would certainly have contrived to write them less well. This natural sense of language — this turn for saying things lightly and yet touchingly, picturesquely yet simply, and for infusing a gently colloquial tone into matter of the most unfamiliar import — he had evidently cultivated with great assiduity. I have spoken of the anomalous character of his Note-Books — of his going to such pains often to make a record of incidents which either were not worth remembering, or could be easily remembered without its aid. But it helps us to understand the Note-Books if we regard them as a literary exercise. They were compositions, as school-boys say, in which the subject was only the pretext, and the main point was to write a certain amount of excellent English. Hawthorne must at least have written a great many of these things for practice, and he must often have said to himself that it was better practice to write about trifles, because it was a greater tax upon one's skill to make them interesting. And his theory was just, for he has almost always made his trifles interesting. In his novels his art of saying things well is very positively tested; for here he treats of those matters among which it is very easy for a blundering writer to go wrong — the subtleties and mysteries of life, the moral and spiritual maze. . . .

Hawthorne's Hester Prynne   William Dean Howells*

From the first there is no affectation of shadowy uncertainty in the setting of the great tragedy of "The Scarlet Letter." As nearly as can be, the scenes of the several events are ascertained, and are identified with places in actual Boston. With a like inward sense of strong reality in his material, and perhaps compelled to its expression by that force in the concept, each detail of the drama, in motive, action, and character, is substantiated, so that from first to last it is visible, audible, tangible. From Hester Prynne in her prison — before she goes out to stand with her unlawful child in her arms and the scarlet letter on her breast before the Puritan magistracy and ministry and people, and be charged by the child's own father, as her pastor, to give him up to like ignominy — to Hester Prynne, kneeling over her dying paramour, on the scaffold, and mutely helping him to own his sin before all that terrible little world, there is the same strong truth beating with equal pulse from the core of the central reality, and clothing all its manifestations in the forms of credible, of indisputable personality.

In its kind the romance remains sole, and it is hard to see how it shall ever be surpassed, or even companioned. It is not without faults, without quaint foibles of manner which strike one oddly in the majestic movement of the story; but with the exception of the love-child or sin-child, Pearl, there is no character, important or unimportant, about which you are asked to make believe: they are all there to speak and act for themselves, and they do not need the help of your fancy. They are all of a verity so robust that if one comes to declare Hester chief among them, it is with instant misgivings for the right of her secret paramour, Arthur Dimmesdale, and her secret husband, Roger Chillingworth, to that sorrowful supremacy. A like doubt besets the choice of any one moment of her history as most specific, most signal. Shall it be that dread moment on the pillory, when she faces the crowd with her child in her arms, and her lover adjures her to name its father, while her old husband on the borders of the throng waits and listens?

> The Rev. Mr. Dimmesdale bent his head, in silent prayer, as it seemed, and then came forward. "Hester Prynne," said he, leaning over the balcony and looking down steadfastly into her eyes, . . . "if thou feelest it to be for thy soul's peace, and that thy earthly punishment will thereby be made more effectual to salvation, I charge thee to speak out the name of thy fellow-sinner and fellow-sufferer! Be not silent from any mistaken pity and tenderness for him; for, believe me, Hester, though he were to step down from a high place, and stand there beside thee, on thy pedestal of shame, yet better were it so, than to hide a guilty heart through life. . . . Heaven hath granted thee an open ignominy, that

---

*Reprinted in part from *Heroines of Fiction*, vol. 1 (New York and London: Harper and Brothers, 1901):161–74.

thereby thou mayest work out an open triumph over the evil within thee, and the sorrow without. Take heed how thou deniest to him — who, perchance, hath not the courage to grasp it for himself — the bitter, but wholesome, cup that is now presented to thy lips!" The young pastor's voice was tremulously sweet, rich, deep, and broken. The feeling that it so evidently manifested, rather than the direct purport of the words, caused it to vibrate within all hearts, and brought the listeners into one accord of sympathy. Even the poor baby, at Hester's bosom, was affected by the same influence; for it directed its hitherto vacant gaze towards Mr. Dimmesdale, and held up its little arms, with a half-pleased, half-plaintive murmur. . . . Hester shook her head. "Woman, transgress not beyond the limits of Heaven's mercy!" cried the Rev. Mr. Wilson, more harshly than before. . . . "Speak out the name! That, and thy repentance, may avail to take the scarlet letter off thy breast." "Never!" replied Hester Prynne, looking, not at Mr. Wilson, but into the deep and troubled eyes of the younger clergyman. "It is too deeply branded. Ye cannot take it off. And would that I might endure his agony, as well as mine!" "Speak, woman!" said another voice, coldly and sternly, proceeding from the crowd about the scaffold. "Speak; and give your child a father!" "I will not speak!" answered Hester, turning pale as death, but responding to this voice, which she too surely recognized. "And my child must seek a heavenly Father; she shall never know an earthly one!" "She will not speak!" murmured Mr. Dimmesdale, who, leaning over the balcony, with his hand upon his heart, had awaited the result of his appeal. He now drew back, with a long respiration. "Wondrous strength and generosity of a woman's heart! She will not speak!"

One could hardly read this aloud without some such gasp and catch as must have been in the minister's own breath as he spoke. Yet piercing as the pathos of it is, it wants the ripened richness of anguish, which the passing years of suffering bring to that meeting between Hester Prynne and Arthur Dimmesdale in the forest, when she tells him that his physician and closest companion is her husband, and that Chillingworth's subtlety has divined the minister's relation to herself and her child. The reader must go to the book itself for a full comprehension of the passage, but no one can fail of its dramatic sense who recalls that Hester has by this time accustomed the little Puritan community to the blazon of her scarlet letter, and in her lonely life of usefulness has conciliated her fellow-townsfolk almost to forgiveness and forgetfulness of her sin. She has gone in and out among them, still unaccompanied, but no longer unfriended, earning her bread with her needle and care of the sick, and Dimmesdale has held aloof from her like the rest, except for their one meeting by midnight, when he stands with her and their child upon the scaffold, and in that ghastly travesty forecasts the union before the people which forms the catastrophe of the tremendous story.

In certain things "The Scarlet Letter," which was the first of Hawthorne's romances, is the modernest and maturest. The remoteness of the time and the strangeness of the Puritan conditions authorize that stateliness of the dialogue which he loved. The characters may imaginably say "methinks" and "peradventure," and the other things dear to the characters of the historical romancer; the narrator himself may use an antiquated or unwonted phrase in which he finds color, and may eschew the short-cuts and informalities of our actual speech, without impeaching himself of literary insincerity. In fact, he may heighten by these means the effect he is seeking; and if he will only keep human nature strongly and truly in mind, as Hawthorne does in "The Scarlet Letter," we shall gratefully allow him a privilege which may or may not be law. Through the veil of the quaint parlance, and under the seventeenth-century costuming, we see the human heart beating there the same as in our own time and in all times, and the antagonistic motives working which have governed human conduct from the beginning and shall govern it forever, world without end.

Hester Prynne and Arthur Dimmesdale are no mere types of open shame and secret remorse. It is never concealed from us that he was a man whose high and pure soul had its strongest contrast in the nature

Mixt with cunning sparks of hell,

in which it was tabernacled for earth. It is still less hidden that, without one voluntary lure or wicked art, she was of a look and make to win him with the love that was their undoing. "He was a person of a very striking aspect, with a wide, lofty, and impending brow; large, brown, melancholy eyes, and a mouth which, unless he compressed it, was apt to be tremulous. . . . The young woman was tall, with a figure of perfect elegance on a large scale. She had dark and abundant hair, so glossy that it threw off the sunshine with a gleam, and a face which, besides being beautiful from the regularity of feature and richness of complexion, had the impressiveness belonging to a marked brow and deep black eyes. She was ladylike, too, after the manner of the feminine gentility of those days; characterized by a certain state and dignity, rather than by the delicate, evanescent, and indescribable grace which is now recognized as its indication." They were both of their time and place, materially as well as spiritually; their lives were under the law, but their natures had once been outside it, and might be again. The shock of this simple truth can hardly be less for the witness, when, after its slow and subtle evolution, it is unexpectedly flashed upon him, than it must have been for the guilty actors in this drama, when they recognize that, in spite of all their open and secret misery, they are still lovers, and capable of claiming for the very body of their sin a species of justification.

We all know with what rich but noiseless preparation the consummate artist sets the scene of his most consummate effect; and how, when Hester and Pearl have parted with Roger Chillingworth by the shore, and then parted with each other in the forest, the mother to rest in the shadow of the trees, and the child to follow her fancies in play, he invokes the presence of Arthur Dimmesdale, as it were, silently, with a waft of the hand. . . .

There is a greatness in this scene which is unmatched, I think, in the book, and, I was almost ready to say, out of it. At any rate, I believe we can find its parallel only in some of the profoundly impassioned pages of the Russian novelists who, casting aside all the common adjuncts of art, reveal us to ourselves in the appeal from their own naked souls. Hawthorne had another ideal than theirs, and a passing love of style, and the meaning of the music of words. For the most part, he makes us aware of himself, of his melancholy grace and sombre power; we feel his presence in every passage, however deeply, however occultly, dramatic; he over-shadows us, so that we touch and see through him. But here he is almost out of it; only a few phrases of comment, so fused in feeling with the dialogue that they are like the voice of a chorus, remind us of him.

It is the most exalted instant of the tragedy, it is the final evolution of Hester Prynne's personality. In this scene she dominates by virtue of whatever is womanly and typical in her, and no less by what is personal and individual. In what follows, she falls like Dimmesdale and Chil-lingworth under the law of their common doom, and becomes a figure on the board where for once she seemed to direct the game.

In all fiction one could hardly find a character more boldly, more simply, more quietly imagined. She had done that which in the hands of a feeble or falser talent would have been suffered or made to qualify her out of all proportion and keeping with life. But her transgression does not qualify her, as transgression never does unless it becomes habit. She remains exterior and superior to it, a life of other potentialities, which in her narrow sphere she fulfils. What she did has become a question between her and her Maker, who apparently does not deal with it like a Puritan. The obvious lesson of the contrasted fates of Dimmesdale and herself is that to own sin is to disown it, and that it cannot otherwise be expropriated and annulled. Yet, in Hester's strong and obstinate endur-ance of her punishment there is publicity but not confession; and perhaps there is a lesson of no slighter meaning in the inference that ceasing to do evil is, after all, the most that can be asked of human nature. Even that seems to be a good deal, and in "The Scarlet Letter" it is a stroke of mastery to show that it is not always ours to cease to do evil, but that in extremity we need the help of the mystery "not ourselves, that makes for righteousness," and that we may call Chance or that we may call God, but that does not change in essence or puissance whatever name we give it.

[Concealment in *The Scarlet Letter*]

William Cary Brownell*

"The Scarlet Letter" is not merely a masterpiece, it is a unique book. It does not belong in the populous category with which its title superficially associates it, and the way in which Hawthorne lifts it out of this and — without losing his hold of a theme that from the beginnings of literature has, in the work of the greatest masters as well as in that of the most sordid practitioners, demonstrated its vitality and significance — nevertheless, conducts its development in a perfectly original way, is indisputable witness of the imaginative power he possessed but so rarely exercised. So multifariously has the general theme that the scarlet letter symbolizes been treated in all literatures and by all "schools" from the earliest to the latest, that however its inexhaustibility may be thus attested — an inexhaustibility paralleled by that of the perennial instinct with which it deals — any further treatment of it must forego, one would have said, the element of novelty, at least. Hawthorne's genius is thus to be credited even in this respect with a remarkable triumph. But that it should not only have thus won a triumph of originality by eluding instead of conquering the banality of the theme — by taking it in a wholly novel way, that is to say — but have produced, in its new departure, a masterpiece of beauty and power, is an accomplishment of accumulated distinction. "The Scarlet Letter," in short, is not only an original work in a field where originality is the next thing to a miracle, but a work whose originality is in no wise more marked than its intrinsic substance.

It is not a story of adultery. The word does not, I think, occur in the book — a circumstance in itself typifying the detachment of the conception and the delicate art of its execution. But in spite of its detachment and delicacy, the inherent energy of the theme takes possession of the author's imagination and warms it into exalted exercise, making it in consequence at once the most real and the most imaginative of his works. It is essentially a story neither of the sin nor of the situation of illicit love — presents neither its psychology nor its social effects; neither excuses nor condemns nor even depicts, from this specific point of view. The love of Hester and Dimmesdale is a postulate, not a presentment. Incidentally, of course, the sin colors the narrative, and the situation is its particular result. But, essentially, the book is a story of concealment. Its psychology is that of the concealment of sin amid circumstances that make a sin of concealment itself. The sin itself might, one may almost say, be almost any other. And this constitutes no small part of the book's formal originality.

*Reprinted in part from *American Prose Masters*, ed. Howard M. Jones (Cambridge: The Belknap Press of Harvard University Press, 1967; original printing by Scribner, 1909), 80–84, by permission of the publisher.

To fail to perceive this is quite to misconceive it. As a story of illicit love its omissions are too great, its significance is not definite enough, its detail has not enough richness, the successive scenes of which it is composed have not an effective enough cohesion. From this point of view, but for the sacred profession of the minister and the conduct this imposes, it would be neither moving nor profound. Its moral would not be convincing. Above all, Chillingworth is a mistake, or at most a wasted opportunity. For he is specialized into a mere function of malignity, and withdrawn from the reader's sympathies, whereas what completes, if it does not constitute, the tragedy of adultery, is the sharing by the innocent of the punishment of the guilty. This inherent element of the situation, absolutely necessary to a complete presentment of it, the crumbling of the innocent person's inner existence, is absolutely neglected in "The Scarlet Letter," and the element of a malevolent persecution of the culpable substituted for it. The innocent person thereby becomes, as I have already said, a device, and though in this way Hawthorne is enabled to vivify the effect of remorse upon the minister by personifying its furies, in this way, too, he sacrifices at once the completeness of his picture and its depth of truth by disregarding one of its most important elements.

He atones for this by concentration on the culpable. It is *their* psychology alone that he exhibits. And though in this way he has necessarily failed to write the *chef-d'œuvre* of the general subject that in the field of art has been classic since monogamy established itself in society, he has produced a perfect masterpiece in the more detached and withdrawn sphere more in harmony with his genius. In narrowing his range and observing its limits he has perhaps even increased the poignancy of his effect. And his effect *is* poignant and true as reality itself. In confining himself to the concealment of sin rather than depicting its phenomena and its results, he has indeed brought out, as has never been done elsewhere, the importance of this fatal increment of falsity among the factors of the whole chaotic and unstable moral equilibrium. Concealment in "The Scarlet Letter," to be sure, is painted in very dark colors. In similar cases it may be a duty, and is, at all events, the mere working of a natural instinct — at worst a choice of the lesser evil. But surely there is no exaggeration or essential loss of truth in the suggestion of its potentialities for torture conveyed by the agony of the preacher's double life. It is true his concealment condemned another to solitary obloquy. But if that be untypically infrequent and also not inherent in the situation as such, it is fairly counterbalanced by consolatory thought of the exceptional havoc confession would have wrought in his case. That is to say, if his remorse is exceptionally acute it is also exceptionally alleviated. On the whole the potential torture of remorse for a life that is flagrantly an acted lie is not misrepresented, either in truth or art, by the fate of Dimmesdale, though it is treated in the heightened way appropriate to the typical.

Concentration upon concealment further contributes to the originality and the perfection of "The Scarlet Letter" by eliminating passion. The sensuous element which might have served to extenuate the offence — since it is of its tragic essence that nothing can excuse it in anything like normal conditions — or if not that to render the story attractive and affecting, is rigidly excluded. There is more sensuousness sighed forth by the unhappy pair[1] of the famous fifth canto of the "Inferno" than in the whole volume. There is but a single reference to the days when Hester and her lover "read no further," and this, though a kindly and catholic touch, is characteristically a moral one.

> With sudden and desperate tenderness she threw her arms around him and pressed his head against her bosom; little caring though his cheek rested on the scarlet letter. . . .
> "Never, never," whispered she. "What we did had a consecration of its own. We felt it so! We said so to each other! Hast thou forgotten it?"
> "Hush, Hester!" said Arthur Dimmesdale, rising from the ground. "No; I have not forgotten."[2]

There is no sensuous, scarcely even an emotional, digression from the steady conduct of the theme. The chill of destiny is sensible even in the chapter called almost mockingly "A Flood of Sunshine," and at the end to the dying minister only doubt redeems eternity itself from despair:

> "Hush, Hester, hush!" said he, with tremulous solemnity. "The law we broke! — the sin here so awfully revealed! — let these alone be in thy thoughts! I fear! I fear! It may be that when we forgot our God — when we violated our reverence each for the other's soul — it was henceforth vain to hope that we could meet hereafter, in an everlasting and pure reunion. God knows: and He is merciful."[3]

To this New England "Faust" there is no "second part." The sombre close, the scarcely alleviated gloom of the whole story are in fit keeping with the theme, — which is the truth that, in the words of the tale itself, "an evil deed invests itself with the character of doom" — and with its development through the torture of concealment to the expiation of confession.

Here, for once, with Hawthorne we have allegory richly justifying itself, the allegory of literature not that of didacticism, of the imagination not of the fancy, allegory neither vitiated by caprice nor sterilized by moralizing, but firmly grounded in reality and nature. Note how, accordingly, even the ways of the wicked fairy that obsessed him are made to serve him, for even the mirage and symbolism so dear to his mind and so inveterate in his practice, blend legitimately with the pattern of his thoroughly naturalistic fabric. The fanciful element is, at least, so imaginatively treated as to seem, exceptionally, to "belong." Hawthorne seems to have been so "possessed" by his story as to have conducted the development of its formal theme for once subconsciously, so to speak, and with the result of decorating rather than disintegrating reality in its exposition. At all events, to this "possession" (how complete it was in material fact all his biographers attest) two notable and wholly exceptional results are due. In the first place he *felt* his theme, as he never felt it elsewhere, and consequently presented it with an artistic cogency he never elsewhere attained. The story, in other words, is real and true. If it is thought to show a bias in pushing too far the doom of evil, to ignore the whole New Testament point of view, as it may be called, epitomized in the Master's "Go and sin no more,"[4] the answer is that though in this way it may lose in typical value, it gains in imaginative realism, since it is a story of that Puritan New England where it sometimes seems as if the New Testament had been either suspect or unknown. Besides, there is enough demonstration of its text on the hither side of what it is necessary to invoke the Puritan *milieu* to justify. Every erring soul may not suffer the extremity of Dimmesdale's agony, but it suffers enough, and the inevitability of its suffering was never more convincingly exhibited than in this vivid picture, softened as it is into a subdued intensity by the artist's poetized, however predetermined, treatment. For, in the second place, it is here alone that Hawthorne seems to have felt his *characters* enough to feel them sympathetically and so to realize them to the full. They are very real and very human. What the imagination of a recluse, even, can do to this end when held to its own inspiration and not seduced into the realm of the fantastic, may be seen in the passage where Hester pleads for the continued custody of her child. Pearl herself is a jewel of romance. Nothing more imaginatively real than this sprite-like and perverse incarnation of the moral as well as physical sequence of her parents' sin exists in romance. Her individuality is an inspiration deduced with the logic of nature and with such happy art that her symbolic quality is as incidental in appearance as it is seen to be inherent on reflection. Mr. James, who objects to the symbolism of "The Scarlet Letter,"[5] nevertheless found her substantial enough to echo in the charming but far less vivid Pansy of his "Portrait of a Lady." Chillingworth, the other symbolic character, is in contrast an embodied abstraction—the one piece of machinery of the book. But it cannot be denied that he performs a needful function and, artistically, is abundantly justified. As a Puritan parallel of Mephistopheles he is very well handled. "The Scarlet Letter" is, in fact, the Puritan "Faust," and its symbolic and allegorical element, only obtrusive in a detail here and there at most, lifts it out of the ordinary category of realistic romance without— *since nothing of importance is sacrificed to it*—enfeebling its imaginative reality. The beautiful and profound story is our chief prose masterpiece and it is as difficult to overpraise it as it is to avoid poignantly regretting that Hawthorne failed to recognize its value and learn the lesson it might have taught him.

Notes

1. I.e., Paolo and Francesca.
2. *The Scarlet Letter*, in *Writings*, VI, 281–82.
3. *The Scarlet Letter*, VI, 371–72.
4. John 8:11.
5. James, *Hawthorne*, p. 113.

Scarlet A Minus   Frederic I. Carpenter*

From the first *The Scarlet Letter* has been considered a classic. It has appealed not only to the critics but to the reading public as well. The young Henry James described the feeling of mystery and terror which it aroused in his childish mind — a feeling not easily definable, but reaching to the depths of his nature. The scarlet letter has seemed the very symbol of all sin, translating into living terms the eternal problem of evil. And in 1850 the book was timely as well as timeless: it specifically suggested the nineteenth-century answer to the eternal problem. "Sin" might sometimes be noble, and "virtue" ignoble. Rousseau himself might have defined the scarlet letter as the stigma which society puts upon the natural instincts of man.

But in modern times *The Scarlet Letter* has come to seem less than perfect. Other novels, like *Anna Karenina*, have treated the same problem with a richer humanity and a greater realism. If the book remains a classic, it is of a minor order. Indeed, it now seems not quite perfect even of its own kind. Its logic is ambiguous, and its conclusion moralistic. The ambiguity is interesting, of course, and the moralizing slight, but the imperfection persists.

In one sense the very imperfection of *The Scarlet Letter* makes it classic: its ambiguity illustrates a fundamental confusion in modern thought. To the question "Was the action symbolized by the scarlet letter wholly sinful?" it suggests a variety of answers: "Yes," reply the traditional moralists; "Hester Prynne broke the Commandments." But the romantic enthusiasts answer: "No; Hester merely acted according to the deepest of human instincts." And the transcendental idealists reply: "In part; Hester truly sinned against the morality which her lover believed in, but did not sin against her own morality, because she believed in a 'higher law.' To her own self, Hester Prynne remained true."

From the perspective of a hundred years we shall reconsider these three answers to the problem of evil suggested by *The Scarlet Letter*. The traditional answer remains clear, but the romantic and the idealistic have

*Reprinted from *College English* 5 (January 1944):173–80, by permission of the journal.

usually been confused. Perhaps the imperfection of the novel arises from Hawthorne's own confusion between his heroine's transcendental morality and mere immorality. Explicitly, he condemned Hester Prynne as immoral; but implicitly, he glorified her as courageously idealistic. And this confusion between romantic immorality and transcendental idealism has been typical of the genteel tradition in America.

I

According to the traditional moralists, Hester Prynne was truly a sinful woman. Although she sinned less than her hypocritical lover and her vengeful husband, she nevertheless sinned; and, from her sin, death and tragedy resulted. At the end of the novel, Hawthorne himself positively affirmed this interpretation:

> Earlier in life, Hester had vainly imagined that she herself might be the destined prophetess, but had long since recognized the impossibility that any mission of divine and mysterious truth should be confided to a woman stained with sin.

And so the traditional critics have been well justified. *The Scarlet Letter* explicitly approves the tragic punishment of Hester's sin and explicitly declares the impossibility of salvation for the sinner.

But for the traditionalists there are many kinds and degrees of sin, and *The Scarlet Letter*, like Dante's *Inferno*, describes more than one. According to the orthodox, Hester Prynne belongs with the romantic lovers of the *Inferno*, in the highest circle of Hell. For Hester sinned only through passion, but her lover through passion and concealment, and her husband through "violating, in cold blood, the sanctity of the human heart."[1] Therefore, Hester's sin was the least, and her punishment the lightest.

But Hester sinned, and, according to traditional Puritanism, this act shut her off forever from paradise. Indeed, this archetypal sin and its consequent tragedy have been taken to symbolize the eternal failure of the American dream. Hester suggests "the awakening of the mind to 'moral gloom' after its childish dreams of natural bliss are dissipated."[2] Thus her lover, standing upon the scaffold, exclaimed: "Is this not better than we dreamed of in the forest?" And Hawthorne repeated that Hester recognized the eternal justice of her own damnation. The romantic dream of natural freedom has seemed empty to the traditionalists, because sin and its punishment are eternal and immutable.

That Hester's sin was certain, and her dream of freedom impossible, traditional Catholicism has also agreed. But the Catholic critics object that Hawthorne's Puritanism denies the Christian doctrine of the forgiveness of sin. They believe that Hester expiated her evil by means of repentance and a virtuous later life. "Hester represents the repentant sinner, Dimmesdale the half-repentant sinner, and Chillingworth the unrepentant sinner."[3] Therefore, Hester individually achieved salvation, even though her sin was clear and her dream of universal freedom impossible.

But all the traditionalists agree that Hester's action was wholly sinful. That Hester herself never admitted this accusation and that Hester is never represented as acting blindly in a fit of passion and that Hester never repented of her "sin" are facts which the traditionalists overlook. Moreover, they forget that Hawthorne's condemnation of Hester's sin is never verified by Hester's own words. But of this more later.

Meanwhile, other faults in Hester's character are admitted by the traditional and the liberal alike. Even if she did not do what *she* believed to be evil, Hester nevertheless did tempt her lover to do what *he* believed to be evil and thus caused his death. And because she wished to protect her lover, she consented to a life of deception and concealment which she herself knew to be false. But for the traditional moralists neither her temptation of her lover nor her deception of him was a cardinal sin. Only her act of passion was.

Therefore Hester's passion was the fatal flaw which caused the tragedy. Either because of some womanly weakness which made her unable to resist evil, or because of some pride which made her oppose her own will to the eternal law, she did evil. Her sin was certain, the law she broke was immutable, and the human tragedy was inevitable — according to the traditional moralists.

II

But, according to the romantic enthusiasts, *The Scarlet Letter* points a very difficult moral. The followers of Rousseau have said that Hester did not sin at all; or that, if she did, she transformed her sin into a virtue. Did not Hawthorne himself describe the radiance of the scarlet letter, shining upon her breast like a symbol of victory? "The tendency of her fate had been to set her free. The scarlet letter was her passport into regions where other women dared not tread." Hester — if we discount Hawthorne's moralistic conclusion — never repented of her "sin" of passion, because she never recognized it as such.

In absolute contrast to the traditionalists, the romantics have described *The Scarlet Letter* as a masterpiece of "Hawthorne's immoralism."[4] Not only Hester but even the Puritan minister becomes "an amoralist and a Nietzschean."[5] "In truth," wrote Hawthorne, "nothing short of a total change of dynasty and moral code in that interior kingdom was adequate to account for the impulses now communicated to the. . . . minister." But Hester alone became perfectly immoral, for "the world's law was no law for her mind." She alone dared renounce utterly the dead forms of tradition and dared follow the natural laws of her own instinctive nature to the end.

Therefore, the romantics have praised *The Scarlet Letter* for preaching *"la mystique de l'Amour."*[6] And especially the French critics, following D. H. Lawrence, have spoken of Hawthorne's "gospel of love." "Hester gave everything to love,"[7] they have repeated:

> Give all to love;
> Obey thy heart;
> Friends, kindred, days,
> Estate, good-fame,
> Plans, credit and the Muse, —
> Nothing refuse.

As Emerson counseled, so Hester acted. In spite of Hawthorne's moralistic disclaimer, his heroine has seemed to renounce traditional morality and to proclaim the new morality of nature and the human heart.

Therefore, according to the romantics, the tragedy of *The Scarlet Letter* does not result from any tragic flaw in the heroine, for she is romantically without sin. It results, rather, from the intrinsic evil of society. Because the moral law imposes tyrannical restraints upon the natural instincts of man, human happiness is impossible in civilization. *The Scarlet Letter*, therefore, becomes the tragedy of perfection, in which the ideal woman is doomed to defeat by an inflexible moral tradition. Because Hester Prynne was so perfectly loyal and loving that she would never abandon her lover, she was condemned by the Puritans. Not human frailty, therefore, or any tragic imperfection of character, but only the inevitable forces of social determinism caused the disaster described by *The Scarlet Letter* — according to the romantic enthusiasts.

III

Between the orthodox belief that Hester Prynne sinned utterly and the opposite romantic belief that she did not sin at all, the transcendental idealists seek to mediate. Because they deny the authority of the traditional morality, these idealists have sometimes seemed merely romantic. But because they seek to describe a new moral law, they have also seemed moralistic. The confusion of answers to the question of evil suggested by *The Scarlet Letter* arises, in part, from a failure to understand the transcendental ideal.

With the romantics, the transcendentalists[8] agree that Hester did wisely to "give all to love." But they insist that Hester's love was neither blindly passionate nor purposeless. "What we did," Hester exclaims to her lover, "had a consecration of its own." To the transcendental, her love was not sinful because it was not disloyal to her evil husband (whom she had never loved) or to the traditional morality (in which she had never believed). Rather her love was purposefully aimed at a permanent union with her lover — witness the fact that it had already endured through seven years of separation and disgrace. Hester did well to "obey her heart," because she felt no conflict between her heart and her head. She was neither romantically immoral nor blindly rebellious against society and its laws.

This element of conscious purpose distinguishes the transcendental Hester Prynne from other, merely romantic heroines. Because she did not deny "the moral law" but went beyond it to a "higher law," Hester transcended both romance and tradition. As if to emphasize this fact, Hawthorne himself declared that she "assumed a freedom of speculation which our forefathers, had they known it, would have held to be a deadlier crime than that stigmatized by the scarlet letter." Unlike her lover, she had explicitly been led "beyond the scope of generally received laws." She had consciously wished to become "the prophetess" of a more liberal morality.

According to the transcendentalists, therefore, Hester's "sin" was not that she broke the Commandment — for, in the sight of God, she had never truly been married. Nor was Hester the blameless victim of society, as the romantics believed. She had sinned in that she had deceived her lover concerning the identity of her husband. And she admitted this clearly.

> "O Arthur," cried she, "forgive me! In all things else, I have striven to be true! Truth was the one virtue to which I might have held fast, and did hold fast, through all extremity; save when thy good. . . . were put in question! Then I consented to a deception. But a lie is never good, even though death threaten on the other side."

Not traditional morality, but transcendental truth, governed the conscience of Hester Prynne. But she had a conscience, and she had sinned against it.

Indeed, Hester Prynne had "sinned," exactly *because* she put romantic "love" ahead of ideal "truth." She had done evil in allowing the "good" of her lover to outweigh the higher law. She had sacrificed her own integrity by giving absolutely everything to her loved one. For Emerson had added a transcendental postscript to his seemingly romantic poem:

> Leave all for love;
> Yet, hear me, yet. . . .
>
> Keep thee to-day,
> To-morrow, forever,
> Free as an Arab
> Of thy beloved.
>
> Heartily know
> When half-gods go,
> The gods arrive.

That is to say: True love is a higher law than merely traditional morality, but, even at best, human love is "daemonic." The highest law of "celestial love" is the law of divine truth.

According to the transcendental idealists, Hester Prynne sinned in that she did not go beyond human love. In seeking to protect her lover by deception, she sinned both against her own "integrity" and against God. If she had told the whole truth in the beginning, she would have been blameless. But she lacked this perfect self-reliance.

Nevertheless, tragedy would have resulted even if Hester Prynne had been transcendentally perfect. For the transcendental ideal implies tragedy. Traditionally, tragedy results from the individual imperfection of some hero. Romantically, it results from the evil of society. But, ideally, it results from a conflict of moral standards or values. The tragedy of *The Scarlet Letter* resulted from the conflict of the orthodox morality of the minister with the transcendental morality of the heroine. For Arthur Dimmesdale, unlike Hester Prynne, did sin blindly through passion, committing an act which he felt to be wrong. And because he sinned against his own morality, he felt himself unable to grasp the freedom which Hester urged. If, on the contrary, he had conscientiously been able to flee with her to a new life on the western frontier, there would have been no tragedy. But:

> "It cannot be!" answered the minister, listening as if he were called upon to realize a dream. "I am powerless to go. Wretched and sinful as I am, I have had no other thought than to drag on my earthly existence where Providence hath placed me."

To those who have never believed in it, the American dream of freedom has always seemed utopian and impossible of realization. Tragedy results from this conflict of moralities and this unbelief.

IV

According to the orthodox, Hester Prynne sinned through blind passion, and her sin caused the tragedy. According to the romantic, Hester Prynne heroically "gave all to love," and tragedy resulted from the evil of society. According to the transcendentalists, Hester Prynne sinned through deception, but tragedy resulted from the conflict of her dream of freedom with the traditional creed of her lover. Dramatically, each of these interpretations is possible: *The Scarlet Letter* is rich in suggestion. But Hawthorne the moralist sought to destroy this richness.

The Scarlet Letter achieves greatness in its dramatic, objective presentation of conflicting moralities in action: each character seems at once symbolic, yet real. But this dramatic perfection is flawed by the author's moralistic, subjective criticism of Hester Prynne. And this contradiction results from Hawthorne's apparent confusion between the romantic and the transcendental moralities. While the characters of the novel objectively act out the tragic conflict between the traditional morality and the transcendental dream, Hawthorne subjectively damns the transcendental for being romantically immoral.

Most obviously, Hawthorne imposed a moralistic "Conclusion" upon the drama which his characters had acted. But the artistic and moral falsity of this does not lie in its didacticism or in the personal intrusion of the author, for these were the literary conventions of the age. Rather it lies in the contradiction between the author's moralistic comments and the earlier words and actions of his characters. Having created living protagonists, Hawthorne sought to impose his own will and judgment upon them from the outside. Thus he described Hester as admitting her "sin" of passion and as renouncing her "selfish ends" and as seeking to "expiate" her crime. But Hester herself had never admitted to any sin other than deception and had never acted "selfishly" and had worn her scarlet letter triumphantly, rather than penitently. In his "Conclusion," therefore, Hawthorne did violence to the living character whom he had created.

His artificial and moralistic criticism is concentrated in the "Conclusion." But it also appears in other chapters of the novel. In the scene between Hester and Arthur in the forest, Hawthorne had asserted:

> She had wandered, without rule or guidance, in a moral wilderness. . . . Shame, Despair, Solitude! These had been her teachers, — stern and wild ones, — and they had made her strong, but taught her much amiss.

And again Hawthorne imputed "Shame" to Hester, and declared that her "strength" was immoral.

This scene between Hester and her lover in the forest also suggests the root of Hawthorne's confusion. To the traditional moralists, the "forest," or "wilderness," or "uncivilized Nature" was the symbolic abode of evil — the very negation of moral law. But to the romantics, wild nature had become the very symbol of freedom. In this scene, Hawthorne explicitly condemned Hester for her wildness — for "breathing the wild, free atmosphere of an unredeemed, unchristianized, lawless region." And again he damned her "sympathy" with "that wild, heathen Nature of the forest, never subjugated by human law, nor illumined by higher truth." Clearly he hated moral romanticism. And this hatred would have been harmless, if his heroine had merely been romantic, or immoral.

But Hester Prynne, as revealed in speech and in action, was not romantic but transcendental. And Hawthorne failed utterly to distinguish, in his moralistic criticism, between the romantic and the transcendental. For example, he never described the "speculations" of Hester concerning "freedom" as anything but negative, "wild," "lawless," and "heathen." All "higher truth" for him seemed to reside exclusively in traditional, "civilized" morality. But Hawthorne's contemporaries, Emerson and Thoreau, had specifically described the "wilderness" (*Life in the Woods*) as the precondition of the new morality of freedom; and "Nature" as the very abode of "higher truth": all those transcendental "speculations" which Hawthorne imputed to his heroine conceived of "Nature" as offering the opportunity for the realization of the higher moral law and for the development of a "Christianized" society more perfectly illumined by the divine truth.

Therefore, Hawthorne's moralistic passages never remotely admitted the possible truth of the transcendental ideal which he had objectively described Hester Prynne as realizing. Having allowed his imagination to create an idealistic heroine, he did not allow his conscious mind to justify — or even to describe fairly — her ideal morality. Rather, he damned the transcendental character whom he had created, for being romantic and immoral. But the words and deeds by means of which he had created her contradicted his own moralistic criticisms.

V

In the last analysis, the greatness of *The Scarlet Letter* lies in the character of Hester Prynne. Because she dared to trust herself and to believe in the possibility of a new morality in the new world, she achieved spiritual greatness in spite of her own human weakness, in spite of the prejudices of her Puritan society, and, finally, in spite of the prejudices of her creator himself. For the human weakness which made her deceive her lover in order to protect him makes her seem only the more real. The calm steadfastness with which she endures the ostracism of society makes her heroic. And the clear purpose which she follows, despite the denigrations of Hawthorne, makes her almost ideal.

Hester, almost in spite of Hawthorne, envisions the transcendental ideal of positive freedom, instead of the romantic ideal of mere escape. She urges her lover to create a new life with her in the wilderness: "Doth the universe lie within the compass of yonder town? Whither leads yonder forest track?" And she seeks to arouse him to a pragmatic idealism equal to the task: "Exchange this false life of thine for a true one! . . . Preach! Write! Act! Do anything save to lie down and die!"

Thus Hester Prynne embodies the authentic American dream of a new life in the wilderness of the new world, and of self-reliant action to realize that ideal. In the Puritan age in which he lived, and in Hawthorne's own nineteenth century, this ideal was actually being realized in practice. Even in our modern society with its more liberal laws, Hester Prynne might hope to live happily with her lover, after winning divorce from her cruel and vengeful husband. But in every century her tragedy would still be the same. It would result from her own deception and from the conflicting moral belief of her lover. But it would not result from her own sense of guilt or shame.

In *The Scarlet Letter* alone among his novels, Hawthorne succeeded in realizing a character embodying the authentic American dream of freedom and independence in the new world. But he succeeded in realizing this ideal emotionally rather than intellectually. And, having completed the novel, he wondered at his work: "I think I have never overcome my adamant in any other instance," he said. Perhaps he added the moralistic "Conclusion" and the various criticisms of Hester, in order to placate his conscience.[9] In any case, he never permitted himself such freedom — or such greatness — again.

Where *The Scarlet Letter* described the greatness as well as the human tragedy which lies implicit in the American dream of freedom, Hawthorne's later novels describe only the romantic delusion which often vitiates it. *The Blithedale Romance* emphasizes the delusion of utopianism, and *The Marble Faun* preaches the falsity of the ideal of "nature" (Donatello). Where Hester Prynne was heroically self-reliant, Zenobia becomes pathetically deluded, and Miram romantically blind. Hawthorne, rejecting the transcendental idealism which Hester Prynne seems to have realized almost in spite of his own "adamant," piously recanted in his "Conclusion" and took good care that his later "dark" heroines should be romantic, unsympathetic, and (comparatively) unimportant.

Notes

1. Cf. Austin Warren, *Hawthorne* (New York, 1934), p. xxxv.

2. H. W. Schneider, *The Puritan Mind* (New York, 1930), p. 259.

3. Yvor Winters, *Maule's Curse* (Norfolk, Conn., 1938), p. 16.

4. Régis Michaud, *The American Novel Today* (Boston, 1928), p. 36.

5. *Ibid.*, p. 44.

6. L. E. Chrétien, quoted in A. Warren, *Hawthorne*, p. lxxviii.

7. Michaud, *op. cit.*, p. 37.

8. Critics suggesting this "transcendental" point of view include the following: Moncure D. Conway, *Life of Nathaniel Hawthorne* (London, 1870); John Erskine, "Hawthorne," in *CHAL*, II, 16–31; and Stuart P. Sherman, "Hawthorne," in *Americans*, pp. 122–52.

9. Cf. Conway, *op. cit.*

Form and Content in
The Scarlet Letter   John C. Gerber*

In any competent literary work, we are often told, form and content are interdependent. And it is added, as a corollary, that the consistency and richness with which the two are adjusted to each other constitute the measure of artistic sophistication in the work. Our present interest is not so much with the theoretical possibilities of these two assertions as with their practical application to Hawthorne's *The Scarlet Letter*. For despite its early position in a substantial American literary tradition, the romance, when appraised by these standards, reveals itself to be a work of rather astonishing sophistication.

Some brief particularization is necessary for terms so general as "form" and "content." Form in *The Scarlet Letter* rises out of a basic division of the whole into four parts, each of which gains its distinctiveness from the character that precipitates or is responsible for the action that takes place within its limits.[1] Furthermore, the order of the parts is determined by the desires and capabilities of the characters. Thus the community, aside from the four main characters, is responsible for the action in the first part (Chapters i–viii); Chillingworth for that in the second (ix–xii); Hester for that in the third (xiii–xx); and Dimmesdale for that in the fourth (xxi–xxiv). Within each part, moreover, there is a noticeable division between cause and effect, between material dealing primarily with the activating agent and material dealing primarily with the person or persons acted upon.

Content in *The Scarlet Letter* consists of those three matters which dominate the thoughts and actions of the characters: sin, isolation, and reunion. Generally speaking, with Hawthorne isolation is inevitably the result of sin, and the desire for reunion is usually the result of isolation. But it is a mistake to suppose that any one of these terms can be employed successfully in a general sense. No one of them is constant in meaning throughout the book.

There is, for example, no such thing as uniformity in the concept of sin. To assume this is to confuse the characters and to misinterpret most of the important speeches. Sin in *The Scarlet Letter* is a violation of only that which the sinner *thinks* he violates. To one character, adultery is transgression against God's law, to another, no more than a violation of the natural order of things. Likewise, to one character hypocrisy is a violation of his own nature, to another, a transgression against the moral code of the community. To speak, therefore, even of adultery or hypocrisy without

*Reprinted from *New England Quarterly* 17 (March 1944):22–55, by permission of the author.

discovering what they mean to each individual is to become hopelessly confused about what Hawthorne is doing. Furthermore, as the nature of the sin differs, so must the nature of the isolation which is its result.

More than anything else, probably, *The Scarlet Letter* is a study of isolation.[2] And just as one cannot generalize about sin in the book, so is it impossible to speak of isolation as though it were always one and the same thing. When a character feels isolated, he feels isolated from someone or something. Isolation, therefore, is a feeling of estrangement from those persons or elements whose code the individual feels that he has violated. By this definition, the study of isolation in *The Scarlet Letter* becomes a matter not only of comparing characters but also of ascertaining the successive degrees of estrangement within a single character.

The problem of reunion is even more complex. Given a sinful act, the consequent chain of cause and effect is something like this: sin brings isolation, isolation creates suffering, and suffering brings the desire to alleviate one's condition through reunion with the element from which one is isolated. At this point, however, an interesting paradox becomes apparent. Reunion in *The Scarlet Letter* is at once both highly individualized and strictly conventionalized. It is individualized in the sense that a character's attempts at reunion are obviously the result of his particular sense of sin and isolation; it is conventionalized in that Hawthorne allows only one pattern for its successful accomplishment. This pattern has three components: a personal sense of responsibility, repentance, and penance.[3] The first of these is essential to the second and third but does not necessarily create them, as Dimmesdale's suffering bears witness. The second is of supreme importance but seldom occurs. In *The Scarlet Letter* there are only three examples of repentance, of which only the least important is presented in detail. The third, penance, is voluntary action designed totally to expiate the wrong. As such, it is not to be confused with the false type of penance which exists apart from repentance and which is wholly ineffectual. True penance must follow and be a manifestation of inward repentance. Ordinarily, it involves both confession and a plea for forgiveness. These, then, are the terms of reunion; and though isolation inevitably follows sin, reunion dispels isolation only when these terms are met.[4]

What should become progressively apparent in the following pages is that Hawthorne has so integrated form and content throughout *The Scarlet Letter* that they exist constantly in a state of interdependence. More specifically, he has so adjusted the two that in the first three parts of the book the activating character serves to multiply sin, intensify isolation, and diminish the hope of reunion. Only in the fourth does he allow the chief character, Dimmesdale, to reverse the process. How complex and yet precise is this adjustment can be realized only by a detailed examination of the book itself.

I

It is not surprising that Hawthorne should have the community directing events as the story opens. Indeed, once he has selected his main characters he can do little else, since none of them can logically create the social situation which is the necessary antecedent to the spiritual complication. Hester is indifferent to what the people think of her baby, Dimmesdale is afraid of what they think, and Chillingworth is too recent a newcomer to affect their thought. Hence, in no case can a social situation be forced unless the community forces it. When the story opens, therefore, the people of the town of Boston are the logical and necessary activators, and they remain such throughout the first eight chapters of the book.[5]

It is not entirely proper, however, to conceive of the community during this time as directly forcing the main characters into further sin. It does force isolation upon Hester. Otherwise, its function is to place the characters into such juxtaposition that new choices between good and evil must be made by each of them. If in every case the character chooses evil, the town can hardly be blamed except as an accessory before the fact. The rich irony of the situation is that the community while in the very act of abetting the spread of sin is complacently certain that it is stemming it.

Specifically, Boston places Hester upon the scaffold where she is seen and recognized by Chillingworth; it compels Dimmesdale to speak about Hester before the entire town, thereby forcing the issue of confession; it throws Hester and Chillingworth together in prison, where Chillingworth, because of his wife's distraught condition, is able to extract a vow to conceal his identity; it requires Hester to wear the scarlet letter; and through a threat against Pearl it brings the main characters together in a scene at the Governor's hall in which Dimmesdale unwittingly betrays his feelings to Chillingworth. The effect of these acts in terms of sin and isolation can best be observed by considering the characters separately.

No one of the three main characters comes into the story guiltless. Of the three, however, Hester has the misfortune of being the only one unable to hide her guilt, and so it is upon her that the penalties of the community fall. It is unnecessary to go into detail about her public humiliation or her subsequent life in the small cottage at the edge of town. What interests us is the reaction which this enforced estrangement has upon her. And to understand this, we must first understand Hester's own attitude toward her misstep.

In the first place, it is evident that Hester does not feel that she has sinned against God. Partly this is so because God has never been a very real presence in her life. But chiefly, we are led to infer, it is because she experiences no new sense of estrangement from Him as the result of her adultery. She attends church "trusting to share the Sabbath smile of the Universal father" and undoubtedly would do so were the minister able to refrain from making her the topic of his sermon. Moreover, though man has punished her for her sin, God has given her "a lovely child, whose place was on that same dishonored bosom, to connect her parent for ever with the race and descent of mortals, and to be finally a blessed soul in heaven!" God, then, has not looked with unkindness upon her deed.

Hester is certain, too, that she has violated no law of her own nature. She is by nature affectionate, even passionate. Her relation with Dimmesdale, consequently, has been the almost inescapable result of her own nature, not a violation of it. As a matter of fact, it is this same affection which now holds her to Boston, even though she concocts for her conscience a pleasantly moral half-truth that she is remaining in order to effect a purification of her soul. Hawthorne does not make all of this completely clear in the first eight chapters. But later, when Hester speaks of her deed as having a "consecration of its own," we can see how firmly she believes that her own nature and the deed have been in harmony.

In the third place, it is plain that Hester does not feel that she has sinned against the community. Indeed, from the very beginning it is evident that the selectmen's attempt to induce inward repentance by outward penance is to result in failure. For though Hester submits to the public exhibition and to the wearing of the scarlet letter, it is clear that her heart has not been touched. Even her dress on that first day seems to express "the desperate recklessness of her mood." With the passing of time, she tones down her dress and softens her attitude, but she continues to manifest rebellion in the bright and imaginative embroidery of the letter which the community intended as a heavy sign of guilt. Pearl, the other symbol of her error, she clothes in the gayest of colors. If any further evidence is needed, it is contained in the statement that she "was patient, — a martyr, indeed, — but she forebore to pray for her enemies; lest, in spite of her forgiving aspirations, the words of the blessing should stubbornly twist themselves into a curse." The plain truth of the matter is that Hester feels she has not sinned against the community, and therefore that the community has no right to inflict penalties. The only real result, then, of the community's action is to isolate Hester from her neighbors in spirit as well as in person.

Yet in spite of all this, Hester knows that her deed has been wrong and that, somehow, the result cannot be good. This is manifest in her anxiety for Pearl, whom she watches constantly, fearful of detecting some "dark and wild peculiarity." Soon she finds it in Pearl's waywardness and unpredictability.

> The child could not be made amenable to rules. In giving her existence, a great law had been broken; and the result was a being whose elements were perhaps beautiful and brilliant, but all in disorder; or with an order peculiar to themselves, amidst which the point of variety and arrangement was difficult or impossible to be discovered.

The great law which Hester feels she has broken, therefore, is the law of order. Not conscious of being a sinner in the orthodox sense of the word, she is nevertheless bitterly aware of the fact that she and Dimmesdale have introduced an act of disorder into an orderly universe. And being aware of this, she can realize that some estrangement from the natural course of life is her due. That this estrangement should be forcibly meted out by the community, however, she can logically resent as being cruelly irrelevant.

The first act of the community with regard to Hester is a distinct failure. Its second is just as wide the mark when, in an attempt to bring some peace to her spirit after her ordeal in the market-place, it makes future peace almost unattainable. For by introducing Chillingworth into her prison apartment, the community through its jailer can be held at least indirectly responsible for the vow of secrecy which Chillingworth is enabled to extract. By natural inclination, Hester scorns deception. Consequently, to have become partner to a plot which surrenders her lover to his worst enemy is for her to commit an act which ultimately she regards as an inexcusable violation of her nature.[6] The immediate result, of course, is to place an additional barrier between her and Dimmesdale; the ultimate result is to create that remorse which is a sign of division and estrangement within the soul.

Like Hester, Chillingworth does not come into the market-place of Boston guiltless. Formerly a brilliant and even kindly man, he erred first when he prevailed upon Hester to marry him. The nature of this act is plain to him. "Mine was the first wrong," he admits, "when I betrayed thy budding youth into a false and unnatural relation with my decay." With sure insight he is quick to see that out of this violation of the natural order only further falsity can result. "Nay, from the moment when we came down the old church steps together, a married pair, I might have beheld the bale-fire of that scarlet letter blazing at the end of our path!" But having admitted this responsibility, Chillingworth is unable or unwilling to go further.

Given the opportunity through the community's manipulation of events, Chillingworth chooses to intensify rather than to expiate his guilt. Hester he simply decides to ignore, and in so doing he sins again by setting up a relation which he, if forced, would have to admit to be false to his marriage vows and unnatural to human affection. To assert to Hester that "between thee and me, the scale hangs fairly balanced" is simply to deny the responsibility which he professed a moment before. One sin in Hawthorne's scheme never checks off another. Hester's lover, moreover, Chillingworth vows to have for himself. To achieve this, he must conceal his identity and thereby set up a false relation between himself and the community. In this fashion he prepares the ground for the "black flower" which is to be his third and greatest sin.

Dimmesdale is not a central figure in the first part of *The Scarlet Letter*; yet the effect of the community upon him is easily discernible and none the less profound. From the first it is obvious that Dimmesdale is a godly person. To his fellow townsmen he is their "godly pastor" or the "godly Master Dimmesdale." It is emphasized, moreover, that "so far as his duties would permit, he trod in the shadowy by-paths, and thus kept himself simple and child-like; coming forth, when occasion was, with a freshness, and fragrance, and dewy purity of thought, which, as many people said, affected them like the speech of an angel." It is not surprising, consequently, that when Dimmesdale finally comes to confess his act of adultery, he should consider it a violation of God's laws. This is, of course, anticipating a later part of the book, but the point to be made here is that when we first see Dimmesdale, we see a man already conscious of having sinned against his Lord. The resulting estrangement has already made its mark upon him.

Unfortunately for Dimmesdale, his sin cannot remain uncomplicated so long as he remains in Boston. For the righteous colony of Massachusetts is a place "where iniquity is dragged out into the sunshine." To hide one's sin is to violate the basic principle of the community's moral code. Thus is a new issue raised for the unhappy minister. To refrain from confessing his adultery is to add sin against the community to sin against God. The issue, in fact, is more than raised; it is forced home. In view of the entire town he is compelled by the Reverend Mr. Wilson to exhort Hester to reveal the identity of the baby's father. Thus, before the whole community, by failing to confess his guilt Dimmesdale breaks the community's cardinal precept. Like Hester and Chillingworth, he becomes twice the sinner and twice the outcast. This is a sorry result, indeed, for the activities of so godly a place as Boston in the seventeenth century!

II

The transition from the first to the second part of *The Scarlet Letter* is so sound in motivation and so subtle in presentation that the reader is likely to be unaware until pages later that a fundamental break in the book has been passed. It occurs in this way. At the conclusion of Chapter VIII, the Reverend Mr. Wilson, as spokesman for the community, closes the case of Boston *versus* the unknown lover of Hester Prynne. In turning down Chillingworth's request for further investigation he says:

> "Nay; it would be sinful, in such a question, to follow the clew of profane philosophy. Better to fast and pray upon it; and still better, it may be, to leave the mystery as we find it, unless Providence reveal it of its own accord. Thereby, every good Christian man hath a title to show a father's kindness towards the poor, deserted babe."

It is abundantly clear, however, that so charitable a disposition of the case is not acceptable to Chillingworth. Not only has he vowed to discover the identity of Hester's lover, but already his mind has been kindled by the possibilities of "a philosopher's research" into the mystery. Confronted with this double urge to investigation on the one hand and the community's withdrawal from the case on the other, the old doctor is placed in a position where he must force the action or give up all but the slenderest hope of revenge. By this time, however, the reader knows enough about Chillingworth to realize that the second alternative is for him not really an alternative at all. The reader, therefore, is not at all surprised that in Chapter IX the responsibility for the main action of the story shifts from the community to him.

The happenings which Chillingworth precipitates in this second part of the book can be quickly summarized. At first by frequent consultations and then by effecting an arrangement whereby he can live in the same house with Dimmesdale, the physician succeeds in becoming a daily and often hourly irritant to Dimmesdale's already sensitive conscience. Cautiously but surely, he succeeds in wearing down the young minister's defenses until in desperation Dimmesdale resorts to flagellation, fasts, and long vigils to ease the increasing torture. Generally, this section is a study of psychological cause and effect, with the victim frantically but ineffectively trying to deal with the effects rather than eliminating the cause. More particularly, it is a rich study in guilt and isolation. Before it is over, Chillingworth forces Dimmesdale into so deep a consciousness of sin that to the distracted minister it seems as if all the bonds which have held him to the forces for right have frayed beyond repair. But in so doing, Chillingworth breaks all his own connections with what Mr. Arvin calls "the redemptive force of normal human relations."[7] and substitutes for them an ineluctable union with evil.

The astounding effects of Chillingworth's activities upon himself are telescoped largely into two chapters. At their beginning he is a learned and not unkind old man; at their end he is a fiend, ecstatic in petty triumph. Between these two extremes is a sequence of deliberately committed acts which can be understood only in terms of his character and beliefs. The main point to keep in mind is that Chillingworth never conceives of his own actions as righteous or sinful, but only as natural or unnatural. In so doing, he submerges moral values in the great physical processes of the universe. Truth for him, we may then infer, lies in these processes, and man's greatest task is to find it out. As we observe the earlier Chillingworth more closely, we discover that there are two means which he believes are essential to this end of man: intellectual zeal and social harmony. Of these the former is the more important, but any departure from either constitutes an unnatural act which is bound in the strict processes of life to bring undesirable consequences. With this in mind, we can turn again to his specific actions and observe how Hawthorne has him err by his own standards, not necessarily by those of Dimmesdale or of Hester or of the good people of Boston.

Several acts in Chapter IX and Chapter X, for instance, result in social disharmony inasmuch as they place Chillingworth in a false relation with those about him. He abandons Hester, his lawful wedded wife; he withdraws his name from "the roll of mankind"; he continues his investigation against the counsel of the authorized representative of Puritan Massachusetts; he practises the outward forms of the local religion with no inward conviction; and he cares ostentatiously for Dimmesdale's ailing body while plotting secretly against his soul. Such a formidable multiplication of "sins," however, seems to give the physician no immediate awareness that his relation with the community is, if anything, more false than that of the man he is tracking down. The reason is simply that a more primary matter — a perversion of his zeal for intellectual truth — has driven these relatively secondary transgressions from his mind.

Once the idea of discovering the identity of Hester's lover takes hold of him, Chillingworth soon loses the "severe and equal integrity" of which he was originally so proud. His concepts, once characterized by "range and freedom," contract and become lost in a single petty, revengeful passion. All the potentialities and satisfactions of the scholar he foregoes for control over the soul of a weak and pathetic minister in the bleak little town of Boston. As a consequence, his moment of greatest triumph occurs when he makes the relatively trivial discovery that Dimmesdale is really the wretched sinner he has suspected him to be. In this sense, his sin is not the triumph of the intellect but the surrender of the intellect. Whatever suffering he eventually endures grows from the knowledge that he has been false to his own intellectual principles.

Hawthorne's handling of Dimmesdale in this second part of *The Scarlet Letter* is a masterpiece of organization and culmination. From the moment when Chillingworth begins his cunning attack upon the young minister, Dimmesdale is forced more and more upon the defensive, until he is driven to the very edge of insanity. For the penetration of the old physician's mind and the insidious method of his approach are far too much for a person hitherto shielded from intellectual combat by theological orthodoxy and from guile by the respect and adulation of his congregation. As a result, Dimmesdale's attempts at parry reveal more of his suffering than of his mental acumen. Chillingworth one day, while examining a bundle of weeds from a nearby graveyard, craftily suggests that "since all the powers of nature call so earnestly for the confession of sin . . . these black weeds have sprung up out of a buried heart, to make manifest an unspoken crime." Dimmesdale, sensing a personal thrust, opposes this idea. Keeping one's sins hidden, he replies, is not an act against the powers of nature. "The heart, making itself guilty of such secrets, must perforce hold them, until the day when all hidden things shall be revealed." Nor is the lack of confession essentially a violation of God's will. Confession on the Judgment Day, he protests, will be required not as retribution but only for the "intellectual satisfaction of all intelligent beings." Forced to speak further, he then defends his hypocrisy on much the same grounds as Hester defends her adultery: truth to his own nature. He and Chillingworth are speaking of sinful men who hide their sins:

> "True; there are such men," answered Mr. Dimmesdale. "But, not to suggest more obvious reasons, it may be that they are kept silent by the very constitution of their nature. Or, — can we not suppose it? — guilty as they may be, retaining, nevertheless, a zeal for God's glory and man's welfare, they shrink from displaying themselves black and filthy in the view of men; because, thenceforward, no good can be achieved by them; no evil of the past be redeemed by better service. So, to their own unutterable torment, they go about among their fellow-creatures, looking pure as new-fallen snow while their hearts are all speckled and spotted with iniquity of which they cannot rid themselves."

If this speech is examined closely, it will be seen that Dimmesdale has devised a three-point defense for his failure to confess: first, his silence is natural to himself; second, his silence will enable him to further God's glory and thus achieve penance for his adultery, which he considers a sin against God; and third, his silence will enable him to promote man's welfare and thus achieve penance for his hypocrisy, which he realizes is a violation of the code of the community. In this last instance, his lack of confession purports to be a means of expiating his lack of confession! This is no argument, and down deep in his heart Dimmesdale knows it. When pressed by Chillingworth, he waives the whole discussion as though indifferent to it. And when confronted with Hester, he admits that she is the better for being free to show her pain.

If his reasoned defense is incapable of coping with Chillingworth's attack, however, his intuitive defense is more successful. For just as his own nature inhibits confession before the community, whose "great heart" would eventually pity and forgive, it prevents confession to Chillingworth, who would do neither. Any "backward rush of sinful thoughts" directed toward the old physician would result only in placing Dimmesdale forever in the power of a malicious scoundrel who is aiming at just such revenge. It is without conscious process, therefore, that Dimmesdale is repelled when Chillingworth drives home his most direct question: "Would you, therefore, that your physician heal the bodily evil? How may this be, unless you first lay open to him the wound or trouble in your soul?" "No! — not to thee! — not to an earthly physician!" cries Mr. Dimmesdale passionately.

Although Chillingworth does not succeed in wringing a confession from the hapless clergyman, he does manage to make him more and more conscious of his sinfulness and loneliness, and by doing so, makes him even more sinful and lonely. For, driven almost to distraction by the physician's proddings, Dimmesdale begins to make frantic attempts at expiation. He tries, for instance, the device of declaring himself before his congregation to be the worst of sinners. But this is only to sin again, for whereas his original silence, involving no overt act, was only a violation of the community's moral code, this specious act of penance becomes a violation of his own nature.

> He had spoken the very truth, and transformed it into the veriest falsehood. And yet, by the constitution of his nature, he loved the truth, and loathed the lie, as few men ever did. Therefore, above all things else, he loathed his miserable self!

On other occasions, he adopts practices which, since they succeed in alienating him from the natural order of things, can be considered only as violations of that order. He beats himself with a bloody scourge, fasts with a rigor unknown to other pious Puritans, and maintains vigils until his brain reels and physical reality becomes illusory.

The depths into which Dimmesdale has been thrust by Chillingworth are best demonstrated in the final chapter of this section, the midnight vigil scene on the scaffold. Here, Hawthorne makes it plain that the minister is not only incapable of changing his sinful course by the action of his own will but has been so weakened that he is incapable of right action even when assistance is offered by outside agents. The vigil itself is another of Dimmesdale's attempts at penance. There might, he feels, be a moment's peace in it. Once on the scaffold, the realization of his isolation sweeps across him, and he involuntarily shrieks aloud. In the moments that follow, three persons appear: Governor Bellingham, Mistress Hibbins, and the venerable Father Wilson. Here are three opportunities for him to break his loneliness and to establish connection with one of the great societies — earthly, hellish, or heavenly. But an involuntary shriek is not enough; before Dimmesdale can be admitted to one of these great companies, a voluntary confession or commitment must be made. One of these three persons must be hailed. For a man of average moral strength, the problem would be to choose among the three. For him the problem is whether he shall choose any. In the end, he cowers silent upon the scaffold and the figures disappear. Thus does Arthur Dimmesdale reach the extreme of his isolation. For the time being, seemingly, earth, hell, and heaven are all closed to him. Had he chosen hell, his eventual fate would have been more terrible, but his immediate suffering could not have been greater.

When his mind begins to give way under the impact of this new sense of alienation, he again reacts involuntarily, this time to burst into a peal of insane laughter. What follows is a series of four rapid occurrences, each of which serves to remind the distracted minister of a source of power which is denied him only because of his failure to expiate his guilt. But in each case, Dimmesdale fails to grasp the opportunity and succeeds only in sinning further. Hester and Pearl, first of all, bring a rush of new life to the collapsing man. Here, presumably, is the perfect reminder of that bond of human affection which strengthens the human heart and enables it to find the path to truth. But when Pearl reminds her father of the expiation which is necessary before the bond can be strong and lasting, he dodges her question by giving it an impersonal and stereotyped answer. Secondly, the meteoric flash across the sky should remind him of strength through union with the tremendous yet wholesome forces of nature. Instead, his diseased mind, extending its "egotism over the whole expanse of nature," sees only a large A, symbol of his guilt. In the third place, the appearance of Chillingworth should remind him of the horror of union with evil and, by contrast, the glory of a courageous stand before God. But though his "soul shivers" at the old physician, he obediently follows him home. Finally, the following morning, his own rich and powerful discourse to his congregation should by its own "heavenly influences" catapult him into giving expression to the truth, that quality which by his nature he loves most of all. Yet when the sexton asks him so simple a question as whether he has heard of the A in the sky the preceding night, Dimmesdale answers, "No, I had not heard of it."

Four decisions are thus forced upon Dimmesdale: he must assert his position in relation to man, to nature, to God, and to his own original and better self. In each case, from sheer weakness and despair of spirit he only adds new falsity to that which already exists. Chillingworth has worked better than he knows. If Dimmesdale is to be saved, aid must come from some outside source.

III

In the transition from part two to part three of *The Scarlet Letter*, content has again created form. Hawthorne once more has brought his story to a point where only one character is in a position to force the action. The community has been provided no reason for reentering the story as an activating force; Chillingworth has rather obviously run his course; and Dimmesdale is clearly lacking in both physical and moral vigor. Only Hester is capable of action. It is Hester, moreover, who wants action. For the first time she has fully comprehended the result of her vow to Chillingworth, and her sense of responsibility for Dimmesdale's condition has thrust all thoughts of her own temporarily from her mind. It is not surprising, therefore, that Chapter xiii should begin with a summary of Hester's activities during the seven years since the scaffold scene and that the following pages should reveal her as the source of whatever action takes place.

The third part of *The Scarlet Letter* extends from Chapter xiii to Chapter xx. In form, it is almost an exact duplicate of the second part. Each sketches the immediate past of the main character, details the present action initiated by that character, and describes the results of that action upon another character. In each case, the other character is Dimmesdale.

Hester is sketched as independent and disillusioned. In some ways her isolation has been almost as complete as Dimmesdale's. For seven years now, heaven and earth "have frowned on her." Even though society has grown more benignant, it has never really accepted her save in time of sickness or death; God, never really a great influence in her life, seems to have become less real; nature's sunlight vanishes on her approach; and her own personality has lost its womanly charm. In brief, shame, despair, and solitude have been her teachers just as they have for Dimmesdale.

Two elements, however, have strengthened her while Dimmesdale weakened: her intellectual speculation and her daughter Pearl. The former has been possible only because her sin has been public and her mind hence not cramped by fears of exposure. It has resulted in a latitude of thought which allows her to picture herself as the prophetess of a new order and which causes her to scorn the institutions of the old: "the clerical band, the judicial robe, the pillory, the gallows, the fireside, or the church." In the second place, Pearl has kept a sense of moral direction in Hester, even though Hester has never fully acted upon it. Once, Pearl saved her mother from the devil in the guise of Mistress Hibbins; constantly, she has saved her from complete surrender, to her own cynicism. In a loose sense, Pearl performs the same service for Hester that Chillingworth does for Dimmesdale, since both serve as pricks to the conscience. When their functions are examined more closely, however, it can be observed that these services have opposite effects. For Dimmesdale, if let alone, might eventually get his spiritual house in order. His natural gravitation is heavenward, and he continues to move toward evil simply because Chillingworth keeps nudging him in that direction. But Hester's inclination is not so dominantly heavenward, and she is kept from an alliance with the Devil largely because Pearl keeps hold of her. Intellectual speculation, stimulating as it has been, has led Hester into moral confusion. It is Pearl who has kept this confusion from collapsing into surrender. This she has done by keeping alive the spark of human affection and by standing rigidly against falsity wherever in her precocious way she has sensed it. Given these complementary sources of power, Hester is easily the strongest character in the book at this point. Even Chillingworth can recognize a quality "almost majestic" which shines through her despair.

Her first act in this part of *The Scarlet Letter* is to extract from Chillingworth a release from her vow of silence. This is the first counter move of the story, and it serves to place the doctor immediately upon the defensive. Just as Dimmesdale had tried to explain away his position to Chillingworth, so the old physician now tries to account for his actions to Hester. Several revealing points come to light as he does so. It becomes clear, for example, that he is thoroughly aware of the cruelty of his actions. He cannot, therefore, be excused, even partly, on the grounds of ignorance. It becomes equally clear that Chillingworth, though he has suffered greatly, has never fully realized the tremendous moral change which has taken place in himself. It is a dramatic and revealing moment in his life, consequently, when he discusses himself before Hester. A look of horror suddenly spreads across his face. "It was one of those moments — which sometimes occur only at the interval of years — when a man's moral aspect is faithfully revealed to his mind's eye." This, if ever, is the time for Chillingworth to repent. Even Hester is moved to beg him to purge himself "and be once more human." That repentance is necessarily impossible for him is apparent to anyone who has read the story closely up to this point.

Chillingworth's intellectual penetration is now nothing more than morbid rationalization. He can still see that events are bound together by a chain of cause and effect; what he cannot do, or refuses to do, is to recognize the beginning and ending of that chain. Once, he confessed that he had started the tragic sequence of circumstances by forcing Hester to marry him. Now, he pins complete responsibility on her and Dimmesdale. His own actions, he feels, have been necessary in order to exact a rightful vengeance. More than that, he could not have avoided them had he desired.

> "Peace, Hester, peace!" replied the old man, with gloomy stern-ness. "It is not granted me to pardon. I have no such power as thou tellest me of. My old faith, long forgotten, comes back to me, and explains all that we do, and all we suffer. By thy first step awry thou didst plant the germ of evil; but since that moment, it has all been a dark necessity. Ye that have wronged me are not sinful, save in a kind of typical illusion: neither am I fiend-like, who have snatched a fiend's office from his hands. It is our fate. Let the black flower blossom as it may!"

It is to be remembered that before his fall Chillingworth's study was not upon theology but upon the processes which make up the natural world. These he had come to see as harmonious yet inexorable: as man discovers increasingly more about them and stays in harmony with them through acts of benignity, these processes lead him to truth and happiness; when man ignores them for selfish pursuits of passion and comes into disharmony with them through acts of cruelty, the processes lead just as relentlessly to suffering and annihilation. These are the main elements of Chillingworth's philosophy, so far as we can discover them from what we are given. When he thinks he finds an explanation for "all that we do" in his "old faith," therefore, he is merely fooling himself. For what he discovers in his "old faith" is simply what he has believed all along. Were it otherwise, the "old faith" would certainly explain to him not only what we do and suffer but also what we can do to terminate that suffering. To put it another way, if Chillingworth can recall the doctrine of predestination, why cannot he also recall such other elements of Calvinism (which is, presumably, his "old faith") as the mediation of Christ, sanctification, and repentance unto life and salvation? The answer is that he has not recalled his "old faith" at all but simply that part of it which enables him to defend and justify his own action. In short, since Chillingworth not only disavows his responsibility for starting the relentless chain of cause and effect but also can envision no possible means of stopping it, he can expect no amelioration of his unhappy state. What Hawthorne has done has been to establish one means of reunion and then to create in Chillingworth a character that can never logically utilize or even consider that means.[8] By Dimmesdale's standards, Chillingworth may be the greatest sinner of them all, but by his own he is understandable in his moral disintegration and wholly consistent in his method of explaining it.

That Hester is able to win release from her vow to Chillingworth is due primarily to his admiration for his wife's cynical independence and to his own surrender to the course of events. The latter is the more important and represents the difference between the second and third parts of the book. In the second part the vow of secrecy was necessary so that he could direct events; now he is content merely to "let the black flower blossom as it may."

Hester's actions from this point break loosely into two lines, that directed toward expiation of her sin of hypocrisy and that directed toward escape from the consequences for her act of adultery. The two lines form an illuminating contrast between the proper and improper methods of dealing with guilt, the one leading to moral triumph and the other to moral failure. Fundamentally, the success of the first line is due to the fact that it arises out of a keen sense of responsibility for wrongdoing. To Hester this sense comes first when she sees Dimmesdale's emaciated figure upon the scaffold at midnight. Her later self-analysis is cuttingly honest. In all things else she has striven to be true. Truth has been the one virtue to which she might have held fast, and did hold fast "in all extremity" save in that one moment of weakness when she consented to deception. But now she finds that "a lie is never good, even though death threatens on the other side." In short, she has been false to her own nature, with the result that Dimmesdale has suffered possibly beyond repair. Realizing all this and recognizing at last the obligation which she owes Dimmesdale because of her love and her share in his crime, Hester becomes deeply and earnestly repentant.

Sincere repentance brings proper action. First, Hester obtains her release from Chillingworth, for any other procedure would merely have substituted one dishonesty for another. Then she waylays Dimmesdale in the forest in order to confess and implore his forgiveness. Confession can rectify the false relation which her silence has created, but only forgiveness from the one who has suffered can bring her peace. "Wilt thou yet forgive me!" she repeats over and over again until her lover at length replies, "I do forgive you, Hester."

Although not generally recognized as such, this is one of the emotional and intellectual climaxes of the book. The emotional effect is definitely one of catharsis, for in a blackening world this is the first experience of purification. With Dimmesdale and Hester, the reader comes through the forgiveness scene feeling suddenly purged of stain. That the experience is not more compelling is due to Hester's inability to follow through on her other and more grievous guilt. Intellectually, the forgiveness scene represents the culmination of a pattern of action which not only is interesting in itself but prefigures the pattern leading up to the final climax of the book. As such it constitutes the only exception to the general statement made previously, that the function of each of the activating characters except the last is to multiply sin, intensify isolation, and reduce the chances for complete and lasting reunion.

Hester's second line of action is related to her sin of adultery and her attempt to overcome the isolation imposed by it. Ironically, the very element which led her to repent for her sin of hypocrisy — truth to her own nature — now provides her with a justification of her act of adultery. When Dimmesdale observes sadly that Chillingworth's sin has been blacker than theirs, Hester is quick to whisper, "What we did had a consecration of its own! We felt it so! We said so to each other!" Confident in this belief, she proposes that they dispel their sense of moral isolation by translating it into physical terms. She and Dimmesdale and Pearl must flee to Europe. And her insistence that Dimmesdale agree represents the highest point in her activities as a directing force in the story.

In the enthusiasm of the moment, Hester takes off her cap and scarlet letter, becoming once more the woman of affection and charm. As if in approval, nature suddenly bursts into sunny radiance. But nature, one should recall, is unsubjugated by human law or unillumined by higher truths in parcelling out its approval. A more accurate moral index of Hester's action is found in Pearl, who as always flatly refuses to countenance a relation based upon falsity. Nature can rejoice at love and ignore immorality; Pearl can see only immorality and ignore the love. Neither, however, has human sympathy or understanding, and both consequently have more in common with each other than either has with Hester or Dimmesdale. Momentarily, it is the moral law which prevails over both human desire and natural law: Pearl forces her mother to reassume her scarlet letter, and the sunshine disappears. But the child's further attempts to bring her parents back to a proper realization of their relationship are deflected, and instead of the confession and the true reunion she is working for, she gets a formal kiss from the minister, a kiss which she immediately and appropriately washes off in the brook. Through Pearl, therefore, it becomes plain that Hester's proposed plan of action is no real solution. This becomes even plainer as one perceives the effects of the suggestion upon Dimmesdale.

As he appears in the early part of the forest scene, he is lonely, cowardly, and naive in the ways of deliberate sin. These attributes should not be taken as co-equal, however, for whereas the first keeps him conscious of the orthodox end of life, the second makes him incapable of employing the orthodox means toward that end, and the third makes him oblivious of alternative means and ends. Dimmesdale's loneliness is never more poignant. He feels himself so far isolated from his God that His choicest gifts have become only "the ministers of spiritual torment," so far removed from his people that their continued adulation brings only "bitterness and agony of heart," and so far torn within himself that his penance has brought not one whit of penitence. Thus do his lonely broodings constantly direct themselves toward that end of life from which sin has isolated him. For if the end of life has meant anything to Dimmesdale, it has meant eternal joy through a righteous union with God, His people, and the things of His universe. But cowardice continues to make it impossible for him to attain this end. Even when Hester divulges the true identity of Chillingworth, Dimmesdale's reaction is not one of compunction inspired by new understanding but one of fear that Chillingworth will betray him. Without the slightest shred of self-respect, he throws himself upon Hester for help. "Be thou strong for me," he pleads.

When Hester suggests a solution involving an easier means and an alternative end—temporal happiness—the solution appears so simple and so breathtaking to Dimmesdale that he wonders why they had never thought of it before. It offers a whole new realm of action, unchristianized and lawless but free and exciting. So exciting is it, in fact, that he is quick to put down any temporary misgivings. Reunion with God? He is irrevocably doomed anyway. Reunion with his people? Hester is all that he needs to sustain him. Union with his own spirit? Already he can feel life coursing through his veins without it. And so for the first time he consents with purpose and deliberation to something that basically he knows to be wrong. The immediate result is a sudden plunge into moral confusion. Like Hester before him, he has sinned against his own better nature.

What before was a depressing conflict between right and wrong has so developed that Dimmesdale is almost literally split in two. To put it another way, Dimmesdale was formerly an individual who had sinned against the synthesis of theology, custom, and personal goodness which made up his own code; now he is two individuals with two different codes. As Hawthorne phrases it, his new impulses can be accounted for by "nothing short of a total change of dynasty and moral code." For the time being, it is the newer and baser nature which initiates action though the older and truer nature never ceases to assert itself in counter-action. The baser nature, for instance, rejoices over the prospect of flight; the truer nature is wistfully glad that flight will not interfere with the Election Sermon. The baser nature gives Dimmesdale unaccustomed physical energy on his walk back to Boston; the truer nature wonders and is frightened at the new aspect of familiar objects. The baser nature suggests shocking remarks to make to his parishioners; the truer nature just manages to keep him from saving them. The baser nature is appealed to by Mistress Hibbins as a kindred perverted spirit; the truer nature is appealed to by the Bible and God's voice. This, however, is the last contrast that can be made between the two. For as Dimmesdale stands within his room, viewing the Bible and the unfinished Election Sermon, the two natures unite. All that remains of the baser one is the knowledge of evil and of his own kinship with it. But that is the key to all that follows. Whatever contrast remains is between the innocent Dimmesdale that existed before Hester accosted him in the forest and the knowing Dimmesdale who is able to greet Chillingworth and tell him firmly that "touching your medicine, kind Sir, in my present frame of body, I need it not." It is out of this same new maturity that Dimmesdale is able to sit down to a new Election Sermon and to write "with earnest haste and ecstasy" throughout the night.

Since Hawthorne refuses to disclose what goes on in Dimmesdale's mind at this point, we are forced back upon deductions based on his actions. Obviously, his truer nature has become ascendant. Obviously, too, he has lost his loneliness, his cowardice, and his naivete about sin and his relation to it. His condition, therefore, has become the exact antithesis of what it was a few hours before. If we can guess at the cause from these results, repentance has presumably taken place. And if this is true, Dimmesdale will spare no effort to perform true penance and hence achieve reunion with the good and true. The expectation is, therefore, that, urged on by high desire and strengthened by spiritual rather than temporal resources, he will wrest the initiative from Hester and become the activating force in the story. In brief, the desires and capabilities of the characters should once more determine the form the book must take. From previous readings we know that they do.

IV

The fourth part of *The Scarlet Letter* offers an interesting variation from the other three parts. Whereas each of these gives immediate attention to the character which is to direct its action, the fourth part withholds such attention for almost two chapters. Indeed, these chapters, "The New England Holiday" and "The Procession," might with some justice be considered a final section of the third part inasmuch as they deal chiefly with the results of Hester's activities as they operate upon Hester herself. There are other and more cogent reasons, however, for considering them as belonging to the fourth part of the book and as a kind of introduction for Dimmesdale's final act. The most obvious is that the background ties these chapters with Chapter XXIII, in which he takes control. Hawthorne is carefully setting the stage for his climax. In terms of content there are other elements to be considered. Dimmesdale's final action must not appear as something opposing Hester's desires but as something evolving from them and sublimating them. Hence, it must be made clear to the reader that Hester has lost confidence in her own scheme and will ultimately be favorably affected by Dimmesdale's expiation rather than antagonized by his seeming disregard for her plans and wishes. Another element is the character of his action. Whereas the community, Chillingworth, and Hester needed days, months, and even years to accomplish their purposes, Dimmesdale needs only moments. Theirs was a series of actions, each carefully plotted and integrated with every other; his is one bold stroke. Their actions created complexities; his removes them. Hence, his can be encompassed and should be encompassed in a much smaller space. But it is equally true that the setting must be carefully prepared, or the action will pass before the reader is prepared to comprehend its full significance. It seems useful and understandable, therefore, that Hawthorne should devote Chapters XXI and XXII to introductory material, Chapter XXIII to Dimmesdale's expiatory action, and Chapter XXIV to the consequences of that action.

By contrast with her previous aggressiveness, Hester's mood in the market place sinks from one of loneliness to one of almost complete despair. Seldom has she seemed so completely isolated. Her frozen calmness, we are told, is due to the fact that she is "actually dead, in respect to any claim of sympathy" and has "departed out of the world, with which she still seems to mingle." The good people of the town sidle away from her and strangers openly gawk. Nor has she come any closer to Pearl. When Pearl keeps asking about the minister, Hester shuts her off with "Be quiet, Pearl! thou understandest not these things." Even Dimmesdale she sees moodily as existing in a sphere remote and "utterly beyond her reach." Indeed, she can hardly find it in her heart to forgive him for "being able so completely to withdraw himself from their mutual world; while she groped darkly, and stretched forth her cold hands, and found him not." Finally, the news that Chillingworth is to take passage on the same ship transforms her loneliness into consternation and despair. "Hester's strong, calm, steadfastly enduring spirit almost sank, at last, on beholding this dark and grim countenance of an inevitable doom, which . . . showed itself, with an unrelenting smile, right in the midst of their path."

Once Dimmesdale begins to direct the action, however, any effort of either Hester or Chillingworth becomes incidental. With a fine sense for dramatic contrast, Hawthorne has Dimmesdale reach his greatest success as a minister a few short minutes before he confesses his crime. Never has he been more uplifting and never more spiritually inclined. Already we know the Election Sermon as something born of new awareness and a sudden stiffening of the spirit. Since the world is no longer illusory or his own heart confused, Dimmesdale apparently has made his peace with the natural order and with himself. But he still feels estranged from God and from the community because of his sins of adultery and hypocrisy. His confession on the scaffold, therefore, is necessary as penance for both these sins, and its dual character Dimmesdale himself makes clear:

> "God knows; and He is merciful; He hath proved his mercy, most of all, in my afflictions. By giving me this burning torture to bear upon my breast! By sending yonder dark and terrible old man, to keep the torture always at red heat! By bringing me hither, to die this death of triumphant ignominy before the people! Had either of these agonies been wanting, I had been lost forever! Praised be his name! His will be done! Farewell!"

In such a manner does Dimmesdale perform true penance and emerge finally at the moment of his death into a true relation with all the elements against which he has sinned. It is vain for him to hope for "an everlasting and pure reunion," but he has made himself worthy of whatever reunion God grants to those who repent.

It remains only to observe the effects of Dimmesdale's action upon the other characters. Pearl, to begin, ceases to be simply a force for rectitude. Since her mission is fulfilled, she is set free to assume a normal place in the human family. Chillingworth, on the other hand, relinquishes whatever slim bonds with that family he still possesses. This does not mean that he becomes a disassociated being, for though *The Scarlet Letter* is a story of isolation Hawthorne never implies even the possibility of complete disassociation. In the end, one is either reunited with the good and true or he becomes the slave of the Devil. And so Chillingworth, now that there is no further material upon which his earthly nature can sustain itself, passes to whatever realms his evil master desires. The people of Boston are bewildered and confused by Dimmesdale's action, first as to the cause of the scarlet letter on the minister's breast, and then as to the reality of the letter itself. In either case, they forget the sin and dwell upon the nature and cause and greatness of the minister's expiation. Had he lived, they might have revered him only the more.

There is no immediate effect upon Hester of any profound significance. Her first reaction is one of despondency and hopelessness. When Dimmesdale asks her whether his solution is not better than what they dreamed of in the forest, she replies, "I know not! I know not! Better? Yea; so we may both die, and little Pearl die with us." Nor does she yet see that any true reunion must ultimately rest upon voluntary expiation of her own. "Surely, surely, we have ransomed one another, with all this woe." But Dimmesdale knows better. "Hush, Hester, hush!" said he, with tremulous solemnity. "The law we broke! — the sin here so awfully revealed! — let these alone be in thy thoughts!"

Years pass in a foreign country before Hester comes to that full sense of personal responsibility which swells into repentance and the desire to do voluntary penance. When that happens, of her own free will she returns to Boston and resumes the scarlet letter. Though even then she does not conceive of her adultery as a sin against the community, she has lost her resentment and has come to feel that her sin can be fully expiated only when it is made known freely in the world, particularly in that part of the world which will recognize it and profit most from the presence of the repentant sinner. "There was a more real life for Hester Prynne here, in New England, than in that unknown region where Pearl had found a home. Here had been her sin; here, her sorrow; and here was yet to be her penitence." And as she still does not conceive of her adultery as a sin against God, she does not repent in the orthodox Calvinistic fashion. Plainly, she still thinks of her guilt in terms of a natural or this-world order. Her vision is of a brighter period when the whole relation between man and woman will be established "on a surer ground of mutual happiness." But her repentant spirit no longer allows her to picture herself as the prophetess of the new order. Rather, she admits that guilt has incapacitated her for such a role and that her penance must be to accept whatever lowly position in the present order she can best fill. In such a manner she finally overcomes — insofar as that is possible for the repentant sinner — the consequences of her act of disorder and wins back a useful and even honorable place in the great scheme of things. That Hester is allowed to overcome her isolation in her own way is Hawthorne's final act of faith in a book in which the integrity of the individual viewpoint is scrupulously maintained. That she should be able to find some peace in so doing comes as the ultimate result of Dimmesdale's confession and represents, therefore, the closing act in *The Scarlet Letter*'s fourth and final section.[9]

Notes

1. Other analyses of the form of *The Scarlet Letter* stress its succession of highly wrought tableaux, its unifying symbol of the scarlet A, and its recurrent scaffold scene. See, for example, George E. Woodberry, *Nathaniel Hawthorne* (Boston, 1902), 189–191; Carl Van Doren, *The American Novel* (New York, 1940), 66–67; and F. O. Matthiessen, *American Renaissance* (New York, 1941), 275. Such technical devices, however, are valuable chiefly because they give coherence to the form, not because they create the form. Mr. Matthiessen comes closer to what seems to me to be the real source of the book's form when he speaks of *The Scarlet Letter* as growing "organically out of the interactions between the characters."

2. Mr. Paul Elmer More makes this even more emphatic in "The Solitude of Nathaniel Hawthorne," *Shelburne Essays*, First Series (New York, 1904), 33: "From the opening scene at the prison door, which, 'like all that pertains to crime, seemed never to have known a youthful era,' to the final scene on the scaffold, where the tragic imagination of the author speaks with a power barely surpassed in the books of the world, the whole plot of the romance moves about this one conception of our human isolation as the penalty of transgression."

3. Mr. Walter Blair mentions these three elements as being involved in Hawthorne's

concept of sin in "Hawthorne's Color, Light, and Shadow," *New England Quarterly*, xv (March, 1942), 82.

4. It must be conceded immediately that these terms do not constitute a process which fully reestablishes the original union. Reunion is not Christian salvation, and the two terms should not be used interchangeably. Indeed, Dimmesdale in his dying moment warns that it is vain to hope to meet even in the hereafter in "an everlasting and pure reunion." It is such a statement that gives support to Mr. Woodberry's assertion in *Nathaniel Hawthorne* (Boston, 1902), 193, that "the idea of salvation, of healing, is but little present and is not felt." To this, Mr. Austin Warren, in *Nathaniel Hawthorne* (New York, 1934), xl, adds: "Certainly Hawthorne has no hope in his creative mind. This is a sorry world; but we can really do nothing about it. Men necessarily sin; but they must be held strictly accountable for their sins all the same. They must repent, but repentance cannot raise the fallen." These gloomy aspects to the story, however, should not blind one to the fact that reunion constitutes a major theme, and that though it does not bring the joy of Christian salvation it does bring relief from suffering in those instances when it is achieved.

5. Henry James, in *Hawthorne* (New York, 1879), 110–111, speaks of the people of *The Scarlet Letter* as being not characters but "representatives, very picturesquely arranged, of a single state of mind." This seems eminently true if one excepts the four main characters. It is this single-mindedness that makes it possible to speak in the singular when referring to the community as an activating force.

6. To avoid confusion, it is necessary to keep in mind that "nature" as applied by Hawthorne to a character's essential constitution refers to the original constitution which the character possesses before sin or circumstance warps it. For Hester to be true to her nature is for her to look, to feel, and to think in harmony with her original attributes: her feminine, almost voluptuous, appearance, her warmly personal affection, and her scrupulous regard for simple truthfulness. None of her later attributes are ever characterized as "natural": her colorless, statuelike appearance, her self-effacing benevolence, her radical speculation. These, according to Hawthorne, are the result of her innate tenderness' being so deeply crushed into her heart that only some "magic" can effect a transformation, *i.e.*, a return to the "natural." The same principle operates with respect to Dimmesdale and Chillingworth. When Hawthorne speaks of the "constitution of his nature" he is referring to Dimmesdale's original nature, in which human affection and timidity are the dominant emotions, and truthfulness, as refined by Calvinistic theology, the dominant trait of his thinking. And, as pointed out later, Chillingworth by "nature" is gifted with kindness and a rigorous scientific integrity.

7. Newton Arvin, *Hawthorne* (Boston, 1929), 189.

8. This may seem to confuse Hawthorne's principle of reunion with the orthodox principle of salvation. At this point, however, we are considering means, not ends, and in means the two are not dissimilar, inasmuch as both involve a personal sense of responsibility, repentance, and voluntary penance or good works. We can justifiably say, therefore, that since Chillingworth refuses to recognize the regenerative elements in his "old faith," he can never win relief from suffering by the process which Hawthorne thinks necessary in order to achieve reunion.

9. Valuable suggestions for this essay came from Gordon Roper, Clarence Faust, and Walter Blair. J. C. G.

Criticism since 1950

The Tongue of Flame:
The Scarlet Letter

Roy R. Male*

I consider *The Scarlet Letter* the most intensely moving and the most beautifully composed work in American fiction. No other book, to use D. H. Lawrence's words, is so deep, so dual, and so complete.[1] It never fails to interest even those uninitiated readers who approach it, as they say, "just for the story." For the reader who seeks something more than an interesting narrative, there is "surface beneath surface, to an immeasurable depth" (VII, 132). This is Hawthorne's comment about Shakespeare's plays, but it applies equally well to his own masterpiece.

The critic faces two major difficulties in discussing the book. Its plot is so lucid that almost every reader thinks he already knows what *The Scarlet Letter* is about. Thus what seem to be the most obvious symbols — Pearl, Roger Chillingworth, the letter itself — are actually the most often misunderstood. Second, the book's texture is so tightly interwoven that any formal or categorical exposition seems fated to produce distortion. To some extent this is true in any analysis of a successful literary work. But the extraordinary unity of *The Scarlet Letter* makes separation of its elements particularly painful.

As it is usually interpreted, the book is said to deal with the consequences of sin upon three individuals. A symmetrical pattern is discerned in which Hester Prynne is the openly repentant sinner, Arthur Dimmesdale the half-repentant sinner, and Roger Chillingworth the unrepentant sinner.[2] Pearl is to be understood as the symbol of the sin, the living embodiment of the scarlet letter. Beyond this point there is less critical agreement — in fact, there is very little agreement at all. Most critics think *The Scarlet Letter* is essentially Hester Prynne's story, but a few, most notably Henry James, have felt that Dimmesdale is really more important. The moral significance of the action has been heatedly argued, with opinions ranging from fervent glorification of Hester's "triumph" as an instance of *felix culpa* to orthodox satisfaction at the inexorable punishment meted out to the sinners.[3]

*Reprinted from *Hawthorne's Tragic Vision* (Austin: University of Texas Press, 1957), 90–118, by permission of the author.

This widespread disagreement among critics has been taken as a tribute to the richness of the book. Doubtless the meaning of any work of art that plumbs the mysteries of human life will be subject to endless debates. Yet, if the book is artistically successful, there ought to be limits to the debate; if the work's broad structure is not clear, we deal not with ambiguity and paradox but with confusion. Now if any work of fiction immediately impresses the reader as having a clean classic structure it is *The Scarlet Letter*, with its symmetrical pillory scenes, its subtle contrasts and massive ironies. Yet even here we find total disagreement. In one of the best interpretations of the book, John C. Gerber has cogently argued that it divides into four unequal parts: In Part I (Chapters I to VIII) it is the community that instigates the action; in Part II (Chapters IX to XII) it is Chillingworth; in Part III (Chapters XIII to XIX), it is Hester; and in Part IV (Chapters XX to XXIV), it is Dimmesdale. Newton Arvin has more tentatively suggested that there are eight scenes that can be grouped into the conventional five acts of a play. Anne Marie MacNamara, who agrees with Henry James that *The Scarlet Letter* is Dimmesdale's story, divides his spiritual growth into four stages: preparation (Chapters I to XVI); communication (Chapters XVII to XIX); transformation (Chapters XX to XXII); and revelation (Chapter XXIII).[4]

None of these divergent outlines can be absolutely rejected; each has a partial validity. The same may be said of the initial premise upon which the conventional interpretations are based — that the book concerns the effects of sin upon the three individuals. This reading is unquestionably accurate as far as it goes, and to encompass something like the full meaning of the book such interpretations as those of Winters, Gerber, and Mark Van Doren should be held in suspension with the version I am about to propose. Fortunately, *The Scarlet Letter* cannot be reduced to any single explication.

Consider, however, some of the questions that the usual reading of the book fails to answer. Why did Hester marry Chillingworth in the first place? Apparently not for money; certainly not for love. Why does Hawthorne spend so much space on Pearl and on the letter if they are merely symbols of sin? Surely Pearl is tedious and sometimes irritating if this is her sole symbolic function. Why does Chillingworth wither and die soon after Dimmesdale confesses? Why does Hawthorne at this point make Pearl the richest heiress in America?

The most damaging flaw in the conventional interpretation is that it fails almost completely to comprehend the language of the book. As one critic remarked years ago, Hawthorne's style is an "intense essence of the language, . . . his words conveying not only a meaning, but more than they appear to mean. They point onward or upward or downward."[5] One of the aims of this chapter will be to elucidate the book's unique language pattern. But before this can be accomplished, several preliminary steps must be taken. After a general statement of the book's subject, the allegorical significance of Pearl and Roger Chillingworth will be established. Once this is clear, the book's structure may be outlined. Only then can we proceed to a consideration of its guiding metaphor, the Tongue of Flame.

Like many great tragedies, *The Scarlet Letter* deals with the quest for truth, the revelation of secrets. First one riddle is solved, then another, until at the close the reader has been drawn up to the ultimate revelation—the secret of man's moral growth. This will remain a mystery, however, because, like the Passion of Christ, it involves an eternal paradox: the mundane wisdom of man is insanity to God, and untempered celestial wisdom is equally insane in the social world. The mature insight of Oedipus coincides with his physical blindness and banishment; Arthur Dimmesdale purifies himself at the terrible human cost of sin, physical decay, and death. The crucial moment occurs when the emotionally involved reader or spectator raises and ennobles his own perspective so that he sees not only the agony but also the purification.

In *The Scarlet Letter* the quest for truth is an effort to know Pearl. As every reader of the book recognizes, she is the scarlet letter incarnate. But as the visible embodiment of truth about the particular sin, she becomes by extension the universal truth about the Original Sin. In a notebook entry, Hawthorne had written in 1841: "Is truth a fantasy which we are to pursue forever and never grasp?" Pearl, whose inscrutable black eyes invest her with a "strange remoteness and intangibility," is a dramatization of this passage. As truth's reflector, she rejects all half-truths, including those of the Puritans. Hawthorne adroitly manipulates the archaisms of the townspeople in order to indicate Pearl's symbolic function. When Chillingworth, for instance, asks a bystander about the identity of Pearl's father, the reply is: "*Of a truth*, friend, that matter remaineth a riddle" (V, 84).

Though Pearl's full significance will emerge only when we see her in relation to other characters, there is another aspect of her role that deserves mention here. She possesses "a native grace." In naming her, Hester has identified the child with the pearl of great price (Matt. 13: 45–46) the *pretiosa margarita*. This pearl has often been interpreted as Christ by the theologians, but it has also been construed as everlasting life or beatitude—the soul, either undefiled or redeemed in baptism. In "The Intelligence Office," Hawthorne had defined the pearl as "the soul of celestial purity" (II, 370). Pearl's name, her attire, and her very being thus sum up the riddle of human existence, in which man's insanity is heaven's sense. "Man had marked this woman's sin by a scarlet letter, which had such potent and disastrous efficacy that no human sympathy could reach her, save it were sinful like herself. God, as a direct consequence of the sin which man thus punished, had given her a lovely child, whose place was on that same dishonored bosom, to connect her parent for ever with the race and descent of mortals, and to be finally a blessed soul in heaven!"

Pearl is a holy spirit, "worthy to have been brought forth in Eden; worthy to have been left there, to be the plaything of angels, after the world's first parents were driven out" (V, 114). But the temporal gap between the sin and the redemption must not be ignored; it is, in fact, at the heart of the story.

As an abstraction, Pearl is inflexible and inexorable. She has a "hard, metallic lustre" that needs grief to melt it and make her human. Both character and type, both natural and preternatural, she is in time and outside of it. She watches her reflection in the forest brook, the stream of time; a little later we are informed that "the soul beheld its features in the mirror of the passing moment" (V, 228). As a growing child, Pearl serves as an index to the passage of time in the narrative; as a symbol, she indicates to Hester and Arthur that truth cannot be perceived outside its temporal context.

These generalizations will derive further support when we see Pearl in relation to the two major characters. Meanwhile, having established as a working hypothesis at least that Pearl signifies truth and grace, we may turn to Roger Chillingworth. He has always been recognized as a personification, but it will not suffice to see him simply as evil incarnate. "Under the appellation of Roger Chillingworth . . . was hidden another name," and the name is not only Prynne—it is Guilt.[6] Hawthorne's portrayal of Chillingworth illustrates how beautifully his imagination could weld the abstract to the concrete. For the physician is interesting in his own right as an alchemist-psychiatrist manqué, who tries to solve the riddle of man's existence by logical or psychological analysis.

As a symbol of guilt, Chillingworth is a leech, draining his patient of nerve, will, and physical energy. But, as the whole book demonstrates, he is also the healer. Only by knowing him, confronting him face to face, is moral growth possible. Not that moral growth is guaranteed or that having this unwelcome guest is "fortunate"—it is simply inevitable in human existence. "The breach which guilt has once made into the human soul is never in this mortal state repaired. It may be watched and guarded; so that the enemy shall not force his way again *into the citadel*, and might even, in his subsequent assaults, select some other avenue, in preference to that where he had formerly succeeded. But there is still *the ruined wall*" (VI, 241). The italicized phrases remove all doubt of Chillingworth's identity. As guilt he invades the dwelling place, which, as we know, is customarily a symbol for the heart in Hawthorne's fiction. "My home," he tells Hester, "is where thou art and where he [the minister] is." Early in the book Chillingworth appears from nowhere to confront Hester in the prison cell of her heart; by the middle of the book he has insinuated himself into Dimmesdale's abode. "A deformed old figure, with a face that haunted men's memories longer than they liked," he gradually shrivels as Hester and Dimmesdale come closer to full recognition of him.

We are now perhaps in a position to understand why Hawthorne makes Pearl "the richest heiress in her day, in the New World." Allegorically, it is clear that the death of Chillingworth would automatically bequeath a massive legacy to Pearl. But the matter is not this simple. In the final pillory scene Pearl becomes humanized. As Dimmesdale ascends, she moves down from her allegorical function and into fully temporal existence. She shifts, as it were, from her role as the universal principle in the spiritual realm — an intuitive or natural language, a vital hieroglyphic — to a key role in the novel, the social world, whose basic medium is money.[7] Hawthorne returns her to the Old World with the riches from the New, giving her a solid social standing.

Once we identify Pearl and Chillingworth, the structural outline of *The Scarlet Letter* is clearly revealed. The first third of the book (Chapters I to VIII) concerns Hester's limited ascension. When she ascends the platform, she stands out in sharp contrast to the flint-faced, manlike women who surround her. Every inch a woman in her dual role as sinner and saint, Hester reaches the peak of her moral development in this section. She openly recognizes her guilt in Chapter III; she accepts the letter as Chillingworth's vital surrogate in Chapter IV; she grasps the truth intuitively through her art in Chapters V and VI; and she educates the leading members of the community in the meaning of that art in Chapters VII and VIII.

The middle third of the book (Chapters IX to XVI) is concerned with the burden of guilt and where it should reside. It is subdivided by the midnight pillory scene in the middle of the book. In Chapters IX to XII we see that guilt has been shifted almost completely from the woman to the man (Chillingworth now lives with Dimmesdale); and in the counterbalancing Chapters XIII to XVI we observe what has happened to the woman as a result of this shifting of responsibility.

The final third (Chapters XVII to XXIV) deals with Dimmesdale's ascension, which begins with the forest interview and ends with the revelation during the New England holiday. Where Hester's ascension was limited, his is complete; where she has been associated (though, as Hawthorne puts it, only "by contrast") with Divine Maternity, Dimmesdale attains the Word Incarnate. The book moves, therefore, from recognition through obscurity to revelation, from the light of Hester's ascension through the dark night of the soul to the final light of Dimmesdale's ascension. And the final symbol, as we shall see, sums up the whole action.

We may now pause to consider what is likely to be the major objection to this interpretation. If Chillingworth represents guilt, it may be asked, what happens to the sin of adultery upon which the whole book is based? The question is not only relevant but of the utmost importance for a grasp of the book's archetypal meaning. The reader may well be asked to see Chillingworth both as wronged husband and as guilt, but he is quite right in insisting that the sin ought to have meaning from both perspectives. The answer is that it does; it has a literal meaning in both senses of the word *literal*: "nonfigurative" and "original." All readers have noticed that the actual sin is prior to the action of the book. Of course it is prior; it is the literal, the Original Sin. Why did Hester marry Chillingworth? Why was Zenobia wedded to Westervelt? Why is Miriam linked to the "model"? Why did Eve allow herself to be seduced by Satan, thus fouling her perfect union with God? Why did all evil spring from Pandora's box? On this archetypal level, the timeless abstractions represented by Pearl and Chillingworth remain constant, but, like the man and the woman, they are stripped of their names and location. The "special reference to New England" is gone, and all that remains is the basic relation between man, woman, and Deity. *The Scarlet Letter* is seen not as romance but as myth — the story of man and woman in a fallen, that is, human, world. Like Rappaccini's garden, life in this "Eden of the present world" is an adulteration of God's original creation. The woman has broken her covenant with God in order to seek the kind of knowledge that is man's province; the man has broken his covenant with God in order to know the woman. As a result, life is such "commixture, and, as it were, *adultery*" that "the production" is "no longer of God's making" (II, 128).

Thus Hawthorne educates us once again in the given conditions of human life. Originally — that is, in his youth and before this book has begun — man's role, as we have seen, is speculation; it is a rootless gamble in space, the discovery of new particulars, the exploration of new fields, physical or intellectual. For maturity, however, man needs to leave this world of the first name and become involved through passion with the woman and her temporal burden. Originally, woman's role is investment; she brings to the man a dowry from the past. Without the man she lingers, literally or figuratively, in the Old World, in the ancestral homestead, buried under the patronymic. Without him she lives in time-drenched darkness; without her he is blanked out in the glare of space. Their union depends upon man's vulnerable area, his heart, and upon woman's, her head. After the union, which is where this book begins, the man wears his hand over his heart; the woman wears a cap over her head. After their union there is an exaggerated inversion of roles: the man, like Milton's Adam, is overwhelmed by a sense of time, of all history; the woman, like Milton's Eve, is blinded by speculation, offering noble but misguided ways of thwarting time. A reassertion of their natural roles, balanced and tempered by their new knowledge, must be effected if they are to find "the oneness of their being" in Pearl and re-establish something like their original relation to God.

Important though it is, we should not become fixed on the archetypal plane of interpretation. On this level all Hawthorne's romances are variants of essentially the same situation. They all involve a man (or his symbolic equivalent), a woman (or her substitute), their guilt, and their possible redemption. These are the given elements in the riddle of moral growth; they are the skeleton upon which all of Hawthorne's best work is based; but to fix our gaze unremittingly upon them is to lose the living letter of the romance. We join Melville's Bartleby and stare at the colorless wall of universals; we are stationary and not particular; we work in the Dead Letter Office.

Perhaps the best way of returning to the flesh and blood of the romance is to consider its guiding metaphor, the Tongue of Flame. Hawthorne derives this figure from the description in Acts 2:3–4 of the descent of the Holy Ghost upon the chosen disciples: "And there appeared unto them cloven tongues like as of fire, and it sat upon each of them. And they were all filled with the Holy Ghost. . . ." However, Hawthorne interprets this gift in his own way. The tongues of flame symbolize not the power of speech in all languages but the ability to address "the whole human brotherhood in the heart's native language" (V, 173). The Tongue of Flame is intuitive communication, the expression of "the highest truths through the humblest medium of familiar words and images."

I call this the crucial metaphor because ultimately the Tongue of Flame comes to be identical with the letter of scarlet, and its revelation consummates a process that goes on throughout the book. The quest for truth in *The Scarlet Letter* takes the specific and time-honored form of seeking to unite the Word and the Light in the Act. The Flame, or the Light, is vision—both insight and, as Sophia called it, "outsight"; it is the ability to see both the old universal patterns and the new particulars; and it is not only vision but revelation. The Word is the utterance and the investment; it comprises the tradition, the rhetorical and moral discipline, the communion, the surname; but it is also the new clothing, the new foliage, the new name. Both categories, therefore, contain the possibility of looking in opposite directions: backward and forward in time, inward and outward in space.

Thus *The Scarlet Letter*, like *Oedipus Tyrannus* and *King Lear*, is about ways of seeing. Many of the chapter titles—"The Interview," "The Interior of a Heart," "The Minister's Vigil," "Another View of Hester"— spring from the effort to gain a better perspective, a clearer view of the truth. Some of the book's key words retain vestiges of their original meaning in expressing this emphasis upon vision: "scene," "witness," "interview," "spectacle," "perspective," "speculation," "spectator," and "re- spectable." From the initial pillory scene, where Hester finds a "point of view," to the end, when she "glanced her sad eyes downward at the scarlet letter," the book deals with different kinds of vision.

But vision alone is insufficient as a means of conversion. To "be true," as the book's moral indicates, one must also "utter," make plain, "show freely" to others the secret of his identity. As the spirit is clothed in flesh and the flesh is clothed in garments, so ideas are clothed in words. The outer garments may be true to the inner reality: Hester's ascension is a mute utterance made manifest by the letter which society has vested upon her and which she has embroidered. Or they may be false covering: Dimmesdale's ascension at the close depends upon his willingness to divest himself of the priestly robe. Most of the garments in the book are accurate reflections of character. The massive women in the first pillory scene are swathed in petticoats and farthingales that match their "boldness and rotundity of speech"; Governor Bellingham's rigid devotion to outward forms may be seen in the hollow suit of armor, and his head and heart are separated by an imposing ruff; Mistress Hibbins wears a triple ruff for the same reason; the sea captain, the sailors, and the Indians express their individuality in their garb of scarlet and gold.

The Light is a process of seeing and disclosing; the Word is a process of uttering and investing; the Act is the intuitive union of both. Truth comes as a reward for intellectual discipline and human sympathy, but the ultimate incarnation that unites light and letter, spirit and flesh can only *be.* This intuition may be simply a sign, like Pearl's gestures, or a facial expression, like Chillingworth's when he discovers the letter on Dimmesdale's breast. More significant expression is achieved in art: Hester's needlework, Chillingworth's psychiatric alchemy, and Dimmesdale's Election Sermon. The highest form of intuitive truth, however, is the life that is patterned as a work of art. To make one's life a parable is to be the word incarnate; from one perspective, Dimmesdale's final symbolic gesture approaches this saintly level.

The action of the book shows how the two major characters are transformed when they join the Word and the Light in their actions and their art. Pearl, of course, does not change except at the end when she loses her allegorical function and becomes humanized. To know her in full context is the object of the quest; as a living hieroglyphic, a "character of flame," she unites language and vision in symbol. In so far as he is a character, Roger Chillingworth seeks to learn her origin and identity. He succeeds by inhumanely uniting his dim but penetrating gaze with amoral lore, both Indian and civilized, to perfect his art. But he is more significant in his allegorical relation to Hester and Arthur than he is as a character.

The main action concerns Hester Prynne and Arthur Dimmesdale as they seek transformation. Hester attains her most nearly complete vision in the first third of the book. She is seen: the object of "universal observation," she feels the "heavy weight of a thousand unrelenting eyes upon her" as she presents a living sermon to those who witness the spectacle. "Transfigured" by the scarlet letter, she discovers that the platform offers perspective in every direction. It enables her to look inward and backward to her parents, her former home, and her guilt; downward to the living realities of her present, the infant and the letter; and, for the only time in the book, upward, to the balcony where authority is seated.

The clarity of her vision at this point in the book is emphasized by the "recognition" scene. Though forced upon her by the community, it is an open recognition of guilt. Standing on her pedestal, Hester squarely faces the stranger who could not be buried in the sea or the wilderness and fixes her gaze upon him—"so fixed a gaze, that, at moments of intense absorption, all other objects in the visible world seemed to vanish, leaving only him and her. Such an interview, perhaps would have been more terrible than even to meet him as she now did, with the hot, mid-day sun burning down upon her face, and lighting up its shame" (V, 85). This lucid "interview" between Hester and Roger Chillingworth is interrupted by one of the preachers of the word, John Wilson, who urges her to "hearken," though he is poorly qualified to "step forth, as he now did, and meddle with a question of human guilt" (V, 87).

Nevertheless, Hester's ascension is limited. She sees the truth, but she will not utter the word. Heeding Chillingworth's gesture of secrecy, she does not publicly identify him. She has been educated under Dimmesdale's "preaching of the word"; she listens to his eloquent appeal for her to reveal her fellow-sinner's identity—an appeal that prompts a half-pleased, half-plaintive murmur from Pearl; but Hester will not utter the name. "She will not speak." And when her actual interview with Roger Chillingworth occurs, not in the mid-day sun but in the dark prison, we have the first clue to what will eventually develop into merely superficial penance. In this "dismal apartment" of her heart, she is confronted by her guilt, who lays his long forefinger on the scarlet letter and makes it his symbolic representative. Chillingworth then enjoins her to keep his identity secret, especially from Dimmesdale. "Recognize me not, by word, by sign, by look!" She determines to recognize only the letter and not the living embodiment of her guilt; and her release from confinement immediately follows.

Hester has thus gained only a partial insight from her plunge into the pit and her consequent ascent. She decides to stay in Boston, reasoning that the scene of her sin should become the scene of her penance. Since her deepest motive, however, is to remain close to her lover, her ideas about expiating the sin are partly rationalization. Nevertheless, she does resist a retreat into space—eastward to Europe or westward into the wilderness. Uniting the perspective gained from the pillory with the word, the letter branded upon her, she puts off the old garments and finds a new self in her art.

Only in her art does Hester begin to find grace and to grasp the truth; that is, only in her art does she come to know Pearl. Her needlework is an "act of penance," a product of delicate imaginative skill, and under other circumstances it might have been the "passion of her life." Through it she becomes involved with birth and death, with the social hierarchy, with all phases of community life (save marriage), adding the hidden sins and wounds of mankind to her own burden. Allowing her imagination full play, she has wrought better than she knew in creating Pearl's attire, and she has been imaginatively right in naming the child.

Unsatisfied with the intuitive vision of her art, however, Hester is tortured by her inability to understand Pearl in any rational medium. Her offspring is fanciful, spritelike, inscrutable; in her wild, bright, deep-black eyes she reflects the truth; but reflection can also foster diabolical illusion. "Brooding over all these matters, the mother felt like one who has evoked a spirit, but, by some irregularity in the process of conjuration, has *failed to win the master-word* that should control this new and incomprehensible intelligence" (V, 117–18). At the end of Chapter VII she makes an abortive effort to grasp the truth intellectually, putting the child through a half-earnest, half-playful catechism. "Art thou my child, in very truth?" she asks. "Tell me, then, what thou art, and who sent thee hither." (We notice, again, how Hawthorne suggests Pearl's fusion of art and truth in the archaisms of the dialogue.) But Pearl is not to be apprehended in this manner, and she further punishes Hester by refusing to admit a heavenly Father so long as the earthly father is concealed.

The superiority of Hester's artistic insight over the hollow rigidity of the orthodox is made clear when she and Pearl educate the highest members of the local hierarchy in the Governor's hall. She goes there to deliver a pair of embroidered gloves—we later learn that "a pure hand needs no glove to cover it" (V, 192)—and to argue for her right to keep Pearl. Bellingham's personality is neatly expressed in his stuccoed house, his gilded volumes, and the suit of armor. His views toward Hester and Pearl reveal themselves in the grotesque, inhuman distortions reflected by the armor. Cut off like Prufrock from spontaneity and fruitful emotion, he appears in an elaborate ruff that causes his head "to look not a little like that of John the Baptist in a charger." His astonishment at seeing the truth incarnate in his house is quite understandable. "I have never seen the like," he says, in unwitting self-criticism. "How gat such a guest into my hall?"

It soon becomes clear that the "truths of heaven and earth" cannot be seen through the catechism. Pearl, though unacquainted with the "out-ward form" of the *New England Primer* or the Westminster Catechism, could have undergone a fair examination in these works. But she naturally evades the question of the clergyman John Wilson about her origin, finally informing him that she had been plucked from the wild rose bush. The stunned Governor asserts that she is "in the dark," thereby provoking Hester into a heated illumination of his own blindness. "*See ye not*, she is the scarlet letter, only capable of being loved, and so endowed with a millionfold the power of retribution for my sin?" Turning to Dimmesdale, she cries: "*Speak for me* . . . thou knowest what is in my heart, and what are a mother's rights, and how much the stronger they are, when that mother has but her child and the scarlet letter! *Look thou to it!*" "There is truth in what she says," answers the minister, who has always been more responsive to the word than to the vision. Upon the Governor's request that he "make that plain," Dimmesdale teaches him what is expressed by Hester's art — namely that Pearl is both burden and blessing.

During the first third of the book, therefore, Hester, her glowing letter, and Pearl are as lights shining in the darkness of the community. The minister, meanwhile, fasts and vigils in the darkness and preaches words that place him in a false light. He attains a new perspective, however, when he begins to live with his guilt. When Chillingworth moves in with him, Dimmesdale finds in the physician's mind a remarkable depth and scope. "It was as if a window were thrown open," but "the air was too fresh and chill to be long breathed with comfort." Later, as Chillingworth keeps probing for "God's own truth," both men hear Pearl's laughter outside. "Looking instinctively from the open window," the minister sees Hester and Pearl in the adjacent burial ground. Here, seen from the new perspective and clearly outlined in the bright sunlight of the summer day, is the very truth that Chillingworth is seeking, but neither man can perceive it. Chillingworth looks at Pearl and asks, "What, in Heaven's name, is she?" And Dimmesdale is unable to explain her "principle of being."

The comprehension and communication of religious truth demands an intuitive fusion of language and vision. Hawthorne suggests that if Dimmesdale had not sinned, his native gifts would have placed him among the group of true saintly fathers whose only fault was their failure to communicate the highest truths to the populace. "All that they lacked was the gift that descended upon the chosen disciples at Pentecost, in tongues of flames; symbolizing, it would seem, not the power of speech in foreign and unknown languages, but that of addressing the whole human brotherhood in the heart's native language. These fathers, otherwise so apostolic, lacked Heaven's last and rarest attestation of their office, The Tongue of Flame. They would have vainly sought — had they ever dreamed of seeking — to express the highest truths through the humblest medium of familiar words and images" (V, 173). But Dimmesdale's burden keeps him on a level with the lowest. His congregation worships him; their adoration intensifies his guilty anguish; and his suffering heightens his fervor. Yet before he can truly speak with the Tongue of Flame, he must not only relate but reveal. He has already *spoken* the truth — confessed his sin — but in such abstract terms that he well knew "*the light* in which his vague confession would be viewed" (V, 176).

So long as they are covert, the minister's gestures are but a mockery of penitence, and his cloistral flagellations, fasts, and vigils are unavailing. The magnificent midnight scaffold scene dramatizes the various degrees of moral blindness in the community and throws the falsity of the minister's rationalizations into sharp relief. Clothed as if he were going to attend public worship, he ascends the platform, which is cloaked in darkness. Much more perceptive than the Governor, who can "see but little further than a mill-stone" in the darkness, he also has a more exalted perspective than John Wilson's. That elderly clergyman approaches the platform, but his glimmering lantern reveals only "the muddy pathway" beneath his feet.

Dimmesdale still persists in his argument, eternally true perhaps, but humanly false, that revelation must wait until judgment day. Hester and Pearl have joined him on the platform; he has been infused with new life as he takes Pearl's hand; but the tableau that follows is a visualization of his argument. For the awesome light of the meteor provides a kind of noon, "as if it were the light that is to reveal all secrets." It is like the day of doom, and in this lurid light the minister sees the ambiguity of his argument without being consciously aware of it. Though he gazes toward the zenith he is at the same time perfectly aware that Pearl is pointing toward Roger Chillingworth, his earthly guilt. He is close to perceiving the relation between the woman, their mutual guilt and their possible salvation; but when he asks Pearl to translate this vision into rational terms, he is unable to understand her natural or intuitive language. She speaks "in a tongue unknown to the erudite clergyman." Nevertheless, his revelation has unconsciously begun. He has divested himself of part of his hollow armor—the black glove.

The middle third of the book is perfectly and ironically balanced, for as the minister is struggling toward outsight and disclosure, Hester is seeking insight and utterance. Her moral predicament during the past few years has been just the reverse of his. Outwardly she has been a penitent sinner, and by her good works she has transmuted the letter into a badge of mercy. To many, the letter has "the effect of a cross on a nun's bosom." But her nominal penance is just as incomplete as Dimmesdale's closeted flagellations. Since the "interview" of Chapter IV she has not acknowledged her connection with Roger Chillingworth, and his symbol, the letter, has ceased being a vital one for her. Without the spirit, the letter killeth: the A may now stand for "Able," but there is "nothing in Hester's bosom, to make it ever again the pillow of Affection," unless another transfiguration occurs. She has become a mannish vagrant, speculating in the gloomy labyrinth of the mind. It is a kind of dissipation in which her natural role as woman has evaporated into space. The Word, outwardly imposed and outwardly worn, has failed in its traditional rhetorical discipline. "The scarlet letter had not done its office."

Thus the midnight scaffold scene has been a dark night of the soul for her as well as for the minister. But as a result of Dimmesdale's changed aspect, she has been given a "new theme for reflection." She resolves to confront her guilt and confess it to the minister. "I would speak a word with you," she says to Chillingworth, "a word that concerns us much." The word amounts to a new acceptance of her responsibility in the sin; and her emotions as she watches Chillingworth depart throw "a dark light" on her state of mind, "revealing much that she might not otherwise have acknowledged to herself." Pearl seems much closer and more earnest than ever before. But Hester is not yet ready for the utterance of the whole truth. To Pearl's relentless questions, Hester can only reply, "Hold thy tongue," and threaten to shut the child in *her* dark closet.

The complex interweaving of utterance and vision, investment and speculation, time and space reaches a peak in the forest interview. Dimmesdale tells Hester of his torture, which has been augmented by his native gifts: "Canst thou deem it, Hester, a consolation, that I must stand up in my pulpit, and meet so many eyes turned upward to my face, as if the *light of heaven* were beaming from it! — must see my flock hungry for the truth, and listening to my words *as if a tongue of Pentecost were speaking!* and then look inward, and discern the black reality of what they idolize?" Hester gently suggests that the sin has been left behind, that penitence is sealed and witnessed by good works. But the pastor knows better. Then she conquers her fears and utters her responsibility for the guilt that now resides with him. "Dost thou not *see* what I would *say?* That old man! — the physician! — he whom they call Roger Chillingworth! he was my husband." Like Milton's Adam, Arthur sternly repels her; and then his heart relents.

At this point Hester offers a way of lightening the burden in their share of woe. Never — not even in the exhortations of Emerson and Thoreau — has the vision of dawn, the promise of America, the dream of a second chance found more deeply felt utterance than in her appeal, as she urges the time-drenched man to recover himself, to put on a new name and leave the ruin behind him. "Preach! Write! Act! Do anything save to lie down and die!" The closing formula of her brief but eloquent sermon is "Up and away!" The fact that this phrase is likely to call up for some modern readers a vision of the gaudily vested Superman may seem unfortunate. But this association is not entirely irrelevant: as we know, one consequence of the doctrine of self-reliance, was its distortion into a grossly materialized version of the superman. And the modern connotations of the phrase, voiced as it is by the woman, simply point up the inversion of roles that climaxes the forest scene. She has grown eloquent while he is now silent; she has lost insight while he is gaining outsight. The parishioner is now preaching to the pastor. Dimmesdale, on the other hand, in whose eyes "a fitful light" has been kindled by Hester's enthusiasm, now gazes upon her with a "look in which hope and joy shone out." She has spoken "what he vaguely hinted at but dared not speak."

As the succeeding events reveal, Hester has preached a half-truth. She has rightly told him to be a man, to exert his protestant function of penetrating into space and conquering new fields. All this he could do — alone. What Hester does not see is that if she is to go with him, he must accept the catholic involvement in guilt-stained time that is the essence of her womanhood. She has usurped the masculine prerogative of speculation, and her intellectual wanderings have been so undisciplined that they have become obscure. In the gloom of the wilderness or the blankness of space, nothing of temporal or moral significance can be seen.

That her proposal is only half valid may be discerned from her symbolic relation to Pearl and the stream of time. Hester would like to retain only the pleasant aspects of the past. She throws off the scarlet letter (it lands, however, on the "hither verge" of the stream of time); she removes the formal cap that confines her hair, resuming "her sex, her youth, and the whole richness of her beauty" from "what men call the irrevocable past." And she tells Arthur: "Thou must know Pearl. . . . Thou hast seen her, — yes, I know it! — but thou wilt see her now with other eyes. She is a strange child. I hardly comprehend her." With his newly discovered vision, the minister can see Pearl, standing a good way off on the other side of the brook. But neither he nor Hester is yet skilled to read "the character of flame," the "oneness of their being." Pearl will not join them, for wholeness is not achieved by drawing a sharp boundary between the worlds of past and present. Her symbolic gestures, reflected in the stream, indicate that their proposed escape from time into motion and space is an unrealizable dream — or at least can be effected only at the cost of leaving their salvation behind.

Though Hester desperately clings to the hope of drowning her guilt in the deep sea, she now recognizes that the forest cannot hide it. The moment of inspiration has passed. By flinging the letter "into infinite space" she had drawn "an hour's free breath," but now the burden must be resumed. The child rejoins her mother, but between Pearl and the minister there is no expression, no communion. He awkwardly impresses a kiss on her brow, which she hastily washes off in the brook.

The precise nature of the minister's transformation in the forest is once again worked out in terms of the Word and the Light. He has stripped away the old words; he has discarded his old self amid the decaying leaves "like a cast-off garment." The scales have dropped from his eyes; he has attained an Emersonian vision. But his old insight has been temporarily obliterated. His condition is indicated by Hawthorne's complex moral topography. The pathway in the woods seems "wilder, more uncouth with its rude natural obstacles, and less trodden by the foot of man, than he remembered it on his outward journey." On the one hand, he is closer to the freedom of individual growth, less hampered by the principles and prejudices of the social system; on the other, he is, as the chapter title indicates, "the minister in a maze" — more deeply involved in a moral wilderness with its "plashy places" and its "clinging underbrush."

In this mood, it is all that Dimmesdale can do to keep from mocking his old words. Intoxicated and unbalanced by the heady wine of the new, he runs into a series of delightfully wrought encounters that anticipate Clifford Pyncheon's escape from his past in *The House of the Seven Gables*. He has temporarily substituted the undisciplined "vision" for communion; thus when he meets a hoary old deacon he has to forcibly restrain himself from "uttering certain blasphemous suggestions that entered his mind, respecting the communion supper. He absolutely trembled and turned pale as ashes, lest his tongue should wag itself, in utterance of these horrible matters." He resists the temptation to blight the innocence of a virgin with "but one wicked look" and the development of evil with "but a word." All his other misadventures stem from his rejection of the old rhetorical discipline. The sinister side of his revolt is cleverly shown by the pompous modern jargon of his conversation with Mistress Hibbins, the embodiment of ubiquitous evil. "I profess, madam," he says, with "a grave obeisance, such as the lady's rank" demands, "I profess, on my conscience and character, that I am utterly bewildered as touching the purport of your words! I went not into the forest to seek a potentate; neither do I, at any future time, design a visit thither, with a view to gaining the favor of such a personage."

After the vision of the forest interview, what Dimmesdale clearly needs now is to be nourished by a communion with the tomb-fed faith and the tome-fed wisdom of the past. In order to grasp the truth in his art form, he must return to the rich intellectual resources of the study, adjacent to the graveyard. "Here he had studied and written; here, gone through fast and vigil, and come forth half alive; here, striven to pray; here, borne a hundred thousand agonies! There was the Bible, in its rich old Hebrew, with Moses and the Prophets speaking to him, and God's voice through all!" White and speechless, he has been able to confront Roger Chillingworth squarely; he has withstood the travail of temptation in the wilderness; and now he is able to join the new vision with the rich utterances of the past. The long fast is over. Partaking of supper, he composes, as if divinely inspired, the flaming rhetoric of the Election Sermon. This is *his* new field; this is his true dawn; and as the golden sunrise beams in his study, he is seen with the pen still between his fingers and "a vast, immeasurable tract of written space behind him."

The Election Sermon itself cannot be rationally reproduced — it is heard and felt. To Hester, who is outside the church, it sounds like the great organ music of "a tongue native to the human heart, wherever educated." In its undertone may be detected the deep ache at the heart of human life itself — a sense of atonement not only for the individual sin but for Original Sin. The crowd inside the church is spellbound at the close of the sermon, profoundly silent as if they had heard "the utterance of oracles." Then they gush forth from the doors, feeling the need of "other breath, more fit to support the gross and earthly life into which they relapsed, than that atmosphere which the preacher had converted into *words of flame.*" The subject of the sermon, as it is later revealed, is akin to the theme of the book: "the relation between the Deity and the communities of mankind, with a special reference to the New England which they were planting here in the wilderness." The minister prophesies a high and glorious destiny for these communities, just as God has providentially transformed his own moral wilderness into glory.

The last ascension scene captures with terse, compelling inevitability the paradox that lies at the heart of tragedy and Christianity. Time and eternity intersect on the platform of the pillory as Dimmesdale, "in the name of Him, so terrible and so merciful, who gives me grace at this last moment," makes the final revelation and is at last united with Pearl. With his vision into eternity, he asks Hester, "Is not this better . . . than what we dreamed of in the forest?" Her answer is the temporal one: "I know not. . . . Better? Yea; so we may both die, and little Pearl die with us." Even her last hope—for a specific reunion in an afterlife—is clothed in earthly terms, and in his dying breath Dimmesdale offers her no encouragement.

The various reactions of the crowd to Dimmesdale's revelation are presented in ascending order from the crude to the spiritual. The first two conjectures about the origin of the letter on his breast—that it was self-imposed torture, or that Roger Chillingworth wrought it with his poisonous drugs—are the most naturalistic and the least valid. A third group—"those best able to appreciate the minister's peculiar sensibility and the wonderful operation of his spirit upon the body"—see the letter as a psychic cancer that gradually manifested itself physically. But the last group is the most interesting. These "highly respectable witnesses" are "spectators of the whole scene," and they see the minister as a saint. They associate his final action with Christ's sympathy for the adulteress, and they think Dimmesdale so shaped the manner of his death as to make of it a parable, illustrating "that in the view of Infinite Purity, we are sinners all alike."

Having stated this view in more detail than any of the others, Hawthorne then explicitly questions it in the light of common sense. A clue to the ambiguity here is offered by the meanings of the word *respectable*. In its usual sense, the adjective tells us that these witnesses were among the more pious and pompous members of the community, stubbornly refusing to see any evil in the high representatives of their society. Yet in a book where the language itself points back to the original—a book dealing with vision and language, where words like "spectator" and "speculation" are extremely significant—we begin to wonder about our easy rejection of these "respectable" witnesses. Etymologically, these are the spectators who *look back*; and from this point of view their version of the minister's life is the most original, the most spiritual of all.

Considerable evidence supporting their view may be found in Hawthorne's description of the New England holiday. Despite its sable tinge, there is an aura of hope. "For today," as Hester tells Pearl, "a new man is beginning to rule over them; and so—as has been the custom of mankind ever since a nation was first gathered—they make merry and rejoice; as if a good and golden year were at length to *pass over* the poor old world." The new man is really Arthur Dimmesdale. Having achieved individuation in the forest, he now returns to join the procession only to rise above it. "The spiritual element took up the feeble frame, and carried it along, unconscious of the burden and converting it to spirit like itself."

But the whole truth is not distilled in the refined perception of the respectable witnesses. Their view must be considered along with the crude ideas of the materialists; and the composite of the two is represented by those firmly grounded in the temporal life who nevertheless appreciate the minister's sensibility, the interaction of flesh and spirit. The "moral," which at first sight seems to be an oversimplification, should be read in this light. To "be true," one must not mean but be. The truth, that is to say, can only be grasped in its total living context; and since this comprehensive view is impossible from any single human perspective, the closest we can come to it is through "expression" — art, symbol, gesture, or parable — a showing "of some trait" from which the totality may be inferred.

At the end we are left with the symbol into which the whole meaning of the book has been distilled. Around the letter have gathered not only the explicit associations of Adultress, Able, Affection, and Angel but also the myriad subtle suggestions of art, atonement, ascension, and the Acts of the Apostles. Here is the A, each limb of which suggests an ascension, with Pearl the link between the two; here is the sable background of the Puritan community; and fused in the entire symbol are the flesh and the spirit, the word and the light, the letter *A*, gules. Hawthorne seized upon the heraldic wording partly because of its rich poetic associations but also because "gules" is the perfect word with which to conclude the book. It means "scarlet," of course, but it originates from the Latin *gula*, meaning "throat." Here condensed in one word is the Tongue of Flame; here, joining the language patterns of vision and eloquence, is the perfect capstone for Hawthorne's symbolic structure.

Notes

1. *Studies in Classic American Literature*, p. 111. Lawrence refers only to Hawthorne's fiction in this judgment.

2. See Yvor Winters, *Maule's Curse* (New Directions, New York, 1938), p. 16.

3. These conflicting views are summarized by Frederic I. Carpenter, "Scarlet A Minus," *College English*, V (January, 1944), 173–80.

4. John C. Gerber, "Form and Content in *The Scarlet Letter*," *New England Quarterly*, XVII (March, 1944), 25–55; Newton Arvin, ed., *The Scarlet Letter* (Modern Classics Series, Harper & Brothers, New York, 1950), p. xii; Anne Marie MacNamara, " 'The Character of Flame': The Function of Pearl in *The Scarlet Letter*," *American Literature*, XXVII (January, 1956), 537–53. I am indebted to Miss MacNamara's article at several points in my interpretation of Dimmesdale's relation to Pearl.

5. Quoted in George P. Lathrop, *A Study of Hawthorne* (Houghton Mifflin Company, Boston, 1876), p. 229.

6. This interpretation of Chillingworth's role was first suggested to me by Hillel Chodos and John L. Murphy.

7. The philosopher whose writings furnish one of the closest parallels to Hawthorne's thought is Johann Georg Hamann. Note, for instance, this passage:

"*Money* and *language* are two subjects whose investigation is as profound and abstract as their use is universal. Both stand in a closer relationship than one might presume. The theory of one explains the theory of the other; therefore they seem to flow from common sources. The wealth of all human knowledge rests on the exchange of words. . . . On the other hand, all the goods of civil or social life have reference to money as their universal standard." (Hamann's italics.) Quoted in James C. O'Flaherty, *Unity and Language: A Study in the Philosophy of Johann Georg Hamann* (University of North Carolina Press, Chapel Hill, N.C., 1952), p. 30.

The Ruined Wall   Frederick C. Crews*

> The golden sands that may sometimes be gathered (always, perhaps, if
> we know how to seek for them) along the dry bed of a torrent, adown
> which passion and feeling have foamed, and past away. It is good,
> therefore, in mature life, to trace back such torrents to their source.
> —Hawthorne, *American Notebooks*

Hester Prynne and Arthur Dimmesdale, in the protective gloom of the forest surrounding Boston, have had their fateful reunion. While little Pearl, sent discreetly out of hearing range, has been romping about in her unrestrained way, the martyred lovers have unburdened themselves. Hester has revealed the identity of Chillingworth and has succeeded in winning Dimmesdale's forgiveness for her previous secrecy. Dimmesdale has explained the agony of his seven years' torment. Self-pity and compassion have led unexpectedly to a revival of desire; "what we did," as Hester boldly remembers, "had a consecration of its own" (*C*, I, 195),[1] and Arthur Dimmesdale cannot deny it. In his state of helpless longing he allows himself to be swayed by Hester's insistence that the past can be forgotten, that deep in the wilderness or across the ocean, accompanied and sustained by Hester, he can free himself from the revengeful gaze of Roger Chillingworth.

Hester's argument is of course a superficial one; the ultimate source of Dimmesdale's anguish is not Chillingworth but his own remorse, and this cannot be left behind in Boston. The closing chapters of *The Scarlet Letter* demonstrate this clearly enough, but Hawthorne, with characteristic license, tells us at once that Hester is wrong. "And be the stern and sad truth spoken," he says, "that the breach which guilt has once made into the

*Reprinted from *The Sins of the Fathers: Hawthorne's Psychological Themes* (New York: Oxford University Press, 1966), 136–53; © 1966 by Frederick C. Crews. Reprinted by permission of Oxford University Press.

human soul is never, in this mortal state, repaired. It may be watched and guarded; so that the enemy shall not force his way again into the citadel, and might even, in his subsequent assaults, select some other avenue, in preference to that where he had formerly succeeded. But there is still the ruined wall, and, near it, the stealthy tread of the foe that would win over again his unforgotten triumph" (*C*, I, 200f.).

This metaphor is too striking to be passed over quickly. Like Melville's famous comparison of the unconscious mind to a subterranean captive king in Chapter XLI of *Moby-Dick*, it provides us with a theoretical understanding of behavior we might otherwise judge to be poorly motivated. Arthur Dimmesdale, like Ahab, is "gnawed within and scorched without, with the infixed, unrelenting fangs of some incurable idea," and Hawthorne's metaphor, inserted at a crucial moment in the plot, enables us to see the inner mechanism of Dimmesdale's torment.

At first, admittedly, we do not seem entitled to draw broad psychological conclusions from these few sentences. Indeed, we may even say that the metaphor reveals a fruitless confusion of terms. Does Hawthorne mean to describe the soul's precautions against the repetition of overt sin? Apparently not, since the "stealthy foe" is identified as *guilt* rather than as the forbidden urge to sin. But if the metaphor means what it says, how are we to reduce it to common sense? It is plainly inappropriate to see "guilt" as the original assailant of the citadel, for feelings of guilt arise only in *reaction against* condemned acts or thoughts. The metaphor would seem to be plausible only in different terms from those that Hawthorne selected.

We may resolve this confusion by appealing to Arthur Dimmesdale's literal situation. In committing adultery he has succumbed to an urge which, because of his ascetic beliefs, he had been unprepared to find in himself. Nor, given the high development of his conscience and the sincerity of his wish to be holy, could he have done otherwise than to have violently expelled and denied the sensual impulse, once gratified. It was at this point, we may say — the point at which one element of Dimmesdale's nature passed a sentence of exile on another — that the true psychological damage was done. The original foe of his tranquility *was* guilt, but guilt for his thoughtless surrender to passion. In this light we see that Hawthorne's metaphor has condensed two ideas that are intimately related. Dimmesdale's moral enemy is the forbidden impulse, while his psychological enemy is guilt; but there is no practical difference between the two, for they always appear together. We may understand Hawthorne's full meaning if we identify the potential invader of the citadel as a libidinal impulse, *now necessarily bearing a charge of guilt.*

This hypothesis helps us to understand the sophisticated view of Dimmesdale's psychology that Hawthorne's metaphor implies. Dimmesdale's conscience (the watchful guard) has been delegated to prevent repetition of the temptation's "unforgotten triumph." The deterrent weapon of conscience is its capacity to generate feelings of guilt, which are of course painful to the soul. Though the temptation retains all its strength (its demand for gratification), this is counterbalanced by its burden of guilt. To readmit the libidinal impulse through the guarded breach (to gratify it in the original way) would be to admit insupportable quantities of guilt. The soul thus keeps temptation at bay by meeting it with an equal and opposite force of condemnation.

But let us consider the most arresting feature of Hawthorne's metaphor. The banished impulse, thwarted in one direction, "might even, in his subsequent assaults, select some other avenue, in preference to that where he had formerly succeeded." Indeed, the logic of Hawthorne's figure seems to assure success to the temptation in finding another means of entrance, since conscience is massing all its defenses at the breach. This devious invasion would evidently be less gratifying than the direct one, for we are told that the stealthy foe would stay in readiness to attack the breach again. Some entry, nevertheless, is preferable to none, especially when it can be effectuated with a minimum resistance on the part of conscience. Hawthorne has set up a strong likelihood that the libidinal impulse will change or disguise its true object, slip past the guard of conscience with relative ease, and take up a secret dwelling in the soul.

In seeking to explain what Hawthorne means by this "other avenue" of invasion, we must bear in mind the double reference of his metaphor. It describes the soul's means of combating both sin and guilt—that is, both *gratification* of the guilty impulse and *consciousness* of it. For Dimmesdale the greatest torment is to acknowledge that his libidinous wishes are really his, and not a temptation from the Devil. His mental energy is directed, not simply to avoiding sin, but to expelling it from consciousness—in a word, to repressing it. The "other avenue" is the means his libido chooses, given the fact of repression, to gratify itself surreptitiously. In psychoanalytic terms this is the avenue of compromise that issues in a neurotic symptom.

Hawthorne's metaphor of the besieged citadel cuts beneath the theological and moral explanations in which Dimmesdale puts his faith, and shows us instead an inner world of unconscious compulsion. Guilt will continue to threaten the timid minister in spite of his resolution to escape it, and indeed (as the fusion of "temptation" and "guilt" in the metaphor implies) this resolution will only serve to upset the balance of power and enable guilt to conquer the soul once more. Hawthorne's metaphor demands that we see Dimmesdale not as a free moral agent but as a victim of feelings he can neither understand nor control. And the point can be extended to include Chillingworth and even Hester, whose minds have been likewise altered by the consequences of the unforgotten act, the permanent breach in the wall. If, as Chillingworth asserts, the awful course of events has been "a dark necessity" from the beginning, it is not because Hawthorne believes in Calvinistic predestination or wants to imitate Greek tragedy, but because all three of the central characters have been ruled by motives inaccessible to their conscious will.

The implications we have drawn, perhaps over-subtly, from Hawthorne's metaphor begin to take on substance as we examine Arthur Dimmesdale in the forest scene. His nervousness, his mental exhaustion, and his compulsive gesture of placing his hand on his heart reveal a state that we would now call neurotic inhibition. His lack of energy for any of the outward demands of life indicates how all-absorbing is his internal trouble, and the stigma on his chest, though a rather crass piece of symbolism on Hawthorne's part, must also be interpreted psychosomatically. Nor can we avoid observing that Dimmesdale shows the neurotic's reluctance to give up his symptoms. How else can we account for his obtuseness in not having recognized Chillingworth's character? "I might have known it!" he murmurs when Hester forces the revelation upon him. "I did know it! Was not the secret told me in the natural recoil of my heart, at the first sight of him, and as often as I have seen him since? Why did I not understand?" (C, I, 194) The answer, hidden from Dimmesdale's surface reasoning, is that his relationship with Chillingworth, taken together with the change in mental economy that has accompanied it, has offered perverse satisfactions which he is even now powerless to renounce. Hester, whose will is relatively independent and strong, is the one who makes the decision to break with the past.

We can understand the nature of Dimmesdale's illness by defining the state of mind that has possessed him for seven years. It is of course his concealed act of adultery that lies at the bottom of his self-torment. But why does he lack the courage to make his humiliation public? Dimmesdale himself offers us the clue in a cry of agony: "Of penance I have had enough! Of penitence there has been none! Else, I should long ago have thrown off these garments of mock holiness, and have shown myself to mankind as they will see me at the judgment-seat" (C, I, 192). The plain meaning of this outburst is that Dimmesdale has never surmounted the libidinal urge that produced his sin. His "penance," including self-flagellation and the more refined torment of submitting to Chillingworth's influence, has failed to purify him because it has been unaccompanied by the feeling of penitence, the resolution to sin no more. Indeed, I submit, Dimmesdale's penance has incorporated and embodied the very urge it has been punishing. If, as he says, he has kept his garments of mock holiness *because* he has not repented, he must mean that in some way or another the forbidden impulse has found gratification in the existing circumstances, in the existing state of his soul. And this state is one of morbid remorse. The stealthy foe has re-entered the citadel through the avenue of remorse.

This conclusion may seem less paradoxical if we bear in mind a distinction between remorse and true repentance. In both states the sinful act is condemned morally, but in strict repentance the soul abandons the sin and turns to holier thoughts. Remorse of Dimmesdale's type, on the other hand, is attached to a continual re-enacting of the sin in fantasy and hence a continual renewal of the need for self-punishment. Roger Chillingworth, the psychoanalyst *manqué*, understands the process perfectly: "the fear, the remorse, the agony, the ineffectual repentance, the backward rush of sinful thoughts, expelled in vain!" (*C*, I, 139). As Hawthorne explains, Dimmesdale's cowardice is the "sister and closely linked companion" (*C*, I, 148) of his remorse.

Thus Dimmesdale is helpless to reform himself at this stage because the passional side of his nature has found an outlet, albeit a self-destructive one, in his present miserable situation. The original sexual desire has been granted recognition *on the condition of being punished*, and the punishment itself is a form of gratification. Not only the overt masochism of fasts, vigils, and self-scourging (the last of these makes him laugh, by the way), but also Dimmesdale's emaciation and weariness attest to the spending of his energy against himself. It is important to recognize that this is the same energy previously devoted to passion for Hester. We do not exaggerate the facts of the romance in saying that the question of Dimmesdale's fate, for all its religious decoration, amounts essentially to the question of what use is to be made of his libido.

We are now prepared to understand the choice that the poor minister faces when Hester holds out the idea of escape. It is not a choice between a totally unattractive life and a happy one (not even Dimmesdale could feel hesitation in that case), but rather a choice of satisfactions, of avenues into the citadel. The seemingly worthless alternative of continuing to admit the morally condemned impulse by the way of remorse has the advantage, appreciated by all neurotics, of preserving the status quo. Still, the other course naturally seems more attractive. If only repression can be weakened — and this is just the task of Hester's rhetoric about freedom — Dimmesdale can hope to return to the previous "breach" of adultery.

In reality, however, these alternatives offer no chance for happiness or even survival. The masochistic course leads straight to death, while the other, which Dimmesdale allows Hester to choose for him, is by now so foreign to his withered, guilt-ridden nature that it can never be put into effect. The resolution to sin will, instead, necessarily redouble the opposing force of conscience, which will be stronger in proportion to the overtness of the libidinal threat. As the concluding chapters of *The Scarlet Letter* prove, the only possible result of Dimmesdale's attempt to impose, in Hawthorne's phrase, "a total change of dynasty and moral code, in that interior kingdom" (*C*, I, 217), will be a counter-revolution so violent that it will slay Dimmesdale himself along with his upstart libido. We thus see that in the forest, while Hester is prating of escape, renewal, and success, Arthur Dimmesdale unknowingly faces a choice of two paths to suicide.

Now, this psychological impasse is sufficient in itself to refute the most "liberal" critics of *The Scarlet Letter* — those who take Hester's proposal of escape as Hawthorne's own advice. However much we may admire Hester and prefer her boldness to Dimmesdale's self-pity, we cannot agree that she understands human nature very deeply. Her shame, despair, and solitude "had made her strong," says Hawthorne, "but taught her much amiss" (C, I, 200). What she principally ignores is the truth embodied in the metaphor of the ruined wall, that men are altered irreparably by their violations of conscience. Hester herself is only an apparent exception to this rule. She handles her guilt more successfully than Dimmesdale because, in the first place, her conscience is less highly developed than his; and secondly because, as he tells her, "Heaven hath granted thee an open ignominy, that thereby thou mayest work out an open triumph over the evil within thee, and the sorrow without" (C, I, 67). Those who believe that Hawthorne is an advocate of free love, that adultery has no ill effects on a "normal" nature like Hester's, have failed to observe that Hester, too, undergoes self-inflicted punishment. Though permitted to leave, she has remained in Boston not simply because she wants to be near Arthur Dimmesdale, but because this has been the scene of her humiliation. "Her sin, her ignominy, were the roots which she had struck into the soil," says Hawthorne. "The chain that bound her here was of iron links, and galling to her inmost soul, but never could be broken" (C, I, 80).

We need not dwell on this argument, for the liberal critics of *The Scarlet Letter* have been in retreat for many years. Their place has been taken by subtler readers who say that Hawthorne brings us from sin to redemption, from materialistic error to pure spiritual truth. The moral heart of the novel, in this view, is contained in Dimmesdale's Election Sermon, and Dimmesdale himself is pictured as Christ-like in his holy death. Hester, in comparison, degenerates spiritually after the first few chapters; the fact that her thoughts are still on earthly love while Dimmesdale is looking toward heaven is a serious mark against her.

This redemptive scheme, which rests on the uncriticized assumption that Hawthorne's point of view is identical with Dimmesdale's at the end, seems to me to misrepresent the "felt life" of *The Scarlet Letter* more drastically than the liberal reading. Both take for granted the erroneous belief that the novel consists essentially of the dramatization of a moral idea. The tale of human frailty and sorrow, as Hawthorne calls it in his opening chapter, is treated merely as the fictionalization of an article of faith. Hawthorne himself, we might repeat, did not share this ability of his critics to shrug off the psychological reality of his work. *The Scarlet Letter* is, he said, "positively a hell fired story, into which I found it almost impossible to throw any cheering light."

All parties can agree, in any case, that there is a terrible irony in Dimmesdale's exhilaration when he has resolved to flee with Hester. Being, as Hawthorne describes him, "a true religionist," to whom it would always remain essential "to feel the pressure of a faith about him, supporting, while it confined him within its iron framework" (*C*, I, 123), he is ill-prepared to savor his new freedom for what it is. His joy is that of his victorious libido, of the "enemy" which is now presumably sacking the citadel, but this release is acknowledged by consciousness only after a significant bowdlerization:

> "Do I feel joy again?" cried he, wondering at himself. "Methought the germ of it was dead in me! O Hester, thou art my better angel! I seem to have flung myself — sick, sin-stained, and sorrow-blackened — down upon these forest leaves, and to have risen up all made anew, and with new powers to glorify Him that hath been merciful! This is already the better life! Why did we not find it sooner?" (*C*, I, 201f.)

Hawthorne's portrayal of self-delusion and his compassion are nowhere so powerfully combined as in this passage. The Christian reference to the putting on of the New Man is grimly comic in the light of what has inspired it, but we feel no more urge to laugh at Dimmesdale than we do at Milton's Adam. If in his previous role he has been only, in Hawthorne's phrase, a "subtle, but remorseful hypocrite" (*C*, I, 144), here he is striving pathetically to be sincere. His case becomes poignant as we imagine the revenge that his tyrannical conscience must soon take against these new promptings of the flesh. To say merely that Dimmesdale is in a state of theological error is to miss part of the irony; it is precisely his theological loyalty that necessitates his confusion. His sexual nature must be either denied with unconscious sophistry, as in this scene, or rooted out with heroic fanaticism, as in his public confession at the end.

On one point, however, Dimmesdale is not mistaken: he has been blessed with a new energy of body and will. The source of this energy is obviously his libido; he has become physically strong to the degree that he has ceased directing his passion against himself and has attached it to his thoughts of Hester. But as he now returns to town,[2] bent upon renewing his hypocrisy for the four days until the Election Sermon has been given and the ship is to sail, we see that his "cure" has been very incomplete. "At every step he was incited to do some strange, wild, wicked thing or other, with a sense that it would be at once involuntary and intentional; in spite of himself, yet growing out of a profounder self than that which opposed the impulse" (*C*, I, 217). The minister can scarcely keep from blaspheming to his young and old parishioners as he passes them in the street; he longs to shock a deacon and an old widow with arguments against Christianity, to poison the innocence of a naïve girl who worships him, to teach wicked words to a group of children, and to exchange bawdy jests with a drunken sailor. Here, plainly, is a return of the repressed, and in a form which Freud noted to be typical in severely holy persons.[3] The fact that these impulses have reached the surface of Dimmesdale's mind attests to the weakening of repression in the forest scene, while their perverse and furtive character shows us that repression has not ceased altogether.

Hawthorne's own explanation, that Dimmesdale's hidden vices have been awakened because "he had yielded himself *with deliberate choice*, as he had never done before, to what he *knew* was deadly sin" (*C*, I, 222; my italics), gives conscience its proper role as a causative factor. Having left Hester's immediate influence behind in the forest, and having returned to the society where he is known for his purity, Dimmesdale already finds his "wicked" intentions constrained into the form of a verbal naughtiness which he cannot even bring himself to express.

Now Dimmesdale, presumably after a brief interview with the taunting Mistress Hibbins, arrives at his lodgings. Artfully spurning the attentions of Roger Chillingworth, he eats his supper "with ravenous appetite" (*C*, I, 225) and sits down to write the Election Sermon. Without really knowing what words he is setting on paper, and wondering to himself how God could inspire such a sinner as himself, he works all night "with earnest haste and ecstasy" (*C*, I, 225). The result is a sermon which, with the addition of spontaneous interpolations in the delivery, will impress its Puritan audience as an epitome of holiness and pathos. Nothing less than the descent of the Holy Ghost will be held sufficient to account for such a performance.

Yet insofar as the Election Sermon will consist of what Dimmesdale has recorded in his siege of "automatic writing," we must doubt whether Hawthorne shares the credulous view of the Puritans. Dimmesdale has undergone no discernible change in attitude from the time of his eccentric impulses in the street until the writing of the sermon. Though he works in the room where he has fasted and prayed, and where he can see his old Bible, he is not (as Male argues) sustained by these reminders of his faith. Quite the contrary: he can scarcely believe that he has ever breathed such an atmosphere. "But he seemed to stand apart, and eye this former self with scornful, pitying, but half-envious curiosity. That self was gone! Another man had returned out of the forest; a wiser one; with a knowledge of hidden mysteries which the simplicity of the former never could have reached" (*C*, I, 223). In short, the Election Sermon is written by the same man who wants to corrupt young girls in the street, and the same newly liberated sexuality "inspires" him in both cases. If the written form of the Election Sermon *is* a great Christian document, as we have no reason to doubt, this is attributable not to Dimmesdale's holiness but to his libido, which gives him creative strength and an intimate acquaintance with the reality of sin.

Thus Dimmesdale's sexual energy has temporarily found a new alternative to its battle with repression—namely, sublimation. In sublimation, we are told, the libido is not repressed but redirected to aims that are acceptable to conscience. The writing of the Election Sermon is just such an aim, and readers who are familiar with psychoanalysis will not be puzzled to find that Dimmesdale has passed without hesitation from the greatest blasphemy to fervent religious rhetoric.

There is little doubt that Dimmesdale has somehow recovered his piety in the three days that intervene between the writing of the sermon and its delivery. Both Hester and Mistress Hibbins "find it hard to believe him the same man" (*C*, I, 241) who emerged from the forest. Though he is preoccupied with his imminent sermon as he marches past Hester, his energy seems greater than ever and his nervous mannerism is absent. We could say, if we liked, that at this point God's grace has already begun to sustain Dimmesdale, but there is nothing in Hawthorne's description to warrant a resort to supernatural explanations. It seems likely that Dimmesdale has by now felt the full weight of his conscience's case against adultery, has already determined to confess his previous sin publicly, and so is no longer suffering from repression. His libido is now free, not to attach itself to Hester, but to be sublimated into the passion of delivering his sermon and then expelled forever.

The ironies in Dimmesdale's situation as he leaves the church, having preached with magnificent power, are extremely subtle. His career, as Hawthorne tells us, has touched the proudest eminence that any clergyman could hope to attain, yet this eminence is due, among other things, to "a reputation of whitest sanctity" (*C*, I, 249). Furthermore, Hester has been silently tormented by an inquisitive mob while Dimmesdale has been preaching, and we feel the injustice of the contrast. And yet Dimmesdale has already made the choice that will render him worthy of the praise he is now receiving. If his public hypocrisy has not yet been dissolved, his hypocrisy with himself is over. It would be small-minded not to recognize that Dimmesdale has, after all, achieved a point of heroic independence — an independence not only of his fawning congregation but also of Hester, who frankly resents it. If the Christian reading of *The Scarlet Letter* judges Hester too roughly on theological grounds, it is at least correct in seeing that she lacks the detachment to appreciate Dimmesdale's final act of courage. While she remains on the steady level of her womanly affections, Dimmesdale, who has previously stooped below his ordinary manhood, is now ready to act with the exalted fervor of a saint.

All the moral ambiguity of *The Scarlet Letter* makes itself felt in Dimmesdale's moment of confession. We may truly say that no one has a total view of what is happening. The citizens of Boston, for whom it would be an irreverent thought to connect their minister with Hester, turn to various rationalizations to avoid comprehending the scene. Hester is bewildered, and Pearl feels only a generalized sense of grief. But what about Arthur Dimmesdale? Is he really on his way to heaven as he proclaims God's mercy in his dying words?

> "He hath proved his mercy, most of all, in my afflictions. By giving me this burning torture to bear upon my breast! By sending yonder dark and terrible old man, to keep the torture always at red-heat! By bringing me hither, to die this death of triumphant ignominy before the

people! Had either of these agonies been wanting, I had been lost for ever! Praised be his name! His will be done! Farewell!" (C, I, 256f.)

This reasoning, which sounds so cruel to the ear of rational humanism, has the logic of Christian doctrine behind it; it rests on the paradox that a man must lose his life to save it. The question that the neo-orthodox interpreters of *The Scarlet Letter* invariably ignore, however, is whether Hawthorne has prepared us to understand this scene only in doctrinal terms. Has he abandoned his usual irony and lost himself in religious transport?

The question ultimately amounts to a matter of critical method: whether we are to take the action of *The Scarlet Letter* in natural or supernatural terms. Hawthorne offers us naturalistic explanations for everything that happens, and though he puts forth opposite theories — Pearl is an elf-child, Mistress Hibbins is a witch, and so on — this mode of thinking is discredited by the simplicity of the people who employ it. We cannot conscientiously say that Chillingworth *is* a devil, for example, when Hawthorne takes such care to show us how his devilishness has proceeded from his physical deformity, his sense of inferiority and impotence, his sexual jealousy, and his perverted craving for knowledge. Hawthorne carries symbolism to the border of allegory but does not cross over. As for Dimmesdale's retrospective idea that God's mercy has been responsible for the whole chain of events, we cannot absolutely deny that this may be true; but we can remark that if it *is* true, Hawthorne has vitiated his otherwise brilliant study of motivation.

Nothing in Dimmesdale's behavior on the scaffold is incongruous with his psychology as we first examined it in the forest scene. We merely find ourselves at the conclusion to the breakdown of repression that began there, and which has necessarily brought about a renewal of opposition to the forbidden impulses. Dimmesdale has been heroic in choosing to eradicate his libidinal self with one stroke, but his heroism follows a sound principle of mental economy. Further repression, which is the only other alternative for his conscience-ridden nature, would only lead to a slower and more painful death through masochistic remorse. Nor can we help but see that his confession passes beyond a humble admission of sinfulness and touches the pathological. His stigma has become the central object in the universe: "God's eye beheld it! The angels were for ever pointing at it! The Devil knew it well, and fretted it continually with the touch of his burning finger!" (C, I, 255). Dimmesdale is so obsessed with his own guilt that he negates the Christian dogma of original sin: "behold me here, the one sinner of the world!" (C, I, 254). This strain of egoism in his "triumphant ignominy" does not subtract from his courage, but it casts doubt on his theory that all the preceding action has been staged by God for the purpose of saving his soul.

However much we may admire Dimmesdale's final asceticism, there are no grounds for taking it as Hawthorne's moral ideal. The last developments of plot in *The Scarlet Letter* approach the "mythic level" which redemption-minded critics love to discover, but the myth is wholly secular and worldly. Pearl, who has hitherto been a "messenger of anguish" to her mother, is emotionally transformed as she kisses Dimmesdale on the scaffold. "A spell was broken. The great scene of grief, in which the wild infant bore a part, had developed all her sympathies; and as her tears fell upon her father's cheek, they were the pledge that she would grow up amid human joy and sorrow, nor for ever do battle with the world, but be a woman in it." (*C*, I, 256) Thanks to Chillingworth's bequest — for Chillingworth, too, finds that a spell is broken when Dimmesdale confesses, and he is capable of at least one generous act before he dies — Pearl is made "the richest heiress of her day, in the New World" (*C*, I, 261). At last report she has become the wife of a European nobleman and is living very happily across the sea. This grandiose and perhaps slightly whimsical epilogue has one undeniable effect on the reader: it takes him as far as possible from the scene and spirit of Dimmesdale's farewell. Pearl's immense wealth, her noble title, her lavish and impractical gifts to Hester, and of course her successful escape from Boston all serve to disparage the Puritan sense of reality. From this distance we look back to Dimmesdale's egocentric confession, not as a moral example which Hawthorne would like us to follow, but as the last link in a chain of compulsion that has now been relaxed.

To counterbalance this impression we have the case of Hester, for whom the drama on the scaffold can never be completely over. After raising Pearl in a more generous atmosphere she voluntarily returns to Boston to resume, or rather to begin, her state of penitence. We must note, however, that this penitence seems to be devoid of theological content; Hester has returned because Boston and the scarlet letter offer her "a more real life" (*C*, I, 262) than she could find elsewhere, even with Pearl. This simply confirms Hawthorne's emphasis on the irrevocability of guilty acts. And though Hester is now selfless and humble, it is not because she believes in Christian submissiveness but because all passion has been spent. To the women who seek her help "in the continually recurring trials of wounded, wasted, wronged, misplaced, or erring and sinful passion" (*C*, I, 263), Hester does not disguise her conviction that women are pathetically misunderstood in her society. She assures her wretched friends that at some later period "a new truth would be revealed, in order to establish the whole relation between man and woman on a surer ground of mutual happiness" (*C*, I, 263). Hawthorne may or may not believe the prediction, but it has a retrospective importance in *The Scarlet Letter*. Hawthorne's characters originally acted in ignorance of passion's strength and persistence, and so they became its slaves.

"It is a curious subject of observation and inquiry," says Hawthorne at the end, "whether hatred and love be not the same thing at bottom. Each, in its utmost development, supposes a high degree of intimacy and heart-knowledge; each renders one individual dependent for the food of his affections and spiritual life upon another; each leaves the passionate lover, or the no less passionate hater, forlorn and desolate by the withdrawal of his object" (C, I, 260). These penetrating words remind us that the tragedy of *The Scarlet Letter* has chiefly sprung, not from Puritan society's imposition of false social ideals on the three main characters, but from their own inner world of frustrated desires. Hester, Dimmesdale, and Chillingworth have been ruled by feelings only half perceived, much less understood and regulated by consciousness; and these feelings, as Hawthorne's bold equation of love and hatred implies, successfully resist translation into terms of good and evil. Hawthorne does not leave us simply with the Sunday-school lesson that we should "be true" (C, I, 260), but with a tale of passion through which we glimpse the ruined wall — the terrible certainty that, as Freud put it, the ego is not master in its own house. It is this intuition that enables Hawthorne to reach a tragic vision worthy of the name: to see to the bottom of his created characters, to understand the inner necessity of everything they do, and thus to pity and forgive them in the very act of laying bare their weaknesses.

Notes

1. All textual references are to the *Centenary Edition of the Works of Nathaniel Hawthorne*, ed. William Charvat, et al. Columbus: Ohio State University Press, 1962–. [Ed. note].

2. Note, incidentally, the implicit sexuality of his cross-country run, as he "leaped across the plashy places, thrust himself through the clinging underbrush, climbed the ascent, plunged into the hollow . . ." (C, I, 216).

3. See, for example, *Collected Papers*, III, 331, 599f.

Dimmesdale's Ultimate Sermon   Terence Martin*

When Arthur Dimmesdale leaves the forest after his meeting with Hester Prynne (in Chapter XX of *The Scarlet Letter*), he walks energetically back to town, resists a series of grotesque temptations to shock parishioners whom he sees, disavows further need of Chillingworth's assistance, and writes a new Election Day sermon with such "an impulsive flow of thought and emotion" that he works through the night until sunrise. We next see him (two chapters later) moving toward the church in the procession — walking with "an unaccustomed force." After delivering his Election sermon, he leaves the church, pale, debilitated, and hesitant,

*Reprinted from *Arizona Quarterly* 27 (Autumn 1971):230–40, by permission of the journal and the author.

then summons Hester and Pearl onto the scaffold with him for the climactic revelation of the scarlet letter.

Hawthorne gives no account of any mental or spiritual process by means of which Dimmesdale comes to the scaffold; there are no sentences informing us that Dimmesdale has repudiated the plan of escape discussed in the forest, no hints which might indicate that he has thought about the matter in any way. His confession comes suddenly, surprisingly, astonishing not only the Puritan multitude in the market place but also Hester and Chillingworth, each of whom has a special knowledge of the situation. The dramatic logic of *The Scarlet Letter*, of course, calls for Dimmesdale's public confession in the third scaffold scene. Obviously, however, one expects something interior and ongoing in the novel to support its formal order. It is, I believe, a matter of some significance to see how Hawthorne's presentation of Dimmesdale functions to set up the third scaffold scene — how, finally, self-delusion, pride, and a capacity for eloquence (energized by passion) evoke the ultimate sermon which not even Dimmesdale can withstand. To put that matter in perspective, we must attend to the details of the concluding chapters.

I

From the time of his forest interview with Hester Prynne to the delivery of the Election sermon, Dimmesdale acts with astonishing vitality. Not only does he rush back into town — a striking contrast to his usual self-searching stumble — but once alone in the privacy of his study he calls for food and eats "with ravenous appetite" — the only time in the novel that such a detail is mentioned. Moreover, he is now able to meet Chillingworth's guile with dissembling of his own. When Chillingworth offers him medical aid, for example, Dimmesdale can reply, "I think to need no more of your drugs, my kind physician, good though they be, and administered by a friendly hand." This is a familiar kind of remark for the minister to make to the physician. But now, of course, Dimmesdale knows who Chillingworth is, and his new awareness gives the conversation an ironic bite. Unaware as yet of the minister's plan to flee with Hester, Chillingworth mentions the fear of the people that another year may find their pastor gone: "Yea, to another world," replied the minister, with pious resignation. "Heaven grant it be a better one; for . . . I hardly think to tarry with my flock through the flitting seasons of another year." Only Dimmesdale (and the reader) can appreciate the ambiguity of the remark. Hawthorne's gloss that Dimmesdale spoke these words "with pious resignation" gives us an added insight into Dimmesdale's new-found ability as an actor. The minister is a different man during his conversation with Chillingworth, careful, crafty, capable of private jokes. And once Chillingworth has departed and the meal has been eaten, Dimmesdale throws "the already written pages" of one Election sermon into the fire and writes another "with such an impulsive flow of thought and emotion, that he fancied himself inspired; and only wondered that Heaven should see fit to transmit the grand and solemn music of its oracles through so foul an organ-pipe as he."

The narrative has moved from the forest to the study with sustained emotional force: the Dimmesdale who feels a surge of life as he is united with Hester and Pearl is the same Dimmesdale who sits down to write the new Election sermon. In the forest, it is important to remember, Hester has lent her strength to Dimmesdale; in the lending, we see that seven years of public penance have not touched the image she has of her action with him: "What we did had a consecration of its own. We felt it so! We said so to each other!" Believing this, Hester has no grounds for penitence. Her act with Dimmesdale was different, she affirms, uniquely consecrated and hence not within the province of ordinary law. Hester's seven years of penance have had surprising consequences. ("The scarlet letter," Hawthorne says simply, "had not done its office.") She has wandered "without rule or guidance, in a moral wilderness"; she has criticized human institutions, "whatever priests or legislators had established." Shame, despair, and solitude have been her teachers, "and they had made her strong, but taught her much amiss."

Hester has lived through these years with unshaken faith in the passion which won for her—in the eyes of the community—a badge of dishonor. Made to live according to the letter of the law, she remains aloof from and comes ultimately to be opposed to the spirit of the law. For she believes, as indeed she must, in the supremacy of her passion. And it is Hawthorne's achievement to make her appeal to passion the persuasive outgrowth of her uncomplaining silence. In the forest with Dimmesdale, Hester removes her *A*, lets her dark hair tumble down, and demonstrates that seven years of ignominy have left her the resolute priestess of a private cult. "As regarded Hester Prynne," Hawthorne tells us, "the whole seven years . . . had been little other than a preparation for this very hour."

An act of passion, nursed by a memory of its sacredness, has blossomed into a principle of conduct. Hester has virtually been preparing for this moment in the forest. But Dimmesdale, broken and ensnared by hypocrisy, has never in his wildest dreams contemplated running away. His earlier sin (and Hawthorne makes the point explicit) had been a sin of passion and "not of principle, nor even purpose." Instinctively, he recoils from Hester's passionate memory of their sin as something consecrated; but, paralyzed by the disclosure of Chillingworth's identity, he cries out at the next moment, "Think for me, Hester! Thou art strong. Resolve for me!" The resolution to flee is radical in its implications for Dimmesdale; he embraces his sin once again, now willfully, with the ardor of a convert to a new faith.

Dimmesdale's conversion experience in the forest is of a deep and revolutionary character. It brings to him "a glow of strange enjoyment"—

"the exhilarating effect — upon a prisoner just escaped from the dungeon of his own heart — of breathing the wild, free atmosphere of an unredeemed, unchristianized, lawless region." Such an atmosphere is intoxicating. On his way from the forest to the study, as we have noted, his actions are extravagant and bizarre. We have been told before that Dimmesdale seldom ventured intellectually or imaginatively beyond the limits set by the traditions of his profession. Now he has leaped at a bound into a patternless world in which he is a new, untutored, wildly erratic citizen. But — Hawthorne points out — his sense of freedom and energy is contaminated at its source. If he had not sold himself to the devil, "he had made a bargain very like it! Tempted by a dream of happiness, he had yielded himself with deliberate choice, as he had never done before, to what he knew was deadly sin. And the infectious poison of that sin had been thus rapidly diffused throughout his moral system" — tempting and frightening him.

Now one might well wonder what kind of a sermon will issue from a mind vibrating with such turmoil. Within the "interior kingdom" of Dimmesdale's "thought and feeling" a "revolution" has occurred — "nothing short of a total change of dynasty and moral code." No longer is he simply the hypocritical minister; he is now the apostate minister, who stands in need of a counter-conversion if he is to be numbered among the elect. What, then, is he writing with "such an impulsive flow of thought and emotion" now that he has thrown his already written pages into the fire? Why, indeed, is he rewriting the sermon at all?

The paragraph which describes Dimmesdale writing his new sermon (the last of Chapter XX) raises again the paradox of heavenly ideas coming through a polluted medium but reveals no evidence that Dimmesdale changes his mind about escaping. Indeed, as we shall see, his decision to flee is the very reason he must write a new sermon. The possibility that his sin in the forest (deliberate and deadly as never before) has beneficent effects, among them the transcending of his self-centeredness, must be considered in the multiple context of his immediate temptations to shock innocent people, of his amazing ability to play the old Dimmesdale to Chillingworth, and especially of Hawthorne's pitying statement about the developing relation between Dimmesdale's weakness and Dimmesdale's pride. For after agreeing to run away with Hester, the minister inquires of her when the ship is scheduled to depart. He considers it "most fortunate" that it will not leave for four days. With a posture of reluctance, Hawthorne interprets Dimmesdale's thoughts — in order "to hold nothing back from the reader." Dimmesdale considers the departure date "very fortunate" because in three days he is to preach the Election Day sermon, "and, as such an occasion formed an honorable epoch in the life of a New England clergyman, he could not have chanced upon a more suitable mode and time of terminating his professional career. 'At least, they shall say of me,' thought this exemplary man, 'that I leave no public duty unperformed, nor ill performed!' " Hawthorne laments the fact that the minister could be "so miserably deceived."

> We have had, and may still have, worse things to tell of him; but none, we apprehend, so pitiably weak; no evidence, at once so slight and irrefragable, of a subtle disease, that had long since begun to eat into the real substance of his character. No man, for any considerable period, can wear one face to himself, and another to the multitude, without finally getting bewildered as to which may be the true.

This is strong language, controlled by a tone of sadness at having to admit the extent of the minister's self-delusion. As the final step in a developing process, Hawthorne has shown us an absolutely stunning doubleness in the minister's character. Having chosen to breathe "the wild, free atmosphere of an unredeemed, unchristianized, lawless region," having undergone a "total change of dynasty and moral code," Dimmesdale reaffirms to himself (he does not mention it to Hester) the importance of the Election Day sermon. He wants to have it both ways, to leave, but to leave with his duty well performed — which is to say, with the congregation marveling at their saintly, inspired minister. And not only that: Dimmesdale's motive here is characteristically secret. No sooner is he converted to Hester's cult than he has an immediate private life outside it which gives him latitude to plan by himself, for himself. The psychological keenness informing Dimmesdale's transformation is of a high order. No matter what "religion" the minister professes, he serves ultimately the interests of one master — himself. Thus, in keeping with the brilliant economy of *The Scarlet Letter*, the moment at which Dimmesdale commits himself consciously to deadly liberating sin becomes the moment at which he secretly wishes to cap his public life with a final burst of eloquence on the most important occasion the Puritan community can offer. He is prepared, as a good preacher should be; he has some pages (perhaps all) already written. But now the significance of the Election Day sermon is heightened by the idea that he will be "terminating his professional career." It will be his last sermon in New England; accordingly, all his powers must go into it. He will rewrite it to make it the final, the greatest, the ultimate, sermon.

Dimmesdale succeeds, of course, in making his sermon the most powerful his auditors have ever heard. Writing energetically, with a hunger for success, he molds his idiom of anguish into a commanding statement. The cadences of Hawthorne's prose describe the sound of the sermon as it falls on Hester's ears: forever present is "an essential character of plaintiveness"; even when the minister's tone grows high and authoritative, there is a "cry of pain." This "profound and continual undertone . . . gave the clergyman his most appropriate power" — the cry of "a human heart, sorrow-laden, perchance guilty, telling its secret . . . to the great heart of mankind; beseeching its sympathy or forgiveness, — at every moment, — in each accent, — and never in vain!"

Dimmesdale manages this personal note of pain while discoursing upon the most orthodox of subjects for an Election Day sermon. His subject is "the relation between the Deity and the communities of mankind, with a special reference to the New England which they were here planting in the wilderness." Toward the end he prophesies "a high and glorious destiny for the newly gathered people of the Lord."

The minister's desire to give one last sermon, formed in the forest, formed out of, as a very part of, his decision to run away with Hester Prynne, has been fulfilled. The consequences of performing his duty so well are all that he (and we) might have expected: "He stood, at this moment, on the very proudest eminence of superiority, to which the gifts of intellect, rich lore, prevailing eloquence, and a reputation of whitest sanctity, could exalt a clergyman in New England's earliest days, when the professional character was of itself a lofty pedestal." When the procession emerges from the church, a great and spontaneous shout engendered by Dimmesdale's eloquence goes up from the people. "Never, on New England soil, had stood the man so honored by his mortal brethren as the preacher."

Dimmesdale has had his way with the sermon. Already the spiritual darling of the people, he is now a genuine Puritan hero-saint — the true giver of the true word. Unaware that Chillingworth has booked passage on the ship he is to flee on with Hester and Pearl, Dimmesdale would seem to have a clear path out of the community. But the energy he brought from the forest is drained. The happy victim of his own eloquence, he stumbles from the procession, beckons to Hester and Pearl, and goes to the scaffold. Dimmesdale's desire to "terminate" his public career by giving the Election Day sermon, a symptom of extreme weakness and delusion, has resulted in a statement so powerful and so persuasive that he cannot withstand it. The sermon, that important force for Puritan salvation, becomes at the end of *The Scarlet Letter* the instrument for self-conversion.

II

The question of how Dimmesdale comes to the scaffold can be answered most effectively, and should be, in terms that have the greatest resonance for *The Scarlet Letter* as a whole. My suggestion that he converts himself by means of his ultimate sermon is, I believe, reinforced by a consideration of some points established earlier in the novel, including evidence that might appear to support an alternative view.

Dimmesdale's demeanor as he walks toward the church in the procession, for example, might seem to indicate a change of mind. As he walks briskly along he gives Hester no glance, no sign of recognition. They had known each other deeply in the forest, she feels; yet "she hardly knew him now!" Dimmesdale seems "unattainable in his worldly position, and still more so in that far vista of his unsympathizing thoughts." This intent, remote Dimmesdale, I believe, is the product of his desire to give one last sermon. Although Hester did know him deeply in the forest, she had no knowledge of why he inquired about the date of the ship's departure, no knowledge that he considered the date "most fortunate," no knowledge that the Puritan face of Arthur Dimmesdale would require a final stamp of Puritan approval on Election Day. We recall, too, that he moves in the procession with energy, and that energy and vitality have been his only since the forest meeting with Hester. "Never, since Mr. Dimmesdale first set foot on the New England shore, had he exhibited such energy. . . . There was no feebleness of step, as at other times; his frame was not bent; nor did his hand rest ominously on his heart." His strength, Hawthorne tells us, seems internal, the result of a vast marshalling of intellectual power.

Having taken a great vitality from Hester and from their decision to run away, Dimmesdale has converted it to the ends of his sermon, investing it in the rich lore of his profession, immersing it in the anguish that gives such a plaintive note to all his sermons. An association between Hester and Dimmesdale's eloquence has been established at other important places in *The Scarlet Letter*. In the first scaffold scene, Dimmesdale must appeal to Hester to name her partner in sin. To the people gathered about, the appeal seems irresistible, powerful beyond withstanding. Proof against its power in this case, however, is the man who has it in him to frame it. The second scaffold scene, at midnight, witnesses Dimmesdale indulging himself with a "vain show of expiation." Hawthorne stresses the egotism of the minister's guilt and mocks him for such a futile show of repentance. Yet Dimmesdale does take vitality from Hester and Pearl when he clasps their hands. And the next morning he preaches a sermon that is held to be the best that has ever come from his lips; souls, more souls than one, says Hawthorne, were converted by that sermon, among them that of the pure young maiden whom Dimmesdale later is tempted to shock upon his return from the forest. Dimmesdale is not brought to public confession either by his initial appeal to Hester or by the powerful sermon he preaches after the midnight scaffold scene. As long as there are other sermons to give he will not achieve his ultimate eloquence. Hawthorne has, nonetheless, established an association between Dimmesdale's contact with Hester and his ability to speak with special power and also between Dimmesdale's sermons and the idea of conversions.

To argue that Dimmesdale converts himself only with the giving of his sermon might seem to be insisting on a fine distinction. But I think that it is both important and possible to incorporate this point precisely in our reading of *The Scarlet Letter*. It would probably be correct to say that

Dimmesdale is writing the sermon that will convert him (though he does not know it) or that as he walks to the church he has something in his mind that will change it (though he does not know that). But the actual preaching of the sermon is necessary for Dimmesdale to convert himself. Writing the sermon is a private act; in the forest with Hester, Dimmesdale does not look forward to *writing* his sermon but to *preaching* it—and preaching it in a church packed with people on Election Day. (We cannot imagine him being satisfied with leaving a written, unpreached, sermon behind as the performance of his duty.) The efficacy of the spoken word is important here, not only in the specific dramatic setting of the Election Day sermon but throughout the novel as a whole. According to the "united testimony" of those who heard the sermon, "never had man spoken in so wise, so high, and so holy a spirit" as Dimmesdale spoke that day:

> nor had inspiration ever breathed through mortal lips more evidently than it did through his. Its influence could be seen, as it were, descending upon him, and possessing him, and continually lifting him out of the written discourse that lay before him, and filling him with ideas that must have been as marvellous to himself as to his audience.

The statement is not without its ambiguity. Yet, at the very least, it suggests that the giving of the sermon is of dramatic significance and, further, that something of great spiritual import is happening ("as it were") as Dimmesdale speaks. Clearly and literally, the minister must preach his way to public confession.

Dimmesdale's self-intentness is by no means confined to the final stages of the novel. Throughout *The Scarlet Letter* the minister suffers from an excess of self. Self-condemnation, self-abnegation, and self-loathing are the stimulants of his psychic life; they are the price he must pay if he is to retain the public image of himself which he so painfully relishes. In preaching about the iniquity of man, Dimmesdale preaches essentially about himself; he gains converts, is revered all the more for his sanctity, and, as a consequence, reviles himself all the more. For he will not surrender his public image or tarnish his public face. That, of course, is why he thinks to ask if he will have time to give the Election Day sermon before he flees. Then, faced with the prospect of one final sermon, the man who has done everything else to himself converts himself.

That Dimmesdale's confession is stimulated more by his sense of imminent death than by his overwhelming eloquence (or by his tortured conscience) is perhaps most readers' response to the final scaffold scene. But this explanation squares almost too well with that of the Puritans themselves, who interpret the pathos of Dimmesdale's sermon as "the natural regret of one soon to pass away." There is simply more to the picture, more to relate to what is going on in the narrative than what we can get from Hawthorne's Puritan spectators. The patterns of the novel are definable, and Dimmesdale's self-conversion is consonant with them.

Irony, paradox, and a presentation of reality as ambivalent and multivalent work powerfully and continually in *The Scarlet Letter*. The Puritans, for example, are presented as harsh and somber; yet Hawthorne says repeatedly that Dimmesdale's only chance for human understanding and forgiveness lies in trusting the great warm heart of the people. Hester Prynne wears a "halo of misfortune." The imposed penance forces her toward attitudes which the Puritans would deem far worse than the sin for which they punished her. Chillingworth's revenge victimizes himself — so that after seven years of consummate vengeance he cries out (to Hester) that Dimmesdale has but increased the debt. And nowhere are such patterns of irony and paradox more in evidence than in Hawthorne's portrayal of Arthur Dimmesdale.

The idea, then, that Dimmesdale's decision to flee reinforces his desire to give the Election Day sermon, that from the hour of his most deadly sin and his most pitiable weakness comes the eloquence that will bring him to public confession and salvation (to a death of "triumphant ignominy" on the scaffold) is part and parcel of the mode of *The Scarlet Letter*. All aspects of Dimmesdale's life contribute to the resolution: the minister has taken the passion and energy of Hester's solitary faith to the forms of Puritan public worship; on the scaffold he reveals the self he has hidden so long, the private shrine of his scarlet *A* (which one is tempted now to interpret as *Arthur*). Admittedly, the idea that Dimmesdale converts himself (or elects himself, on Election Day) might pose some problems of orthodoxy for a strict Puritan. But with *The Scarlet Letter* as our evidence, we can say that it is better, after all, to have Hawthorne be a great writer and an indifferent Puritan than to have it the other way around.

[Isolation and Interdependence as Structure in *The Scarlet Letter*]   Arne I. Axelsson*

It seems fairly obvious that *The Scarlet Letter* is more a story about isolated people than about sinners. Attempts to interpret the romance as being about three different types of sinners, or even three different types of people — with or without allegorical overtones — are unsatisfactory since they ignore the fact that the romance contains *four* major characters. Especially from a structural point of view Pearl's role in the book must be considered, and a critical approach which pays no or little attention to her

*Reprinted in part from "Isolation and Interdependence as Structure in Hawthorne's Four Major Romances," *Studia Neophilologica* 45 (1973):392–402, by permission of the journal.

part can never be convincing. Because of the difficulties arising from Pearl's amoral innocence in a romance which many critics take to deal only with the problem of sin and guilt, it has even been assumed that Hawthorne failed to create the kind of character he intended in Pearl. Thus, interpretations based on moralistic concerns alone easily reach the conclusion that *The Scarlet Letter* would be a better work of art without her. However, all such difficulties disappear if we suppose instead that what Hawthorne had in mind was a romance about human isolation and interdependence rather than one about sin and sinners.

The four major characters then emerge as types of human "isolatoes" — to borrow Melville's word — who occur frequently in Hawthorne's writing: Hester, the proud and passionate idealist who trusts her own feelings more than the laws of society, but who also makes emotional mistakes which lead to isolation; Dimmesdale, the sensitive and passive man prone to withdrawal, and isolated as a result of an indissoluble inner tension; Chillingworth, the villain, whose inhuman occupation leads to his separation from humanity; Pearl, the innocent victim, whose isolation from society and play-mates is the result of the negligence, mistakes or sins of the people about her, in particular her mother's sin. Around these four persons and a central scaffold of ignominy Hawthorne builds the three key scenes which form the structural backbone of the romance. The same scenes also mark phases of development in the main plot, the theme of which is the gradual reunion of the dispersed Hester–Dimmesdale–Pearl family in spite of the powerful counterinfluence from Chillingworth. In the first of these scaffold scenes Hester and Pearl are alone on the platform. Dimmesdale is completely separated from the two, morally and physically. In the second scene, half-way through the book, all three stand together on the scaffold, but their union is only temporary and they all know that Dimmesdale will not recognize its existence in broad daylight. In the third scene the reunion is effected, although the author leaves the question open as to its final validity in heaven. Chillingworth is naturally present on all these occasions as a representative of the separating forces.

If we look more closely at the division into parts of *The Scarlet Letter* and the underlying structure on which it rests, we find that the first half of the romance is largely taken up by Hawthorne's definition of his four major characters' positions in respect to each other and to society. Generally, Hester's isolation from society, her former husband and her lover is developed in chapters 1 through 5. That situation is also the point of departure for the plot of the romance, which is not so static as has often been supposed. There follows a section of three chapters which deal with Pearl, first in her relations to her mother and then to society and to Dimmesdale. Chapters 9 and 10 concentrate on the Chillingworth–Dimmesdale relationship and they lead up to a special study of the clergyman in chapter 11. That chapter is also a preparation for the second scaffold scene in chapter 12, which ends the first half of the book. On the plot level, we see how the attitude of society gradually softens. At the beginning of the book Hester and her child are total outcasts from the Puritan community, but as time passes Hester is at least partially accepted by society — for example, nobody questions her place by the Governor's death bed. Although Hester still avoids the Puritans and seems to regard them with almost the same bitterness as before, her isolation generally tends to decrease. At the same time Dimmesdale and Chillingworth steadily become more and more alienated from society. Towards the middle of the book, however, some hope seems to emerge for Dimmesdale, as he becomes aware of the power of sympathy and the bond of mutual dependence which exist between him and Hester and Pearl as they stand in the night, joining hands.

The second half of the romance starts like the first one. After an introductory chapter entitled "Another View of Hester," there follows Hester's second meeting with Chillingworth, which Hawthorne contrasts with the first meeting in the earlier part of the romance, and then two chapters, number 15 and 16 — corresponding to 6 and 7 in the first half — are devoted to the relationship between Hester and Pearl. Then the symmetry between the two parts is partly broken, as we now have no Chillingworth section following. Instead Hawthorne goes on to develop the Hester–Dimmesdale–Pearl triangle of interrelations in chapters 17–19. Chapter 20, like chapter 11, deals only with Dimmesdale. The following chapters, which lead up to the final scaffold scene in 23, again treat Hester and Pearl and their relations to society. The final chapter has the form of a coda and gives a summary of later events and Hester's final position. At first, the plot during this second part continues to move toward a possible familial reunion, as Hester defies Chillingworth and decides to reveal his true identity to Dimmesdale. But then Hawthorne creates a diversion of the action and the development toward increased integration is broken. Dimmesdale and Hester are temporarily united, but in the wrong way, as is made evident by Pearl's negative attitude. Consequently, shortly before the final scaffold scene we find Hester and Pearl still as isolated as ever before, separated from society and from Dimmesdale, and Dimmesdale himself, for all his eloquence, is still as much morally apart from his parishioners as before. And when the three of them finally do unite, it is only for a short time, and the only one whom we definitely know to be saved through that union is Pearl. Nevertheless, there is no doubt that the last scaffold scene represents a higher degree of fulfillment and inter-dependence than the second one, and so we evidently have a development of the plot, both in the second part and in the romance as a whole. If there remains some doubt about Hester's and Dimmesdale's final restoration to the chain of humanity, there is also a corresponding doubt about Chillingworth's final exclusion from that chain. Actually, Hawthorne seems to say, Chillingworth was not totally isolated — even a bond of hate is better than no bond at all, and who knows what may come of that hate in another existence? Thus even the arch-fiend is allowed a kind of post-humous movement in the direction of interdependence.

To summarize: the isolation–interdependence motif seems to function well as a structural basis for *The Scarlet Letter*. From a generally shattered and isolated position with respect to society and each other, the characters move towards more coherence and greater interdependence. The three scaffold scenes illustrate stages in that development. The main course of the development changes only once, as the isolation of the characters temporarily increases toward the end of the romance, before the final reunion. The outcome is Pearl's total integration with humanity and a most positive relationship with her mother. Hester and Dimmesdale remain cases of doubtful but possible integration, whereas Chillingworth's possibilities of joining the chain of humanity are only facetiously suggested by the author.

[The Major Phase I, 1850: *The Scarlet Letter*]

Nina Baym*

Hawthorne took his post at the Salem Custom House under the impression that the position had been removed from the patronage rolls and that it would be his regardless of the results of future elections. When, after the Democratic defeat in 1848, the local Whigs determined to turn him out, they raised questions about his administrative competence as a means of justifying their action and removed him from the post. Hawthorne detested his work in the Custom House, but it was a living. To lose it—especially in a publicly humiliating way—was a traumatic experience. As long as the Whigs remained in office he could not expect another political appointment; he had no profession but writing, and writing had failed to support him at the Manse. In the period immediately following his dismissal the Hawthorne family lived on such household money as Sophia Hawthorne had saved, on the sale of her hand-decorated lamp-shades and hand screens, and on the contributions of friends. Hawthorne was poor, out of work, unfairly disgraced—and his terrible crisis was exacerbated yet further by the death of his mother (to whom he was deeply tied despite the emotional reserve that characterized their relationship) on July 31, 1849. *The Scarlet Letter* was written in a mood of grief and anger and seems to have had a therapeutic effect on him. "He writes immensely," Sophia reported in a letter to her mother. "I am almost frightened about it. But he is well now and looks very shining."[1]

*Reprinted from *The Shape of Hawthorne's Career* (Ithaca: Cornell University Press, 1976), 123–51. © 1976 by Cornell University. Used by permission of the publisher, Cornell University Press.

Before he finished *The Scarlet Letter*, he set it aside to compose "The Custom-House," so that in effect the two were written concurrently.[2] He designed "The Custom-House" for many purposes: to balance the mood and tone of *The Scarlet Letter*, which, he feared, was monotonous in its single effect; to increase the length of the volume in which *The Scarlet Letter* would be published; to take revenge on the politicians who had caused his removal from the Custom House. But above all he wrote it as a commentary on, and a frame for, *The Scarlet Letter*. The essay tells the story of how Hawthorne came to write *The Scarlet Letter* and in so doing tells us a good deal about how to read it. If "The Custom-House" makes an introduction to *The Scarlet Letter*, so does *The Scarlet Letter* provide the conclusion for "The Custom-House."

In *The Scarlet Letter* Hawthorne defined the focus of all four of his completed long romances: the conflict between passionate, self-assertive, and self-expressive inner drives and the repressing counterforces that exist in society and are also internalized within the self. In this romance he also formulated some of the recurrent elements in his continuing exploration of this theme. In Hester he developed the first of a group of female representatives of the human creative and passionate forces, while in Dimmesdale he created the first of several guilt-prone males, torn between rebellious and conforming impulses. These two characters operate in *The Scarlet Letter* in a historical setting, which was not repeated in any of Hawthorne's later romances, but the historical setting is shaped according to thematic preoccupations that do recur. Nominally Puritan, the society in *The Scarlet Letter* in fact symbolizes one side of the conflict.

None of his many treatments of the Puritans depicted them in their own terms — that is, as a group bound together by a covenant among themselves and with God, to establish "a due form of government both civil and ecclesiastical," in accordance with "a special overruling providence." (The words are John Winthrop's, from "A Model of Christian Charity.") The historical first generation of Puritans made constant reference out from their every act to the divine purpose for which they acted and the greater will they were bound to serve. Hawthorne, however, always treated the Puritans within an entirely secular framework. His early works constantly balance their punitive intolerance against their strong sense of their own rights and their hardy endurance. "Main-street" manifested, for the first time, a discrimination between them and their descendants on the grounds of their pure religious faith, but his treatment did not operate *within* that faith. The formulation in *The Scarlet Letter* is different from both of these, but retains the same secularity.

In *The Scarlet Letter*, unlike Hawthorne's stories about Ann Hutchinson, the Quakers, Roger Williams, or the Salem witches, the Puritans are not punishing a heresy but an act that in its essence does not appear to quarrel with Puritan doctrine. What Hester and Dimmesdale have done is not a crime against belief but against the law. Many critics have maintained that, since the act violates one of the Ten Commandments, it is necessarily seen by Hawthorne as a crime against Divine Law. But in *The Scarlet Letter* he considers the act entirely as a social crime. Precisely because he does not take up the issue of whether the law broken is a divine law, the issues center on the relations of Hester and Dimmesdale to their community and to themselves as they accept or deny the judgment of the community on them. They differ from one another, not as beings more or less religious, more or less "saved," but as beings differently bound to the community and differently affected by it.

Such a thematic situation is created in *The Scarlet Letter* by the virtual absence of God from the text, and in this respect the romance is a very poor representation of the Puritan mental life as the Puritan himself would have experienced it. Divinity in this romance is a remote, vague, ceremonially invoked concept that functions chiefly to sanction and support the secular power of the Puritan rulers. And — another difference from Hawthorne's earlier formulation of Puritan psychology — these rulers are not transfigured by the zeal of a recovered faith burning like a lamp in their hearts. Remove the sense of communal purpose and service in behest of God, and a self-satisfied secular autocracy remains; this is what we find in *The Scarlet Letter*. The Puritans of this community are sagacious, practical, realistic; they are lovers of form and display; they even tend toward luxury — consider Hester's many opportunities for fancy embroidery, and the elegance of Governor Bellingham's residence.

The ruling group is composed of old males, aptly epitomized in the Governor, "a gentleman advanced in years, and with a hard experience written in his wrinkles. He was not ill fitted to be the head and representative of a community, which owed its origin and progress, and its present state of development, not to the impulses of youth, but to the stern and tempered energies of manhood, and the sombre sagacity of age; accomplishing so much, precisely because it imagined and hoped so little."[3] This patriarchy surrounds itself with displays of power, and when Hawthorne writes that this was "a period when the forms of authority were felt to possess the sacredness of divine institutions" (p. 64), he makes the point, crucial for his story, that the Puritans venerate authority, not because it is an instrument in God's service, but because they believe secular authority itself to be divine.

What Hawthorne says of this group at the beginning of the romance he repeats at the end. In the final scene we see them as men of "long-tried integrity," of "solid wisdom and sad-colored experience," with "endowments of that grave and weighty order, which gives the idea of permanence, and comes under the general definition of respectability" (p. 238). The portrait is by no means wholly unfavorable (although respectable or authoritarian types will become increasingly unattractive in the subsequent romances) because Hawthorne feels, as he felt in *Grandfather's*

Chair, that men of this type were required to establish a new nation: "They had fortitude and self-reliance, and, in time of difficulty or peril, stood up for the welfare of the state like a line of cliffs against a tempestuous tide" (p. 238). But such men are totally unfit to "meddle with a question of human guilt, passion, and anguish" (p. 65) — to meddle, that is, with the private, inner, imaginative life of the person. They are purely formal, purely public men; the society they devise accordingly recognizes no private life, and it is against this obtuseness that Hester and Dimmesdale must try to understand their own behavior and feelings.

A community that embodies the qualities of aging public males must necessarily repress those of the young and female. Dimmesdale is a brilliant young minister who, in order to maintain himself as a favorite among the oligarchs, has repressed himself — made himself prematurely old by resolutely clinging to childhood. He "trode in the shadowy by-paths, and thus kept himself simple and childlike; coming forth, when occasion was, with a freshness, and fragrance, and dewy purity of thought, which, as many people said, affected them like the speech of an angel" (p. 66). In this dewy innocent we recognize faint traces of Hawthorne's earlier men of fancy, and like them Dimmesdale does not so much want power as approval. He is a dependent personality. But he is still a young man, and to forgo the engagement with life characteristic of youth he must continually hold himself back. His "sin" is an impulsive relaxation of self-restraint and a consequent assertion of his youthful energies against the restrictions established by the elders. He does a passionate, thoughtless, willful thing. Precipitated out of his protected security as much by fear as by guilt, he must now confront the conflicts of adulthood. It is not only that he has been initiated into sex; it is less the sexual than the mental and emotional that interests Hawthorne, the inner rather than the outer aspects of the experience. Dimmesdale must now recognize and deal with previously hidden, subversive, and disobedient parts of himself.

Hester begins from no such position of security as Dimmesdale, and her relative lack of protection is at once a disadvantage and a blessing. He is the darling insider while she is in many ways an outsider even before her deed exposes her to public disgrace. She has been sent to Massachusetts by her husband, there to await his arrival; her own will is not implicated in her residence in the community. She thus has nothing like Dimmesdale's tie to the group at the outset. If, as the unfolding of the romance demonstrates, she is a far more independent character than Dimmesdale, her independence may be partly the effect of her relative unimportance in and to society and her consequent paradoxical freedom within it. To judge by the development of a certain feminist ideology in Hester's thinking over the years, it would seem that Hawthorne intended to represent a basic difference in the status of men and women within a patriarchal structure. Since women are of less account than men — are not fully members of the society—they are coerced physically rather than psychologically. Forced to wear a symbol of shame in public, Hester is left alone behind that symbol to develop as she will.

The story of *The Scarlet Letter* evolves from the sin of omission that has occurred before the narrative begins to a much more important sin of commission that takes place in the same place seven years later. The original sexual encounter between Hester and Dimmesdale was an act neither of deliberate moral disobedience nor of conscious social rebellion. The characters had forgotten society and were thinking only of themselves. But seven years later when they meet again, they deliberately reject the judgment society has passed upon them. "What we did had a consecration of its own," Hester says, and "what hast thou to do with all these iron men, and their opinions?" (pp. 195, 197). Deciding to leave the community, they in effect deny its right to punish them. Hester is mainly responsible for this decision; seven years of solitude have made of her a rebel and a radical. The consequent catastrophe originates with Dimmesdale, whose fragile personality cannot sustain the posture of defiance once Hester's support has been removed and he is back in the community. He reverts—rather quickly—to the view that society has the right to judge and therefore that its judgment is right. His dying speech does not convince Hester. "Is not this better," he demands, "than what we dreamed of in the forest?" "I know not! I know not!" she replies (p. 254). She undertakes alone the journey they had planned together and secures the fruit of her sin from the consequences of a Puritan judgment. Then, surprisingly, she returns.

But by returning, even though she takes up the scarlet letter and wears it until her death, she does not acknowledge her guilt. Rather, she admits that the shape of her life has been determined by the interaction between that letter, the social definition of her identity, and her private attempt to withstand that definition. Her life is neither the letter nor her resistance—neither the inner nor the outer—but the totality. But by again wearing the letter after her return—a gesture nobody would have required of her after so many years—and thus bringing the community to accept that letter on her terms rather than its own, Hester has in fact brought about a modest social change. Society expands to accept her with the letter—the private life carves out a small place for itself in the community's awareness. This is a small, but real, triumph for the heroine.

Hester and Dimmesdale work through their seven-year purgatory accompanied by alter egos, partly supernatural and parasitic beings related in several symbolic ways to their hosts: for Hester, Pearl; for Dimmesdale, Chillingworth. These subsidiary figures embody the sin that has been committed as it is felt and understood by each of the two actors; they are figures of the imagination made real. Since Hester and Dimmesdale imagine their act quite differently, the deed assumes a radically different shape in each one's inner life. Hester perceives her "sin" in the shape of the beautiful child, wild, unmanageable, and unpredictable, who has been created from it; Dimmesdale sees his in the form of the vengeful and embittered husband who has been offended by it.

Splintered off from the characters with whom they are associated, Pearl and Chillingworth indicate disharmony and disunity within Hester's and Dimmesdale's emotional lives, a direct result of the conflict between their sense of themselves and their awareness of how the community perceives them. Each character is alienated from a different part of his nature; crudely, Hester is tormented by her passions and Dimmesdale by his conscience. At the end of the romance the two shattered personalities become whole again and the symbolic characters disappear. Dimmesdale dies and so does Chillingworth; Hester, free at last from social stigma, becomes a whole person and so does Pearl.

For the seven solitary years that she remains in the community, Hester tries to come to terms with its judgment. She actually wants to accept that judgment, for, if she can, she will see purpose and meaning in her suffering. But her attempts cannot shake her deepest conviction that she has not sinned—that is, that the social judgment is not a divine judgment: "Man had marked this woman's sin by a scarlet letter, which had such potent and disastrous efficacy that no human sympathy could reach her, save it were sinful like herself. God, as a direct consequence of the sin which man thus punished, had given her a lovely child, whose place was on that same dishonored bosom, to connect her parent for ever with the race and descent of mortals, and to be finally a blessed soul in heaven!" (p. 89).

As an embodiment of Hester's sin, Pearl is a kind of variant of the scarlet letter. Hester perceives her as such, and dresses her to bring out the identity, "arraying her in a crimson velvet tunic, of a peculiar cut, abundantly embroidered with fantasies and flourishes of gold thread. . . . It was a remarkable attribute of this garb, and indeed, of the child's whole appearance, that it irresistibly and inevitably reminded the beholder of the token which Hester Prynne was doomed to wear upon her bosom. It was the scarlet letter in another form; the scarlet letter endowed with life!" (p. 102). In dressing Pearl to look like the letter, Hester appears to be trying to accept the Puritan idea that Pearl is a creature of guilt. But her behavior is subversive and cunning, for she has already transformed the letter into a work of art with her gorgeous embroidery, and it is to this transfigured symbol that she matches Pearl.

Hester's art—and that she is an artist, Hawthorne leaves no doubt—though ornamental in form, must not be confused with the delicate prettiness of Owen Warland's butterfly or the cold fragility of the snow-image. Her art is not pretty but splendid, and not cold but fiercely passionate, for it stems directly from the passionate self that engendered Pearl and is now denied all other expression: "She had in her nature a rich, voluptuous, Oriental characteristic,—a taste for the gorgeously beautiful, which, save in the exquisite productions of her needle, found nothing else, in all the possibilities of her life, to exercise itself upon" (p. 83). Now this expressive activity, which is fundamentally nonsocial, must be realized in shapes that are perceived and classified and judged by society. Hester's activity is permissible when it is employed in giving "majesty to the forms in which a new government manifested itself to the people," that is, by creating "deep ruffs, painfully wrought bands, and gorgeously embroidered gloves" (p. 82). With these items her gift is brought into the service of authority. But when Hester employs this same activity on her own letter, it is quite another matter. By making the letter beautiful, Hester is denying its literal meaning and thereby subverting the intention of the magistrates who condemn her to wear it. Moreover, by applying this art to her own letter, she puts her gift to work in the service of her private thoughts and feelings rather than in support of public rituals. The Puritan women understand at once what she has done: "She hath good skill at her needle, that's certain . . . but did ever a woman, before this brazen hussy, contrive such a way of showing it! Why, gossips, what is it but to laugh in the faces of our godly magistrates, and make a pride out of what they, worthy gentlemen, meant for a punishment?" (p. 54). Fortunately for Hester — fortunately for the artist — the magistrates lack this ironic perception. They are not imaginative men, and if this failing has led them to deny expression to the imagination, it also prevents them from recognizing it when it manifests itself in subtle or indirect forms.

But in a society that does not recognize and provide forms for imaginative expression, the artist of the private must always make her statement covertly by distorting the available public forms of expression. The executed product therefore involves a compromise, sometimes a very radical one, between the conception and its final shape. In the interplay between Pearl and the letter, Hawthorne and Hester both wrestle with the problem of bringing together the artist's "idea," which is nonsocial and even nonverbal, and the eventual product. At the most basic level the writer must use language, a social construct, for his expression. Thereby his product becomes social even if his idea is not. Pearl, the antisocial creature, must be transformed into the letter A. Ultimately, artistic conceptions that are expressive but perhaps not meaningful in a declarative sense must acquire meanings through the form in which they are expressed, meanings that may be irrelevant to and even at odds with the conception. The undecorated scarlet letter would certainly be a form false to Hester's conception of what she has done. Her recourse is to play with that form in order to loosen it, expand it, undercut it, and thereby make it capable of a sort of many-layered communication. Her artist's activity is directly contrasted to the operation of the Puritan mind, forever anxiously codifying the phenomena of its world into the rigid system of its alphabet.

If Pearl is Hester's imagination of her sin, she also symbolizes the sinful part of Hester's self—the wild, amoral, creative core. Hester is at odds with this part of herself (though she probably would not be if society had not judged as it did) and, until she comes to some sort of resolution, is a divided personality. Truly to assent to her punishment, Hester must come to judge her own nature, or that part of it, as society has judged it. She does try to feel guilty, and hopes that by behaving like a guilty person she will eventually create a sense of guilt within her. She tries to restrain and discipline the child according to society's judgments, but her passionate nature—pushed by ostracism into defiance—continues to assert itself. Pearl expresses all the resentment, pride, anger, and blasphemy that Hester feels but may not voice, and perhaps does not even admit to feeling. One recalls the famous catechism scene where Pearl, to Hester's mortification, proclaims that "she had not been made at all, but had been plucked by her mother off the bush of wild roses, that grew by the prison-door" (p. 112). Pearl repudiates all patriarchs: God, the magistrates, her actual father. Boldly, the child aligns her mother with the persecuted and martyred, for the rosebush is said to have sprung from the footsteps of "sainted" Ann Hutchinson (p. 48).[4] Pearl locates herself within a world inhabited entirely by women, figuring her birth as an event that occurred without men. She confirms the conflict in Hester's case as one between a woman and a patriarchal social structure.

Hester's ultimately unshakable belief in the goodness of this wild and nonsocial core of her being, frightening though it may sometimes be, saves her from taking the readily available and far less imaginative route of witchcraft. This path, which leads straight from the governor's door in the person of his sister, Mistress Hibbens, is in fact a legitimate Puritan social institution. The witches are rebels, but their rebellion arises from accepting the Puritan world view and defining themselves as evil. Yes, they say, we are indeed terribly wicked creatures, and we rejoice in our badness. Because they view themselves as society views them, the witches indirectly validate the social structure. Hester's defiance is another thing entirely.

Alone, her emotions repressed, she does her needlework and thinks. She "assumed a freedom of speculation . . . which our forefathers, had they known of it, would have held to be a deadlier crime than that stigmatized by the scarlet letter" (p. 164). Had she spoken her thoughts, she probably would "have suffered death from the stern tribunals of the period, for attempting to undermine the foundations of the Puritan establishment" (p. 165). Naturally, her mind dwells much on her condition as a woman, especially because caring for a girl-child forces her to see her situation in more general terms: "Was existence worth accepting, even to the happiest among [women]?" Pursuing her thought, she is overwhelmed by the magnitude of the changes that must occur before woman's lot becomes generally tolerable. There is certainly no individual solution; there is only individual escape into happy love.[5] But love for Hester is the instrument of misery rather than an escape into bliss, for it is love that keeps her in Boston close to Dimmesdale all those long, sad years. And when she proposes to leave, it is not for herself but for him that she is concerned. The limitation imposed by love on freedom is an aspect of woman's (as distinct from the general human) condition, and this is partly why Hester, returned to Boston, hopes for the revelation of a new truth that will "establish the whole relation between man and woman on a surer ground of mutual happiness" (p. 263).

Hester, labeled guilty by society, gradually rejects the meaning of that label although she cannot reject the label itself. Dimmesdale, thought to be innocent, eventually displays himself in public as a guilty man. His character contrasts completely with Hester's, except in one crucial respect: both of them must ultimately, at whatever cost, be true to the imperatives of their own natures. No matter how she tries to assent to it, Hester cannot help but reject the judgment of the letter. Dimmesdale must finally stigmatize himself no matter how much a part of him longs to concur in the idea of his innocence. As I have already briefly observed, Hester is naturally independent and romantic, Dimmesdale dependent and conservative, and these tendencies are reinforced by their different places in the social structure.

"Mr. Dimmesdale," Hawthorne writes, "was a true priest, a true religionist, with the reverential sentiment largely developed, and an order of mind that impelled itself powerfully along the track of a creed, and wore its passage continually deeper with the lapse of time. In no state of society would he have been what is called a man of liberal views; it would always be essential to his peace to feel the pressure of a faith about him, supporting, while it confined him within its iron framework" (p. 123). Observe how, characteristically for Hawthorne, the particular content of a creed is seen as irrelevant to its essential purpose of satisfying the psychological needs of a certain kind of personality. In any society, Dimmesdale would have been a "religionist" because he is a reverent person—that is, he requires authority over him. Although he happens to be a Puritan, Dimmesdale's type is not confined to the Puritan community or bounded by the specific nature of Puritan doctrines. This is a psychological, and not an ethical or philosophical, portrait.

Because of his dependent nature, Dimmesdale is profoundly sincere in his wish to conform. He has apparently remained ignorant of his own passions until his encounter with Hester reveals them. But the passion has been there all the time. Hester must not be misread, as D. H. Lawrence so egregiously misread her, as a dark lady with an appetite for corrupting pure men. She occasions Dimmesdale's passion but does not create it. There are physical signs of struggle in Dimmesdale—his perpetual paleness, the tremor of his mouth denoting both "nervous sensibility and a vast power of self-restraint" (p. 66). In fact, Hawthorne shows what the minister can never accept: the true source of his power over the people is not the spirituality to which he sincerely attributes his success but his denied and despised passionate nature.

Dimmesdale reaches his audience not by argument but by emotion. His instrument is the music of his voice: "This vocal organ was in itself a rich endowment; insomuch that a listener, comprehending nothing of the language in which the preacher spoke, might still have been swayed to and fro by the mere tone and cadence. Like all other music, it breathed passion and pathos, and emotions high or tender, in a tongue native to the human heart, wherever educated." It ranges from a "low undertone, as of the wind sinking down to repose itself," through "progressive gradations of sweetness and power" to a climax of "awe and solemn grandeur. And yet, majestic as the voice sometimes became, there was for ever in it an essential character of plaintiveness" (p. 243). The voice bypasses language to become a direct expression of unmediated feeling.

After his encounter with Hester, Dimmesdale becomes a much more effective preacher, because his feelings have surfaced and cannot entirely be suppressed thereafter. Dimmesdale's congregation is no more aware than he of the source of his power: "They deemed the young clergyman a miracle of holiness. . . . The virgins of his church grew pale around him, victims of a passion so imbued with religious sentiment that they imagined it to be all religion, and brought it openly, in their white bosoms, as their most acceptable sacrifice before the altar" (p. 142). The passionate man arouses passion in others. In spite of himself, Dimmesdale has become an artist. But an artist is not what he intended to be. He is bewildered and horrified by his success. A man like this, deeply committed to the furthering of the social aims of permanence and respectability, who yet finds himself possessed of this subversive power, is necessarily a psychologically ravaged human being. Before he knew Hester, his profession had provided him with a refuge. Afterward, the refuge becomes his prison. Unable to identify his "self" with the passionate core he regards as sinful, he is even less able to admit that this sinful core can produce great sermons. He is obsessed with a feeling of falseness. His act with Hester almost immediately becomes loathsome to him. The part of him that is Puritan magistrate, and which he thinks of as his "self," condemns the sinful "other."

The guiltiness of his act, as it appears to him, is well expressed in the hideous figure of Chillingworth, who materializes out of thin air and, after establishing a superficial connection with Hester, moves on to his true mission of persecuting Dimmesdale. This monster becomes his constant companion and oppressor. If Pearl, to borrow a Freudian metaphor, may be seen as representing Hester's "id," so Chillingworth can be interpreted as Dimmesdale's "superego." That he is intended as a part of Dimmesdale's personality is made clear not only by the magical ways in which he appears on the scene and disappears from it, and his unrealistic fixation (for a cuckolded husband) on the guilty *man*, but also by the spatial disposition of the two together in a single dwelling, just as Hester and Pearl are housed together. Chillingworth is the watchful eye of the personality, linked with both intellect and conscience.

Fearing the punishment of society, and yet afraid of going unpunished, Dimmesdale has substituted an internal for a social punishment. The replacement of his kindly, benevolent mentor Reverend Wilson by this malevolent inner demon symbolizes the self-imposed punishment. Chillingworth's cruelty represents Hawthorne's idea that the internal judge, freed (exactly as Pearl at the other end of the spectrum is freed) from "reference and adaptation to the world into which it was born" (p. 91), is unmitigatedly merciless: "All that guilty sorrow, hidden from the world, whose great heart would have pitied and forgiven, to be revealed to him, the Pitiless, to him, the Unforgiving!" (p. 139).

By virtue of his age and relation to Hester, Chillingworth invites a classical Freudian explanation for Dimmesdale's feelings of guilt. In a larger, more mythic framework, to characterize Chillingworth as a sort of father is to establish his connection to the patriarchal structure of the Puritan society. Dimmesdale feels guilty because he has offended the "fathers," the male gods of his universe. But he did not offend them by stealing one of their women, for they are all men without women and do not appear to covet Hester for themselves. His offense is to have repudiated their rule by acknowledging her dominion. In the forest she is, like the great Squaw Sachem in "Main-street," an alternative to the patriarchy: "O Hester, thou art my better angel! I seem to have flung myself—sick, sin-stained, and sorrow-blackened—down upon these forest-leaves, and to have risen up all made anew, and with new powers to glorify Him that hath been merciful! This is already the better life! Why did we not find it sooner?" (pp. 201–2). Here Hester fulfills the image of "Divine Maternity" that she suggested at the scaffold (p. 56). Here is the precivilized nature goddess opposing western civilization, the impulsive heart defying the repressive letter of the law. Here, in brief, is a profoundly romantic mythology.

The protracted relationship with Chillingworth during the seven-year span of the romance represents Dimmesdale's strategy to keep from confessing. Nothing frightens him more than the idea of public exposure. He pacifies his inner thirst for punishment by self-castigation. Of course, he fails to confess partly because he cannot bear the thought of social ostracism. For a being who defines himself largely by the image he sees reflected back from the watching eyes around him, loss of social place implies loss of identity. It would be far more difficult for him than for Hester to survive a public disgrace. But confession would mean more than this. It would be a final capitulation to his sense of guilt. No matter how he persecutes himself, no matter what masochistic free rein he allows his overbearing conscience, he does not fully assent to his guilt until he admits it openly, because open admission has irreversible consequences.

Observe that public confession has in fact never been demanded of Hester. She has never had to say "I am guilty," because, for the Puritans, to have done the deed and to be guilty are synonymous, and Hester has obviously done the deed. Dimmesdale has no such escape. If he confesses, he must confess his guilt. Chillingworth as a substitute for social judgment actually forestalls that judgment and protects Dimmesdale from an ultimate condemnation. Once he confesses, he has no psychological alternative but to die. Quite literally, Chillingworth the physician has kept him alive all these years, even if only to torment him.

Dimmesdale's resistance is roundabout and neurotic, but it keeps him functioning and is appropriate to his deep internal divisions. The aftermath of the forest scene breaks his will to resist, convincing him that he is as evil as he had feared. Leaving the forest, Dimmesdale is possessed by a flood of impulses, which, although amusingly puerile to the reader, are horrifying to him. He wants to teach obscene words to a group of little boys, blaspheme before a devout old woman, and solicit the sexual favors of a maiden in his congregation. At long last freeing his passionate self, he finds freedom expressed in a series of silly, wicked wishes. Lacking Hester's long evolution of thought and independence, the "free" Dimmesdale is no more than a naughty boy. In his own eyes he is a monster. He ceases, therefore, to resist social judgment. He turns his new burst of life into the writing of his greatest sermon, still not recognizing the source of his power, still bewildered that "Heaven should see fit to transmit the grand and solemn music of its oracles through so foul an organ-pipe as he" (p. 225). He delivers the sermon to great approbation and, at the height of his triumph, confesses. By that confession, he executes himself.

The final scene on the scaffold seems to suggest that the public institutions of society and the private needs of the personality are irreconcilable. Dimmesdale, revealing his inner nature, has died. Hester, in order to express herself at last and to permit Pearl to develop freely, must leave the community. But her return to Boston and the consequent loosening of the community to accommodate her lighten the gloomy conclusion. A painfully slow process of social relaxation may, perhaps, be hoped for. The human heart may not need to be an outcast forever.

The Puritan community in *The Scarlet Letter* is a symbol of society in general. It is portrayed as a set of institutions unresponsive to personal needs and deliberately repressive of the private experience. Puritan institutions define the human being as all surface, all public. So far as the inner life is made public, it must be submitted to social definitions. Social institutions, however, may not be defined in the language of individual needs. The Puritan magistrates are not hypocrites. For them, the business of establishing and perpetuating a society demands the full energies of all the members of the community; there is no time for the indulgence of a private dimension of the personality. Self-expression is therefore a threat to the community.

Since the magistrates believe that self-expression is a threat, they make it a crime. Thereby, of course, they make it a threat as well. *The Scarlet Letter* asks whether this state of opposition between passion and authority is necessary; it expresses the hope that a society allowing greater individual expression might evolve, but it does not commit itself to a certain conclusion. It makes clear, however, that in a society such as the romance describes, the relationship of the artist who speaks for passion to the social institutions that suppress it can only be one of estrangement, duplicity, or subversion. Dimmesdale's voice and Hester's letter enunciate and undermine the social creed. Disguised as a social document, the work of art secretly expresses the cry of the heart. Doing this, it covertly defies society in response to hidden but universal needs.

Two questions arise: what relation does the situation depicted in *The Scarlet Letter* bear to Hawthorne's idea of his own contemporary society? And what relation does the thematic design of the romance bear to his own function as an artist? Clearly, *The Scarlet Letter* is quite different from all of Hawthorne's earlier work, which had argued that the individual finds rich fulfillment when integrated into society, that society expresses the personality. Now although Hawthorne does not suggest in *The Scarlet Letter* that there is any joy in isolation, he does show that the individual pays a very high price to be a member of the group. The earlier fictions and sketches exhibited the imagination at work in the service of society; *The Scarlet Letter* makes it clear that imagination serves the self. The earlier works tended to define serving the self as obsession, egotism, or eccentricity; *The Scarlet Letter* asserts that the self has needs and claims that must be satisfied. The earlier works restricted the exercise of imagination to the surface of events, while *The Scarlet Letter* ties imagination to the life beneath appearances. Evidently, Hawthorne jettisoned the whole load of commonsense assumptions about imagination and art and replaced them with a romantic vision.

If the vision of *The Scarlet Letter* is romantic, then Hawthorne must be presenting his own role and function in an entirely new way. One wonders whether Hawthorne actually underwent some sort of conversion or simply adopted another in a long series of authorial stances designed to find favor with an audience. Clearly, a romantic view was more up-to-date than the late eighteenth-century ideology his works had been expressing. And Hawthorne was too great a realist ever to publish a work that he thought might actually harm his reputation. One might conclude that in *The Scarlet Letter* he was accommodating himself to the taste of the times. The conception of art, imagination, and the artist implicit in this romantic formulation is nevertheless intellectually and aesthetically far richer and more vigorous than the formulation he had abandoned; consequently, it might have given him the support and justification for his professional commitment that he had not found before. Since it propelled him into the most productive decade of his career and thrust him immediately into the forefront of living American authors, this romantic vision certainly was usable.

"The Custom-House" invites us to view it as a deeply held belief as well. The essay tells the story of a conversion to the idea of literature as self-expression, in defiance of external and introjected social demands. It suggests that the psychological survival of the "I" depended upon that conversion. A product, Hawthorne says, of the same "autobiographical impulse" that motivated "The Old Manse," "The Custom-House" takes up his story where the earlier essay left it. Ignoring what we know to have been the economic imperatives that took him back to Salem, Hawthorne projects a psychological story in the conventions of romance. Appropriately, then, we may label "The Custom-House" an autobiographical romance.

Hawthorne interprets his return to Salem and his employment at the Custom House as the answer to psychological longings that his life at the Manse failed to satisfy and in part created. After three years of living in a transcendental cloudland, it was time to return to solid earth. He needed to participate in the ongoing work of the world, to prove himself a contributing member of society. He had to confront what might be called the persisting influence of Salem on his artistic life. By "Salem" is meant the combined environmental and personal pressures that made him think writing an idle and sinful craft.

Hawthorne personifies Salem in his Puritan ancestry, whose imagined judgment on him as a writer survives all his attempts to overcome it: "What is he? . . . A writer of story-books! What kind of a business in life, — what mode of glorifying God, or being serviceable to mankind in his day and generation, — may that be? Why, the degenerate fellow might as well have been a fiddler!" (p. 10). Hawthorne's attempts to resist these imagined strictures by castigating his ancestors in turn for their bitter persecuting spirit and hard severity (p. 9) have no effect, because these Puritan ancestors, of course, represent a part of Hawthorne himself. "And yet, let them scorn me as they will, strong traits of their nature have intertwined themselves with mine" (p. 10). There is nothing to do but accede to the pressures they exert and return to Salem.

So far as these ancestors (or that part of Hawthorne they represent) are concerned, the sojourn in the Custom House has a twofold benefit. To work there is to satisfy their demand that he be serviceable. And the Custom House may provide Hawthorne with materials for a literature to mediate between the requirement of service and his self's need for imaginative expression. It is implicit in Hawthorne's treatment of life at the Custom House that a successful literature would likely be realistic, with imagination subordinated to external reality and dedicated to the service of the other. At the outset of "The Custom-House" Hawthorne leaves open the question of retiring from the surveyorship eventually to translate his experiences into literature or remaining in the position permanently. Ultimately, the decision is never made because he is dismissed from office.

Hawthorne makes no attempt to hide the fact that he did not choose to leave his position, but we are never meant to think that he enjoyed it. We know from the biographies that he stayed because he could not afford to go; in "The Custom-House," however, Hawthorne presents himself as remaining because he sincerely wants to do what the ancestors expect of him. Like Dimmesdale, he is trying to be socially acceptable. But he is increasingly miserable, and the dismissal, he says, is fortunate. Far from plunging him into the midst of social life, the Custom House thoroughly isolates him. Everybody there appears to exist in a state of suspended animation. All are old men, of torpid imaginations and emotionally atrophied. The work itself is trivial, monotonous, and dispiriting.

The Custom House building, Uncle Sam's institution, quickly becomes a metaphorical prison. Working for society instead of himself, the Custom House officer loses his manhood:

> While he leans on the mighty arm of the Republic, his own proper strength departs from him. He loses, in an extent proportioned to the weakness or force of his original nature, the capability of self-support. . . . Uncle Sam's gold — meaning no disrespect to the worthy old gentleman — has, in this respect, a quality of enchantment like that of the Devil's wages. Whoever touches it should look well to himself, or he may find the bargain go hard against him, involving, if not his soul, yet many of its better attributes; its sturdy force, its courage and constancy, its truth, its self-reliance, and all that gives the emphasis to manly character.
>
> [Pp. 38–39]

The ejected officer, left "to totter along the difficult footpath of life as best he may," is one who "forever afterwards looks wistfully about him in quest of support external to himself" (p. 39), and sounds a good deal like Arthur Dimmesdale. The iron framework of the Puritan oligarchy has been replaced by a more benevolent but ultimately equally debilitating kind of paternalism.

Hawthorne represents his romance, *The Scarlet Letter*, as originating in the attempts of his imagination to make itself felt and keep itself alive in the deadly atmosphere of the Custom House. His withdrawal from the tedium of the first-floor routine into the cluttered chambers of the upper story signifies Hawthorne's withdrawal into his own mind, his escape into fantasy. But in these circumstances, fantasy is an escape to freedom rather than a retreat from life. It is an affirmative rather than a denying gesture. In one of his flights of fancy, Hawthorne comes upon a roll of parchment enclosed within "a certain affair of fine red cloth" wrought "with wonderful skill of needlework" and "intended, there could be no doubt, as an ornamental article of dress" (p. 31). Examination proves it to be a fabric representation of the letter *A*.

"My eyes fastened themselves upon the old scarlet letter, and would not be turned aside. Certainly, there was some deep meaning in it, most worthy of interpretation, and which, as it were, streamed forth from the mystic symbol, subtly communicating itself to my sensibilities, but evading the analysis of my mind" (p. 31). Impulsively, Hawthorne puts the letter to his breast and experiences "a sensation not altogether physical, yet almost so, as of burning heat; and as if the letter were not of red cloth, but red-hot iron" (p. 32). In this electric moment, which many critics have recognized as central to both "The Custom-House" and *The Scarlet Letter*, Hawthorne senses with a mixture of fear and excitement that he has found his subject. The letter—a verbal sign, a symbol, and the channel of inspiration—becomes the type of Art.

Because in *The Scarlet Letter* the A signifies a social crime, Hawthorne suggests that the writing of his romance is in some sense an analogously guilty act. My analysis of *The Scarlet Letter*, stressing the self-expressive and passionate nature of Hester's and Dimmesdale's act, indicates why there is an analogy. For Hawthorne, the romance originated as expression of his own feelings of social defiance and discontent, as a reaction to the stifling position of surveyor in the Custom House at Salem. The decision to write the romance, or to try to write it, involves a transference of Hawthorne's allegiance from his Puritan conscience to his imagination, personified in "The Custom-House" by Surveyor Pue. Adopting this figure as his "official ancestor," Hawthorne accepts the former surveyor's charge that he publicize Hester's story.

Now Hawthorne discovers that to generate a fantasy is not the same thing as to give it body. As he attempts in his free hours to compose his tale, he becomes aware in a frighteningly new way of the terrible effect the Custom House is having on his imaginative faculties. And he realizes how profoundly he values these faculties. "My imagination was a tarnished mirror. . . . The characters of the narrative would not be warmed and rendered malleable, by any heat that I could kindle at my intellectual forge. . . . 'What have you to do with us?' [they] seemed to say. 'The little power you might once have possessed over the tribe of unrealities is gone! You have bartered it for a pittance of the public gold. Go, then, and earn your wages!' " (pp. 34–35).

> I had ceased to be a writer of tolerably poor tales and essays, and had become a tolerably good Surveyor of the Customs. That was all. But, nevertheless, it is any thing but agreeable to be haunted by a suspicion that one's intellect is dwindling away; or exhaling, without your consciousness, like ether out of a phial. . . . I began to grow melancholy and restless; continually prying into my mind, to discover which of its poor properties were gone, and what degree of detriment had already accrued to the remainder. I endeavoured to calculate how much longer I could stay in the Custom-House, and yet go forth a man.
> [Pp. 38–40]

Clearly, then, it is impossible for Hawthorne to continue to be a writer of romances while placating the inner Puritan. The unexpected fruits of the Custom House interlude are the authentication of just those theories he laid aside when he left Concord for Salem and the validation of a definition of happiness as living throughout the whole range of one's faculties and sensibilities (p. 40) — in brief, living the fullest inner life.

Yet Hawthorne, in accepting Hester as his subject, does not return to the transcendentalists so much as go beyond them. She represents everything the transcendentalists believe and more besides, for in her Emerson's "Spirit" is transformed into Eros and thus allied to sex, passion, eroticism, flesh, and the earth. The Puritans seek to repress Spirit not only because of their dedication to permanence and form, but also because as shrewd men of hard experience they are aware of its sexual sources. Thus, the sin in *The Scarlet Letter* is sexual, and a sexual sin can symbolize Hawthorne's writing of romances. This is why Hawthorne epitomizes Puritan severity in a depiction of their persecution of women. In women they see the occasion of a dangerous passion. Their opposition to sex is not prudish but pragmatic. As he goes beyond transcendentalism in his rejection of the concept of an unearthly spiritualism, Hawthorne goes beyond most of his earlier work, but echoes some of the themes expressed in "The Birthmark," "Drowne's Wooden Image," and, ironically, "The Artist of the Beautiful." In *The Scarlet Letter* he also presents an advocate of unearthly spiritualism, Dimmesdale.

Hawthorne's servitude in the Custom House generated, as a reactive defense, the fantasy of the scarlet letter; his dismissal led to its creation. In both idea and execution, the romance is related to maladjustment between Hawthorne and his society. Miserable as Hawthorne had been in the Custom House, to be forced out of it represented an evident failure: "The moment when a man's head drops off is seldom or never, I am inclined to think, precisely the most agreeable of his life. . . . In view of my previous weariness of office, and vague thoughts of resignation, my fortune somewhat resembled that of a person who should entertain an idea of committing suicide, and, altogether beyond his hopes, meet with the good hap to be murdered" (pp. 41–42). Observe the ambivalence of the images. Hawthorne's thoughts of resigning from the Custom House are like thoughts of suicide. Why should this be, if the Custom House is so unpleasant? Obviously Hawthorne is torn.

Like Hester, he becomes a rebel because he is thrown out of society, by society: "Meanwhile, the press had taken up my affair, and kept me, for a week or two, careering through the public prints, in my decapitated state. . . . So much for my figurative self. The real human being, all this time, with his head safely on his shoulders, had brought himself to the comfortable conclusion, that everything was for the best; and, making an investment in ink, paper, and steel-pens, had opened his long-disused writing-desk, and was again a literary man" (pp. 42–43). Anxious for so long to "be of some importance in [my good townspeople's] eyes, and to win myself a pleasant memory in this abode and burial-place of so many of my forefathers" (p. 44), Hawthorne has finally accepted his destiny. The Custom House self, the man of affairs and the world, the public servant, becomes a figurative self, and Hawthorne accepts the conjunction of the real being with the literary man. The autobiographical episode has a happy ending, for in composing *The Scarlet Letter* he found himself "happier, while straying through the gloom of these sunless fantasies, than at any time since he had quitted the Old Manse" (p. 43). The direct attack of "The Custom-House" on some of the citizens of Salem adds a fillip of personal revenge to the theoretical rebellion that it dramatizes.

In the current state of biographical knowledge we cannot be sure to what degree the symbolic representation in "The Custom-House" corresponds to the facts. We do not know, for example, whether the germ of *The Scarlet Letter* actually occurred to Hawthorne in the Custom House or was conceived entirely in the months after his dismissal. Many readers have noted the foreshadowing appearance of a beautiful young woman with an embroidered *A* on her bosom in "Endicott and the Red Cross"; it is at least possible that the story had, in some form, been in his mind for years. We also do not know if Hawthorne really tried to write *The Scarlet Letter* before he was dismissed from the Custom House and, failing, actually became distracted and gloomy over the loss of his powers. But if, in fact, the story is not a symbolic representation of the truth, then it is all the more striking that Hawthorne should wish to represent *The Scarlet Letter* as a gesture of insubordination.

Even at his most defiant, Hawthorne could not entirely avoid the tone of self-deprecation. But in "The Custom-House" he almost appears to satirize his own formerly characteristic apologetic mode. "It was a folly," he writes, "with the materiality of this daily life pressing so intrusively upon me, to attempt to fling myself back into another age; or to insist on creating the semblance of a world out of airy matter, when, at every moment, the impalpable beauty of my soap-bubble was broken by the rude contact of some actual circumstance" (p. 37). These are metaphors apt for Owen Warland's butterfly, but not for *The Scarlet Letter*. And he goes on to theorize that it would have been "wiser . . . to diffuse thought and imagination through the opaque substance of to-day, and thus to make it a bright transparency." But "The Custom-House" has shown that it was not folly, but absolute necessity, to turn into his own mind for sustenance. And his humorous portraits of the inhabitants of the Custom House have done the job of diffusing thought and imagination through them. Despite the apparent humility of his conclusion to this paragraph — "A better book than I shall ever write was there" — Hawthorne was never less humble.

This lack of humility is clearly evident in his preface to the second edition of *The Scarlet Letter*, dated March 30, 1850, some two weeks after his romance had been published. The book had already sold well enough to assure Hawthorne that he had, at last, a solid success. He acknowledges the furor caused by "The Custom-House" with evident delight. He has learned the interesting lesson that to create a scandal is not necessarily to hurt sales. For years he had dependently courted public approbation; now he has been rewarded for independence:

> As the public disapprobation would weigh very heavily on him, were he conscious of deserving it, the author begs leave to say, that he has carefully read over the introductory pages, with a purpose to alter or expunge whatever might be found amiss, and to make the best reparation in his power for the atrocities of which he has been adjudged guilty. But it appears to him, that the only remarkable features of the sketch are its frank and genuine good-humor, and the general accuracy with which he has conveyed his sincere impressions of the characters therein described. . . . [The sketch] could not have been done in a better or more kindlier spirit, nor, so far as his abilities availed, with a livelier effect of truth.
>
> [Pp. 1–2]

And then, with relish, he pens his final sentence: "The author is constrained, therefore, to republish his introductory sketch without the change of a word."

Notes

1. Stewart, *Nathaniel Hawthorne*, pp. 91, 93–94; see also Hubert H. Hoeltje, "The Writing of *The Scarlet Letter*," *New England Quarterly*, 27 (1954), 326–46.

2. William Charvat, in his introduction to the Centenary *Scarlet Letter*, shows that "The Custom-House" was completed by January 15, 1850, on which date three chapters of *The Scarlet Letter* remained to be written (p. xxii).

3. *The Scarlet Letter*, p. 64. Subsequent references to the Centenary *Scarlet Letter* and "The Custom-House" are given parenthetically in text.

4. On the basis of Hawthorne's treatment of Ann Hutchinson in the early biographical sketch, some critics have read this passage as ironical. But there is no rhetorical reason for irony in the passage in *The Scarlet Letter*; and, as we have seen, Hawthorne greatly modified his harsh depiction in later accounts of Ann Hutchinson.

5. Some critics have taken Hawthorne's comment that these speculations vanish in a woman's mind "if her heart chance to come uppermost" as a patronizing antifeminist comment which undercuts the validity of Hester's thinking. But such an interpretation is too simple, for it is precisely Hawthorne's point that the existing system very rarely allows the heart to come uppermost. The fact that one woman in a thousand (let us say) is happy and therefore not a radical says nothing to the urgency of the need of the other nine hundred and ninety-nine.

Dark Light on the Letter

Hyatt H. Waggoner*

One way of thinking about why *The Scarlet Letter* continues to move us is by comparing what Hawthorne has to say to us with what Emerson has to say. Is the tragic view of life the only one an intelligent and sensitive person can honestly hold? Is there no way out of the dark maze in which we wander, or is it possible, as Emerson thought, that the darkness is in part of our own making? Is there a way of *seeing* that will permit us to perceive that the "ambiguity of sin and sorrow" in which Hawthorne's characters are enmeshed is not inevitable for us all?

The opening lines of Robert Penn Warren's poem "His Smile" — the first of his series of poems bearing the overall title "Homage to Emerson, on Night Flight to New York" — provide an entry into this central question confronting the reader of *The Scarlet Letter* today. The smile is Emerson's. Emerson's essays lie open in the lap of the speaker in the poem, seeming to say that there is "no sin. Not even error." Illuminated by the reading light that casts a "finger" of brightness down on them, the essays seem to "glow" in the "pressurized gloom" of the cabin while far below a few fields "in the last light gleam" as the plane flies eastward and the earth "slides westward." Outside the window, night "hisses" with a sound "that only a dog's / Ear could catch, or the human heart." The speaker interprets Emerson's smile as meaning that Emerson had "forgiven God everything."

Later poems in the series make clearer what has been implied in the opening lines of "His Smile": that the speaker, presumably the poet himself, is uncertain whether the smile rests on anything more than self-deception, a willed turning-away from the darkness of man's night-flight through life. His uncertainty finds expression in a double-edged use of a colloquialism: "At 38,000 feet Emerson / Is dead right."

The hallmark of Emerson's public writings — though not always of his journals — is his confidence in life, his trust in the ultimate beneficence of the Oversoul — the word he usually preferred to "God" — within and behind us and nature. Positive evil and negative limitation tended to disappear, he felt, when viewed under the aspect of eternity.

Emerson thought that if we would only open ourselves to experience, only approach it in love and trust and with a sense of wonder, we would find that the limits to our moral and spiritual, our personal growth — limits that had seemed so solid to us — would disappear. In effect Emerson's central idea was a reinterpretation of the ancient dictum that all things work for good to him who loves God. If this is true, the tragic view of life results from our own failure of trust and from the inadequacy of our vision.

As Emerson said in the poem "Circles," which he prefixed to his essay

*Reprinted from *The Presence of Hawthorne* (Baton Rouge: Louisiana State University Press, 1979), 67–75, by permission of the publisher.

of the same title, if we could only stand off far enough, in imagination, from the little "ball" of earth to see ourselves as "proud ephemerals" held by gravity to the "outside" of the ball, if we could only "see," in our "mind's eye," the whole "profile" of the "sphere" we inhabit, we would be imaginatively and spiritually reborn. The eschatological vision that would result from such an imaginative movement off into space-time would enable us to see the immanence of the Oversoul, the ultimate spiritual Reality, in the humblest and most ordinary of our immediate circumstances.

Emerson and Hawthorne were contemporaries and for several years neighbors and something like friends in Concord, but the two men could hardly have been more unlike in temperament, in approaches to life, and in their final conclusions about it. It would be oversimplifying both men to say that Emerson saw only the light, Hawthorne only the darkness of life. However, it would not be misleading to find Emerson's chief thrust in his effort to illustrate "human power in every department" of life, and to try to persuade us that this power results from the fact that, as he said, when we achieve the proper angle of vision "we learn that God IS; that he is in me; and that all things are shadows of him"; and, correspondingly, to find that Hawthorne's predominant concern in his fiction is with just those experiences of guilt and limitation that Emerson thought it possible to transcend. "Sin" for Emerson was, as he once said, "the soul's mumps," a childhood disease to be outgrown. For Hawthorne, except during the early years of his marriage, sin seemed the only certainty besides death.

The ultimate question *The Scarlet Letter* poses to us is whether there is ever to be any escape from such tragic conflicts as those the novel presents. In Hester Prynne's story we find society in conflict with the individual's drive for self-realization, religious and moral codes in conflict with natural impulse, and, within individuals, duty in conflict with the desire for pleasure and happiness. For Hester there is no escape, only sublimation and self-control. For Dimmesdale there is only public confession of guilt and submission to a will he conceives as higher than his own. Are suffering and defeat then inevitably and always the law of life?

Fortunately for the lasting power the novel has over us, Hawthorne does not attempt here, as he later would in *The House of the Seven Gables*, to tell us overtly what he thinks, or hopes, the answer is. He lets his story, and the images he finds to tell it, speak for themselves, not distorting his picture to make it suggest the hope he personally entertained, as he so often did in his lesser works, not manipulating what he had imagined but being controlled by it. The one "moral" of his story he felt certain enough of to state for us is not a hopeful one: "Be true! Be true! Show freely to the world, if not your worst, yet some trait whereby the worst may be inferred!"

The complex image with which the tale concludes is as preponderantly dark, despite Hawthorne's wish that he might lighten it, as the images in the first chapter. The inscription on the stone that marks the double grave of Hester and her one-time lover is given us only as a medieval herald might have worded it, not in its Puritan starkness; but even when lifted and rendered legendary — distanced — by the heraldic language, it is dark enough. The words the herald might have written to be placed on the coat of arms of a noble family were, Hawthorne tells us, illuminated "only by one ever-glowing point of light gloomier than the shadow: — 'ON A FIELD, SABLE, THE LETTER A, GULES.' "

The darkness of this ending suggests that life is tragic but not that it is pointless, meaningless, absurd. In the course of the novel, the image of red ("gules," the heraldic term for the color red) has come to suggest both sin and guilt, and also the natural, the passionate, and the beautiful. It has been associated with the rose beside the jail, with Pearl's dress, and with its biblical and traditional uses, all of which point toward prohibited sexual activity. Blackness and darkness have been associated with both secrecy and death. But in the final double image there is no suggestion left of the "positive" (the "natural," the happy) implication of red, only the "negative" — the guilt and the death — and the darkness that began to be apparent in the story's opening sentences is now "relieved" only by a "point" of light that is too gloomy to "glow," like Emerson's pages in Warren's poem. A story in which the action has moved, metaphorically, between the points defined in the first chapter as the cemetery, the prison, and the rose, ends with one of its reference points, the rose, missing. Guilt and death, the prison and the cemetery, appear to be the last words that can be spoken about these lives.

There are of course other ways of reading Hawthorne's "romance," not counting the way of looking for its "latent" meaning — signs in it of Hawthorne's neurosis — hidden beneath the "manifest" content. (Only by radically changing the meaning of the word "meaning" can this way seem to be relevant to literary criticism.) We may, for instance, take more seriously than we have so far what was, as both external and internal evidence attest, Hawthorne's conscious effort to lighten the ending of his dark tale. For example, he allows Pearl to escape the environment (and the moral code?) that prevented her mother from finding fulfillment as a woman and a person. Pearl, after she grows up, lives in Europe, which for Hawthorne, as for Henry James later, ambiguously symbolizes freedom from Puritanic inhibitions.

Or again, we might try to find more light in the ending by seeing Dimmesdale's words and gestures as he approaches the scaffold and faces his death of "triumphant ignominy" as Christlike, and so suggesting not defeat but final triumph, not darkness but, ultimately, light. Hawthorne probably intended that we should notice Dimmesdale's gesture with his arms, his words of forgiveness of Chillingworth, and his way of embracing his fate.

Or we might remember what Hawthorne knew: that the language of heraldry not only distanced, it lifted, enhanced, and ennobled, the deeds of which it spoke in its own peculiar symbolism. Illegitimate birth, for example, ceased to be a disgrace when emblazoned on a feudal coat of arms. An earl descended from a bastard was still an earl: public acknowledgment of the family's "disgrace" on their shield "wiped out" the stigma.

Hawthorne's most obvious attempt to lighten his ending becomes clear when we consider his source for the words he places last in his book. Andrew Marvell's poem "The Unfortunate Lover" concludes with these lines,

> This is the only *Banneret*
> That ever love created yet:
> Who though, by the malignant Starrs,
> Forced to live in Storms and Warrs:
> Yet dying leaves a perfume here,
> And Musick within every Ear:
> And he in Story only rules,
> In a Field *Sable* a Lover *Gules*.

The discoverer of this undoubted "source" of Hawthorne's words at the end of his work[1] saw it as removing the tale to a greater distance from us — as though it were not already distant enough — and as supporting an interpretation that would lay "greater emphasis on aesthetic rather than moralistic intention" — whatever such a dichotomy would mean. But of course Hawthorne's use of Marvell to help him end his story testifies chiefly to his desire — his "hope," as he had put it in the final sentence of his first chapter — that he might find something somewhere in the story he was about to tell that would lighten or "relieve" what he called "the darkening close of a tale of human frailty and sorrow." (Note that he did *not* call it, as some of his interpreters have, a tale of "sin" and merited suffering.)

Marvell had said that love created a flag, to be flown proudly; that the lovers were victims of circumstances; and that yet the unhappy story affects us as perfume and music do: as wholly to be admired, not condemned. The use to which Hawthorne put Marvell's words in his ending reveals the extent to which, in a part of his mind at least, Hawthorne felt that his own doomed lovers were victims. The ending suggests how deeply, how much more deeply than he knew — or at least was able to admit to himself — Hawthorne sympathized with the adulterous lovers of his tale, how close he was to agreeing with the words he put in Hester's mouth, "What we did had a consecration of its own."

For most modern readers, Hawthorne's efforts to relieve the darkness of his ending do not — cannot — succeed. They did not for Hawthorne himself and his wife Sophia either, when they read the story aloud together after he had finished it, and wept. Pearl, after all, exists as an adult and achieves happiness outside the story. The parallels between Dimmesdale's words and actions in the last scaffold scene and Christ's at the time of his crucifixion do not work either — if indeed they really were intended to. They are likely either to go unnoticed by most readers today or to strike them as a mere contrivance on Hawthorne's part. Jesus after all did not wait until he was dying of "natural" causes, and with no other course open to him, to embrace his destiny. As for Marvell's lines, they do not so much effectively "lighten" the tale as reveal Hawthorne's desire that it should be lightened.

For Hawthorne, the focal point of his story, I suspect, was the fate of a young woman married to an old man. Scholars who have uncovered the "sources" of *The Scarlet Letter* in New England's history have found the passages in Hawthorne's favorite reading that probably suggested to him the penalty of having to wear the scarlet letter, the name "Hester" for his heroine, and much more. But the history of Mary Latham, married to an old and (presumably) impotent man, a girl who committed adultery with "divers young men," was probably the story that ignited his imagination. It was very likely her story that prompted his notebook entry in 1844 or 1845, "The life of a woman, who, by the old colony law, was condemned always to wear the letter A, sewed on her garment, in token of her having committed adultery." What was such a person to do, in a society that demanded and enforced repression of sexual impulses except as they could be satisfied in marriage? What "happy" outcome for her *could* there be?

When he finally came to write his novel Hawthorne did everything he could do without committing himself to open approval of her defiance of Puritan morality to make us sympathize with Hester, who knowingly defied the Puritan code and who dreamed of a day in the future, beyond her time, when women would be considered as people, not property. In the beginning of his tale, Hawthorne gave Hester great beauty and vitality, and a halo; at the end, he knew he had made her a tragic heroine who had managed, by the strength of her courage and integrity, to find meaning and purpose in life despite her frustration.

He could think of no "happy ending" for her, no escape that could be made plausible. He did not think her "innocent," but he did consider her a victim. Her tale, when his wife read it to him, moved him more than any of his later novels would have the power to do. Could any escape from frustration be imagined? He thought perhaps it could — at least for those more fortunately placed than Hester and Dimmesdale — and quickly undertook to write a happier work, *The House of the Seven Gables*, which he would later describe as more "representative" of him. In a sense he would be right, but only half: the self it represented was more the ideal self-image, the man he wished to be, than the total man. It better suggested what he believed but less powerfully embodied what he felt.

Hawthorne's sensibility and outlook more closely and clearly fore-shadow Robert Penn Warren's than do those of any other nineteenth-century American writer of fiction. His tensions between desire and belief, feeling and thought, have been Warren's. In theme, image, and situation,

Hawthorne's fiction, especially his short tales, anticipates the fiction of Warren. The "Hawthorne tradition" in American fiction runs through Melville to James (despite James's effort to break free from it) to Faulkner to Warren. What this whole tradition leaves unclear is whether there is any — any conceivable, any possible — escape from the consequences of "human frailty," any emotion possible to conceive besides "sorrow."

For Hawthorne, when he wrote *The Scarlet Letter*, the cemetery and the prison of the opening chapter were undeniably evident in life. The rose, which he hoped might serve to "symbolize some sweet ["fulfilling"? "self-realizing"?] moral [fulfilling but not condemned, not "guilt-producing"?] blossom [flowers, like Hester, are beautiful and, also like her, feel no guilt], that may be found along the track, or relieve the darkening close of a tale of human frailty and sorrow" — for Hawthorne, the rose could only be postulated and hoped for. In this novel at least, Hawthorne's most deeply felt, it could not be found.

Can it be found — and found to be authentic, not just professed or wished for — granted that as we look back through history it seems mostly not to have been found, except perhaps by the mystics and the saints? Can guilty, suffering, and dying man find fulfillment of his confliciting desires to satisfy himself and at the same time love and be loved by others? Can he find a way to be himself and yet live in community with others, to be true at once to "nature" and to "society"?

If he can, he must do so without denying the tragic truths Hawthorne's novel so beautifully embodies. *The Scarlet Letter* is Hawthorne's finest expression of his feeling of "the way life is." Emerson's effort to tell us how it *might* be for the enlightened was not Hawthorne's subject here. As he wrote to his publisher about what he was creating, "*The Scarlet Letter* is positively a hell-fired story, into which I find it almost impossible to throw any cheering light." To most of us today, the story is likely to seem not so much "hell-fired" as true to ordinary experience as most people suffer it most of the time.

Notes

1. Robert L. Brant, "Hawthorne and Melville," *American Literature*, XXX (1958), 366.

The Obliquity of Signs:
The Scarlet Letter

Millicent Bell*

It is not wrong to identify in this famous short novel the subjects that lie so clearly upon its surface — the effect of concealed and admitted sin, or the opposed conditions of isolation and community, or the antithetic viewpoints of romantic individualism and puritan moral pessimism or the dictates of nature and law. But — and perhaps it is the current self-consciousness of literature that makes this so — it may now be possible to find in this work a primary preoccupation with the rendering of reality into a system of signs. Hawthorne may have had similar reasons to our own for questioning — while performing — the interpretation of experience as a species of message. It is a general human impulse to seek coherence — a syntax — in life, but it is the artist above all who does so most heroically, who is the champion of our general endeavor. When that endeavor becomes dubious, art itself becomes questionable. Like ourselves, Hawthorne may have come to feel that the universe at large speaks an incomprehensible babble in which it merely amuses us to suppose we hear communicating voices, explanation — even consolation.

The very title of the book is a sign, the smallest of literary units, the character "standing for" no more than a speech sound. The letter "A" is the first letter, moreover, of the alphabet, which Pearl recognizes as having seen in her horn book, and represents the beginning, therefore, of literacy. Reading will be given the broadest meaning in this novel. It will become a trope for the decipherment of the world as a text. *The Scarlet Letter*, then, is, as much as any work of fiction can be, an essay in semiology. Its theme is the obliquity or indeterminacy of signs. From this source comes an energy present in every part of the book; from it derives the peculiar life of those other themes which might otherwise seem lacking in modern interest.

That the status of signs is especially important to Hawthorne is evident in a peculiar stylistic feature of *The Scarlet Letter*. Though the reader has the impression of a constant encouragement to symbolic interpretation, it turns out, upon examination, that Hawthorne's prose contains only occasional metaphor or simile and no true allegorical cohesion. What in fact happens is something else: we are frequently *asked to consider* things as symbolic; objects, persons and events are *called* signs rather than being silently presented as such. Hawthorne undertakes a narrative putatively historical, to begin with, introducing it in the Custom House Preface as a redaction from a documentary record, to reinforce the sense of a reconstructed literal past. But again and again he deliberately declares that the actualities of his tale are or may be taken as signs, and he

*Reprinted from the *Massachusetts Review* 23, no. 1 (Spring 1982):9–26, by permission of The Massachusetts Review, Inc. © 1982 The Massachusetts Review, Inc.

uses repeatedly such words as "type," "emblem," "token," or "hieroglyph." All these words are used in a sense roughly synonymous.

"Type" is almost invariably employed to mean "that by which something is symbolized or figured; anything having a symbolic signification; a symbol, emblem" (OED), a sense which had been current already in English during the Renaissance and can be found in one of Hawthorne's favorite older writers, Spenser. The word was still used in this way in the mid-nineteenth century when the meaning more common with us, of a general form or of a kind or class, arose, and Hawthorne, who is conservative in language, almost always seems to be employing the older rather than the newer of these two senses. He even occasionally hints the special theological usage which identifies in the Old Testament events in the New of which they are "types" — or rather he employs a reversed adaptation of this which labels something in his story a "type" of a Bible element — as when Hester Prynne is called "a scarlet woman and a worthy type of her of Babylon." But it should be observed that this particular description comes not from the narrator but from one of the tale's seventeenth century Puritans who might be expected to typologize in this way, just as it is the Puritan authority that has affixed upon Hester the signifying letter which is invariably described as being not red but scarlet. She is called a "type" in a non-scriptural sense by the Hawthorne-narrator. At such times she can be associated with traditional figures of moral personification when he comments, "It may seem marvellous that this woman should call that place her home, where, and where only, she must needs be the type of shame" — which still implicitly refers to the viewpoint of the Boston community or, again, when Chillingworth is said to have come home to behold "the woman, in whom he hoped to find embodied the warmth and cheerfulness of home, set up as a type of sin before the people." Other occurrences of the term, however, are closer to the simpler meaning of a symbol. Such is the early designation of the infant Pearl as "a forcible type, in its little frame, of the moral agony which Hester Prynne had borne throughout the day."

"Token," i.e., "something that serves to indicate a fact, event, object, feeling, etc.; a sign, a symbol" (OED) also serves to indicate a sign, with the added implication that the sign is an evidence, even a consequence of the signified. Dimmesdale's distaste for Chillingworth's appearance is "a token, implicitly to be relied on, of a deeper antipathy in the breast of the latter." "Emblem" is another name for a symbolic signifier, more exclusively visual, deriving from the seventeenth century taste for expressing abstractions by means of objects or pictured objects, but since used as another synonym for symbol as well as for an armorial device or even for a badge that might be worn on clothing. Hester's "A" is all these — a badge she wears, a device for the escutcheon on her tombstone — "On a field sable, the letter A, gules" and the "emblem of her guilt."

Finally, there is "hieroglyph," which more than any of the terms just glanced at suggests the art of writing at the same time that it suggests the pictorial figure, in the reference to the picture-writing of the Egyptians. By extension, too, a hieroglyph is "a figure, device, or sign, having some hidden meaning; a secret or enigmatical symbol" (OED), and so more than any of the others expresses Hawthorne's feelings about the signifiers he has marked out in his tale. Such a mystery is the child Pearl, as we shall shortly consider. As Hester and Dimmesdale watch her in the forest, it is observed, "She had been offered to the world, these seven years past, as the living hieroglyphic, in which was revealed the secret they so darkly sought to hide, — all written in this symbol, — all plainly manifest, — had there been a prophet or magician skilled to read the character of flame." Pearl, the animate letter or character, is truly the hieroglyphic figure which hides an elusive meaning.

Like a rhetorician, Hawthorne has, in the examples I have given, labelled his subjects as though they were figures of speech in a spoken or written text. But, of course, these types, emblems, tokens, and hieroglyphs are not really supposed to be products of the human imagination. They belong to the category of privileged signs deriving from a transcendent presence. They are "written" by a spiritual force which expresses itself in the secret language of appearances. To read such texts one must be gifted with a prophet's or a magician's power to see beyond actuality. As Chillingworth says of the "riddle" ("a question or statement intentionally worded in a dark or puzzling manner" [OED]) of the identity of Hester's lover, "the Daniel who shall expound it is yet a-wanting." The surface of life which he beholds is thus compared to the most famous of dark texts, the writing on the wall at Belshazzar's feast.

For us, there may no longer be a center, as Jacques Derrida would call it, to assure to such — or any — appearances the status of signs. With our loss of confidence in the sacred grounding of signs we have lost confidence in their objectivity, and see them only as games of the mind. Hawthorne may have been at the threshold of our condition, though he was still formally committed to older views. The Puritan ontology as well as the Puritan morality haunted the American mind in Hawthorne's day, and haunted his in particular. We think more usually of the moral imperatives of Puritanism as a lingering presence in Hawthorne's writing — and where more than in this tale of transgression and penance? But it is the Puritan understanding of the relation of natural to divine reality that was more important to him. The Puritans regarded reality textually; a long tradition of Christian thought which spoke through them analogized the world as a book which might be compared to scripture as an act of divine writing. What God had written in the creation was a cryptic language, yet one could be confident nonetheless that no phenomenon but had its sacred sense. Such a viewpoint was older than Christianity, having its roots in platonism. It was, too, enjoying a new life in the secularized religion of romantic transcendentalism of which Hawthorne was aware at close hand.

Hawthorne knew perfectly well his difference and distance from the Puritans though "strongs traits of their nature," he said, had "intertwined themselves" with his. He was skeptical as well about the convictions of his Concord neighbors, Emerson and Thoreau. His temperamental nominalism, which is so visible in the determined abstention from all interpretation practiced in his Notebooks with their tireless recording of trivial realities, made him a man for whom the world is exactly what it is and no more. Yet, as for so many mid-nineteenth century minds the loss of the visionary sense, the draining of significance from the mundane, was felt with a certain anguish, at best a wry humor, and the viewpoint of science seemed to him pitiably meager and even morally dangerous. In *The Scarlet Letter* he gives play to all of his mingled feelings — his tenderness for the poetry of a lost faith in essences, his ironic detachment and disbelief, and his fear of such disbelief in himself or others.

The agency of these complex feelings is, in the novel, a persona about whom too little has been said. His divided attitudes are made clear in the Custom House Preface — making the Preface a necessary part of the fictional whole, giving a character to the narrating voice. This narrator appears to us in the Preface as a man undecided in his view of reality between the Puritan-transcendental conviction that the invisible speaks ceaselessly behind the visible and the materialism that finds the explanation of things merely in accident and physical laws. He admits his deviation from the beliefs of his "grave-bearded, sable-cloaked and steeple-crowned" progenitors, yet declares a legitimate descent from them. He values his experiences at the Custom House as an antidote to transcendental associations and inclinations. Even the old inspector, a personality of unillumined materiality, was, he tells us, "desirable as a change of diet, to a man who had known Alcott." Yet his final and most moving words are a tribute to the art that discerns the spirit essence in the quotidian.

In this well-known section of the Preface he discusses his aesthetic problems while striving, in the Custom House, to overcome his creative torpor. But it should be noted that his problem is as much ontological as aesthetic: it involves his unsuccessful struggle to attain the transcendental sense. In the nighttime vigil in the parlor of his Salem house, the moonlight "making every object so minutely visible, yet so unlike a morning or noontide visibility," the homely details of the room were completely seen, he recalls, "yet spiritualized by the unusual light." The room became a neutral territory where "the Actual and the Imaginary may meet." It was the sort of meeting he would have liked to bring about in his writing yet could not, though the "wiser effort would have been, to diffuse thought and imagination through the opaque substance of today . . . to seek, resolutely, the true and indestructible value that lay hidden in the petty and wearisome incidents, and ordinary characters." His failure was no matter merely of skill or of artistic imagination, as it has seemed to most readers. The requisite imagination that he lacked was the prophet or magician's—or if the poet's, then the romantic poet's seer-like power to discern higher truth. Unable to find essence in his surroundings he could only retreat to the unsubstantiality of the past or the fanciful, in which one might play with the idea of significance in the mode of romance.

Nevertheless, nothing is more serious than *The Scarlet Letter*, despite the charge of Henry James that its faults are "a want of reality and an abuse of the fanciful element—of a certain superficial symbolism" which "grazes triviality." James did not see that Hawthorne's method in the book was to express his own profoundest problem. In a way that is seldom understood and seems sometimes merely coy, he offers and withdraws, denies and provides the sense of the spirituality of life—and so suggests the opacity or unreliability of its signs. Many a reader has been irritated by the narrator's reluctance to decide what, if anything, Chillingworth saw on Dimmesdale's bosom, or what, if anything, was seen in the sky during the night-scaffold scene in Chapter XII or what, if anything, was seen on Dimmesdale's bosom, again, by the assembled multitude in the final scaffold scene. These are only the most memorable instances of Hawthorne's reluctance to settle a simple question of appearances. More important, however, is his refusal to help us to assign final significance to these phenomena, even if granted. Repeatedly, he seems only willing to say, as at the conclusion of the final scene after summarizing the conflicting reports of witnesses, "The reader may choose among these theories."

Nowhere is this insistent ambiguity more conspicuous than in the central scaffold scene—which James, it may be noted, particularly disliked. Here are duplicated the conditions of the moonlit chamber of the Preface; the scene is bathed in a supernal light which makes each detail both completely visible and radiant with meaning. In the light cast from the sky during the minister's night-vigil, he sees for the first time that Roger Chillingworth is no friend, he pierces the veil. Yet this is also the occasion for the narrator's most skeptical discussion of the delusiveness of signs. He comments upon the "messages" read into nature by man and the egotism of the assumption that they are addressed to our particular selves. "We impute it, therefore, solely to the disease in his own eye and heart that the minister, looking upward toward the zenith, beheld there the appearance of an immense letter,—the letter A," he seems to conclude. But, immediately after, we hear that the sexton reported the next day that "a great red letter in the sky,—the letter A," was seen by others also, and by them taken to stand for Angel, to signify the governor's passing. So, what are we to make of the reading of signs? The sexton, who has found Dimmesdale's glove on the scaffold, says that Satan must have dropped it there, intending—falsely—to impute that Dimmesdale belongs where evil-doers are set up to public shame. Signs may be only the mischief-making of Satan, then, and no true tokens? Except, of course, that this token *is* well placed!

Hester's letter is the central example of the almost infinite potentialities of semantic variety. A material object, a piece of embroidered cloth held in the finder's hand, it is the one irreducible reality which connects the intangible historic past with the narrator's present sensation; it authenticates, is an evidence of its vanished substantiality. As an abstract sign on Hester's bosom, it purports to speak both for the nature of her past and for the present condition of the wearer. It is a letter of the alphabet, but also, presumably, an initial, a sign of a sign, since it represents a word, the next larger linguistic unit after the letter. But "adultery" is never "spelled out." The word, like the act it designates, is invisible in the text — the act held inaccessibly out of the reader's sight while the word only hovers in his mind. The merely implied word becomes somehow less explicit, and when we are told that the letter is a "talisman" (a magic object generally engraved with figures or characters) of the Fiend, we suspect a more generalized significance. It is said to throb in sympathy with all sin of whatever kind beheld by Hester. It seems to represent an absolute and undenotable evil.

The letter may indicate the presence in Hester of Original Sin, and refer to a common corruption which requires no outward demonstration, which does not manifest itself in true signs, which even the most virtuous in deed must share. The old Calvinist mystery is really the mystery of signs — there is an inner reality that cannot be signified by deed, while deeds, good works or the reverse, are without inner meaning. Trapped in this disjunction the Puritans themselves forget the original significance of Hester's letter and take it to stand for "able" — which is, unlike "adultery," enunciated in the text — because of her good works. But Hester, when the magistrates consider removing the stigma, says, "were I worthy to be quit of it, it would fall away of its own nature, or be transformed into something that should speak a different purport." She seems, still, to insist upon its relation to her inner self. Yet she will try to comfort Dimmesdale by pointing out *his* good works — "Is there no reality in the penitence thus sealed and witnessed by good works?" — until he tells her that *his* scarlet letter still "burns in secret."

On Dimmesdale, where the letter may be guessed to have appeared for a similar signifying function as on Hester, it is, however, as invisible as the act or condition it refers to. Society has placed no token upon him and when Chillingworth opens the sleeping minister's vestment he sees "something" which is not pictured or named for the reader. Even in the final scene when he tears his own garment from his chest we are told only, "It was revealed! But it were irreverent to describe that revelation," and the reader is cheated again of the confirming spectacle. Although some spectators testified to having seen that the minister did bear a letter like Hester's, others saw nothing. And the sign, if it had really been there, might, anyhow, our narrator remarks, have been only the medical symptom of Dimmesdale's psychic distress, "the effect of the ever active tooth of remorse gnawing from the inmost heart outwardly," an instance of psychosomatic symptomology (another sign theory which greatly interested Hawthorne, as we shall see in a moment).

Pearl, the asker of so many preternaturally pertinent questions, asks her mother to explain the meaning of the sign she wears and is not answered — plausibly because the answer would be beyond her grasp but also so that the reader may still not hear the signified, the unutterable. When she asks, "What does the letter mean, mother," Hester says evasively, "I wear it for the sake of its gold thread." Pearl says that she has been told that the scarlet letter is the Black Man's mark, an expression she repeats when she asks if the minister holds his hand upon his bosom because the Black Man has "set his mark" there. "Mark," for which the root sense is, once again, token or sign, implies here, as a special meaning, a signature, the personal sign of a signer set in stead of his name. As such it signifies not the wearer but the writer, the author of all sin. Pearl connects this guessed-at sign with Hester's A when she asks, "Is this his mark?" and extracts from her mother the acknowledgement, "Once in my life I met the Black Man! This scarlet letter is his mark!" And Pearl then guesses, when she sees the minister's hand over his heart, "Is it because, when the minister wrote his name in the book, the Black Man set his mark in that place?"

Both symbol and consequence of Hester's and Dimmesdale's sin, Pearl is herself an instance of the ambiguity of signs. She is the animate letter, the child dressed in gold-embroidered scarlet, "the scarlet letter in another form, the scarlet letter endowed with life." Yet when she dances about in the final scene in the city square, "her dress, so proper was it to little Pearl, seemed an effluence or inevitable development and outward manifestation of her character, no more to be separated from her than the many-hued brilliancy from a butterfly's wing, or the painted glory from the leaf of a bright flower." Her appearance, once the sign, the "effluence" of her parents' sin, is now an exterior organically developed from her own airy nature, as the rest of nature's signs emanate from transcendent being. Earlier, she reverses or nullifies Hester's sign when she places it, made of eel grass, upon herself. It is the color of nature, green, the eidetic image of her mother's token, and Pearl waggishly reflects as though to mock the meaning-searcher, "I wonder if mother will ask me what it means!" But Hester refuses to see it as a sign, and says, "The green letter on thy childish bosom has no purport."

The mystery of meaning is expressed in the obliquity of Pearl's own answers to the question of what she is. Hester wonders, "Child, what are thou?" and is answered, "O, I am your little Pearl," which is no answer for her name is her sign not her significance. Hester asks, "Tell me, then what thou art and who sent thee hither?" and then answers this question herself, but Pearl demurs, "I have no Heavenly Father," the animate sign denying its source in the divine. A little later, the Reverend Wilson asks again, "Who made thee?" and Pearl's answer is that she has not been made but plucked from the prison rose-bush, an answer at once improbably arch and informed with a pantheistic view of nature, dispensing with the myth of express creation. Hawthorne's ironic dubeity can be felt in his presentation of the Governor's shocked, "a child of three years old, and she cannot tell who made her!"—for how many among his readers would have had perfect confidence in the catechism reply? Of course, all the while that we have had this play of alternative semiologies, of Puritan and transcendental explanations of origin, it is obvious that Pearl's pert remarks are naturalistically explicable; she has just seen the roses in the governor's garden, has already been called "red rose" by Wilson himself, who also calls her "little bird of scarlet plumage," the natural creature she will be likened to in the last scene.

Our first view of Hester and her child occurs, nevertheless, when they emerge from the prison door passing the rose-bush and the weeds "which evidently found something congenial in the soil that had so early borne the black flower of civilized society, a prison." Weeds and prison are linked by a resemblance that is not merely metaphor but attributable to the generative force of which they are both products. Nearby, the rose-bush holds up "delicate gems" which "might be imagined to offer" sweetness to the condemned "in token that the deep heart of Nature could pity and be kind to him." Nature, the symbolizer, proffers a token from the realm of spirit in the same way as the Christian godhead has sent Pearl as "emblem and product of sin." But Hawthorne does not assert either source of signification uncontrovertibly: his weak copula, "might be imagined," is a reminder that such symbolizing may be only the result of the human imagination.

It is quite "significant," therefore, that the artistic imagination appears centrally in Hester herself who is an artist of needlework, the only medium available to a woman in her day. Her works are distinguished by their power of symbolic exhibition, her first oeuvre of note having been her letter. She is afterwards called upon to show the meaning of other human situations, the pomp of public ceremonies, the sorrow of funerals which she would "typify by manifold emblematic devices." Her art is also *self*-expressive, "a mode of expressing and therefore soothing the passion of her life." Pearl has something of her mother's instinct: her creativity operates upon "a stick, a bunch of rags, a flower," adapting them to her inner drama. Her art is harmless play. But Hester collaborates with Puritan society in converting Pearl herself into a symbol by clothing her in her symbolizing, signifying costume. She thus does violence to the irreducible being of the child who is shown repeatedly to be a natural phenomenon, a whimsical child and nothing else. All art, all symbolizing, is reductive.

In the mirror of art the truth is distorted from its natural proportions, as Hester's own image is when she sees herself in the polished armor in the Governor's house. The monstrously enlarged "A" upon her breast, her face reduced to insignificance by the convex surface of the breastplate, represent her reduction as the woman behind the scarlet letter. And in time, "all the light and graceful foliage of her character had been withered by this red hot brand, and had long fallen away, leaving a bare and harsh outline," the person *becoming* the symbol. Yet the narrative shows at the same time that Hester resists this simplification, remaining a complex, developing personality. An opposite process takes place in the case of Chillingworth who, as his history advances, becomes more and more an abstract symbol of infernal malice until at the end he simply shrivels to nothing, all his humanity gone.

But Hawthorne does not dismiss or disparage the reading of signs altogether. He continues throughout the narrative to find ways of exploring the relation of phenomenon and meaning, of outerness and inwardness; his narrative discovers and tests other pairs of terms that represent signifier and signified. One example is the theory of disease by which he anticipates psychosomatic medicine. Chillingworth, it will be recalled, ascribes his patient's malady to a spiritual cause. "He to whom only the outward and physical evil is laid open knoweth, oftentimes, but half the evil which he is called upon to cure. A bodily disease, which we look upon as whole and entire within itself, may, after all, be but a symptom of some ailment in the spiritual part . . . a sickness, a sore place, if we may so call it, in your spirit, hath immediately its appropriate manifestation in your bodily frame." Bodily disease, then, is a "manifestation" of spirit, another instance of the sign language of all phenomena. Hawthorne's interest in the general science of signs, extends, logically, to the branch of medicine having to do with symptoms, which is also called semiology. Older medical concepts and even modern ones, of course, imply a dualism in the patient whose disease is defined as a manifestation of some hidden meaning — and a meaning that was truly inaccessible, for the most part, before the germ theory and modern knowledge of physiology. And so the source of disease, though presumed to be spiritual in Dimmesdale's case, will not, after all, be accessible to the probing of his physician-enemy.

Dimmesdale himself subscribes to his physicians' theories when he attributes his own distrust of Chillingworth to his inner spiritual disorder — "the poison of one morbid spot was infecting his heart's entire substance." In fact, his perceptions are accurate. But his inner condition does produce hallucinations, delusive signs. These seem to demonstrate, again, Hawthorne's view of the effects of the Puritan-transcendental view of a superior spiritual reality, his preference for the matter-of-fact: "It is the unspeakable misery of a life so false as his, that it steals the pith and substance out of whatever realities there are around us . . . To the untrue man, the whole universe is false, — and it is impalpable, — it shrinks to nothing within his grasp."

All things hidden and all things exposed become antonyms in the novel to reflect the opposition of outer and inner. The forest, where the lovers meet alone save for little Pearl who does not understand what she sees except by occult instinct, is the place of a seclusive truth, difficult to read; the forest path, like a hard text, is "obscure." The public scenes in which Hester and Dimmesdale are together are the locus of communal truth, that which is perceived by all. "We must not talk in the market-place of what happens to us in the forest," Hester warns Pearl, distinguishing between the unutterable inner world and the world of speech. Hester's "A," Mistress Hibbins says, is a "token" that Hester has been to the forest many times, but the minister's visit is ultimately incommunicable. His election sermon is best understood when, in fact, its *words* are indistinguishable and only the mournful tone of his voice conveys his state to Hester as she stands outside. Language, by implication, misleads us, tells us nothing of the heart, which has no language. Dimmesdale's unintelligible murmur is like Pearl's babble or the gibberish she speaks in his ear in the night scaffold scene—perhaps a sacred speaking in tongues, perhaps the non-sense of a message-less world.

Nature, too, only babbles. The forest keeps its secrets though the babbling brook would seem to want to "speak" them: "All these giant trees and boulders of granite seemed intent on making a mystery of the course of this small brook: fearing, perhaps, that, within its never-ceasing loquacity, it should whisper tales out of the heart of the old forest whence it flowed, or mirror its revelations on the smooth surface of a pool." Pearl asks what the brook says, but Hester replies that if she had a sorrow of her own the brook would tell her of it, "even as it is telling me of mine!" implying that she has understood the brook as the brook has understood her, but also that one hears in Nature's babble what one's own experience suggests. And as Pearl continues to play by the side of the brook her own cheerful babble mingles with its melancholy one, we are told, and "the little stream would not be comforted and still kept telling its unintelligible secret of some mournful mystery."

Hawthorne's antithesis between the solitary soul and society is a variation upon the theme of an inexpressible inner reality. Hester is one of the great American isolatoes, who cannot speak the language of community. At his extremest, this loner is Melville's Bartleby, who withdraws from language altogether. By embracing silence he acknowledges the lapse of a common truth which unites not only men with one another but which, by a language of signs, unites the universe to mankind. Hester's sin is not only unutterable but involves a name, that of her partner, which she refuses to utter. Her sexual history is so private that it cannot be imagined when we gaze at her in the chaste aftermath of Hawthorne's novel. And yet that privacy has its public manifestation, the child Pearl. And Hester's sin is outrageously publicized by her exposure in the most public of places, the town pillory. The opening scene of the novel draws thrilling intensity from this paradox. From the hidden interior of her prison cell, from the secrecy of her own heart, Hester emerges with the child upon her arm, isolated and silent, to stand upon the most public site in Boston. A special piece of cruel machinery, a vise to hold the head upright, is available on the scaffold so that the condemned may be forced to face those who look upon him, and Hawthorne comments, "There is no outrage more flagrant than to forbid the culprit to hide his face for shame." But Hester voluntarily faces her viewers. Nevertheless, her exposure reveals nothing. Indeed, the spectator is prompted to find her an "image of Divine Maternity," to read the scarlet woman as her opposite.

"Secret" is a key word in *The Scarlet Letter*. All the principal personages have secrets — Hester, the identity of her lover, Dimmesdale his sin, Chillingworth his own identity and motive. Chillingworth's name is like Hester's sin in never being enunciated in the text — though we may guess that it is Prynne. Perhaps the most important of these secrets, in terms of the progressive tension of the plot is Dimmesdale's. Chillingworth's struggle to bring to the surface what lies hidden in the minister's heart is the primary conflict of the story (James was right in saying that the essential drama is there, between the two men, and not in Hester). This is also because more is involved in their struggle than the story tells: theirs is the contest between two views of the communicability of meaning. Chillingworth had asked Hester to name her lover and she had refused, eliciting from him the comment, "there are few things, — whether in the outward world, or the invisible sphere of thought — few things hidden from the man, who devotes himself earnestly and unreservedly to the solution of a mystery." By profession a scientist, an investigator of nature and mankind, he is confident that he can compel all mysteries to yield to him. From the "prying multitude," from even the magistrates and ministers, Hester's secret may be hidden, but, Chillingworth declares, "I come to the inquest with other senses than they possess. I shall seek this man as I have sought truth in books, as I have sought gold in alchemy."

Chillingworth is defined as a materialist, one of a species of men who have lost the sense of spiritual meanings. "In their researches into the human frame, it may be that the higher and more subtle faculties of such men were materialized, and that they lost the spiritual view of existence amid the intricacies of that wondrous mechanism which seemed to involve art enough to comprise all of life within itself." The newcomer becomes the community physician, replacing the aged deacon and apothecary, "whose piety and deportment were stronger testimonials in his favor" than a medical diploma, for he is learned in both "antique physic" and the Indians' homeopathic medicine.

He believes, consequently, that the inner condition of his patient, the meaning of his disease can be understood. The narrator seems to agree: "Few secrets can escape an investigator who has opportunity and license to undertake such a quest." Like a researcher into a difficult scientific problem he is described "prying into his patient's bosom, delving among his principles, prying into his recollections, proving everything with a cautious touch, like a treasure-seeker in a dark cavern." Hawthorne even goes on to say, "A man burdened with a secret should especially avoid the intimacy of his physician" for "at some inevitable moment, will the soul of the sufferer be dissolved, and flow forth in a dark and transparent stream, bringing all its mysteries into the daylight." The doctor—more investigator than therapist, is said to be "desirous only of truth, even as if the question involved no more than the air-drawn lines and figures of a geometrical problem, instead of human passions, and wrongs inflicted on himself."

His contest with Dimmesdale, who steadfastly protects his secret, is dramatically illustrated in their conversation in the graveyard in Chapter Ten. Upon a grave without identifying tombstone the physician finds weeds that "grew out of the [buried man's] heart and "typify, it may be, some hideous secret that was buried with him." They have sprung up there, Chillingworth declares, "to make manifest an unspoken crime." Dimmesdale, however, insists upon the inaccessibility and sacredness of the dead man's secrets. "There can be . . . no power, short of the Divine mercy, to disclose, whether by uttered words, or by type or emblem, the secrets that may be buried with a human heart. The heart . . . must perforce hold them, until the day when all hidden things shall be revealed. . . . These revelations . . . are meant merely to promote the intellectual satisfaction of all intelligent beings, who will stand waiting, on that day, to see the dark problem of this life made plain." Not merely, then, does he not choose to tell his secret; it cannot ever be revealed to men until Judgment Day. It is a mystery too profound for us before that. And, Hawthorne's language seems to suggest, it is a mystery which is only part of the general mystery of "hidden things" for which "type or emblem"— the language of appearance—provide no clue. As the methodical indeterminacy of *The Scarlet Letter* suggests, there is no present disclosure of "the dark problem of this life."

To presume otherwise by trying to penetrate the mystery of another soul is Chillingworth's sin, as Dimmesdale tells Hester. He "violated in cold blood the sanctity of a human heart." This statement is not usually understood, though invariably quoted in discussions of the novel. We tend to think that Chillingworth has sinned because he has criminally used the knowledge he has gained in order to manipulate and destroy the minister. But this is not what the words say. The insistence upon illicit discovery, the assault by Chillingworth upon sacred knowledge, is itself illegitimate.

Here perhaps is the pious man's reply to the problem of the obliquity of signs. Hawthorne may have felt that it was his only stay against skepticism to believe in an ultimate revelation, an ultimate deciphering of what is beyond our comprehension in this life. But he may also have entertained the suspicion that no ultimate meanings exist. Perhaps he sometimes felt both enough to share the thought expressed by Melville in a letter he got from him only a year after *The Scarlet Letter* was published: "If any of those other Powers choose to withhold certain secrets, let them; that does not impair my sovereignty in myself; that does not make me tributary. And perhaps after all, there is *no* secret."

New Essays

"Again a Literary Man": Vocation and *The Scarlet Letter*

Rita K. Gollin*

"Shall you want me to be a Minister, Doctor or Lawyer?" (N. H. to his mother, 7 March 1820)

"What do you think of my becoming an Author, and relying for support upon my pen." (N. H. to his mother, 13 March 1821)

"I want my own place! — my own place! — my true place in the world! — my proper sphere! — my thing to do, which nature intended me to perform. . . ." ("The Intelligence Office")

"The real human being . . . was again a literary man." ("The Custom-House")

As Nathaniel Hawthorne composed "The Custom-House" at the end of 1849 and then completed *The Scarlet Letter*, he was taking stock of himself, dramatizing but also masking personal anxieties. The victorious Whigs had dismissed him from his job as Surveyor in the Salem Custom House the previous June, and his mother had died soon after. Now he was acting upon incompatible imperatives — honest self-presentation and protective self-concealment. He was also contemplating his role as a writer. While winding up his first romance, doing his best to earn a living, he was reasserting but also reassessing his resumed identity as "a literary man."

As a teenager trying to decide what to do with his life, Hawthorne had already developed the ironically masked personality that would determine the style and characters of his fiction. None of the careers that would please his family attracted him. He did not want to be a businessman like his Manning uncles, nor could he see himself entering any of the respectable professions open to college graduates. His explanations were at once facetious and serious: ministers led too narrow a life, doctors were parasitical, and there were already too many lawyers. Although he enjoyed writing, he knew writing was not a practical way to earn a living. He became a writer nonetheless, but he was deeply ironic about that choice. If he sometimes said he belonged to a sacred priesthood, he more frequently mocked himself as a scribbler, protesting like Kafka's "Hunger

*This essay was written specifically for this volume and is published here for the first time by permission of the author.

Artist" that he had found nothing better to do. All of this entered into his first romance, empowering it with his own personal experience.

During his childhood, when he lived in the Manning household with his mother and sisters, he turned to books for excitement—to Chaucer, Spenser, Shakespeare, Bunyan, Scott, and Gothic romances. During the adolescent interlude when he lived with his mother and sisters in the wilds of Raymond, Maine, he substituted the adventures of "savagizing" with his fowling-piece and his fishing pole. But on his fifteenth birthday, he was back in Salem with the Mannings and enrolled in a local school. He "sighs for the woods of Raymond, and yet he seems convinced of the necessity of prepairing to do something," his aunt Mary told his mother, assuring her that "we all endeavour to make him as comfortable & happy as we can."[1] As the words "seems," "something," and "as we can" suggest, Hawthorne was unsettled, uncomfortable, and unhappy. He had exchanged the freedom of Raymond for the compromises of Salem.

To make his discontent tolerable, he exaggerated it and donned literary masks, as in his letter to his sister Louisa of September 1819. He quoted Isaiah to express chagrin at being in "a 5 dollar school, I, that have been to a 10 dollar one. 'Oh Lucifer, son of the morning, how art thou fallen!' "; and he quoted Thomas Moore to bemoan his departure from Raymond: "twas light that ne'er shall shine again on lifes dull stream." For excitement, he was reading "*Waverly, The Mysteries of Udolpho, The Adventures of Ferdinand Count Fathom, Roderick Random*, and the first vol. of *Arabian Nights*." But with masked self-revelation, he reported something more important. After writing out two sorrowful quatrains about the evanescence of genius and "earthly pomp," he announced they were his rhymes though "not exactly my thoughts." He complained—and bragged—"I am full of scraps of poetry can't keep it out of my brain." After penning a third stanza, he said "I could vomit up a dozen pages more if I was a mind to"; then after eight more lines, he boasted that his sister Elizabeth was "not the only one of the family whose works have appeared in the papers." Despite the burlesque, he already thought writing was natural for him ("can't keep it out of my brain") yet also a matter of choice ("I could vomit up . . . more), and he wanted his work ratified by publication—in "the papers" as well as in that very letter (114–15).

Even so, neither he nor his family was clear about what he was "prepairing to do." Six months after he had left Raymond, his mother wrote her brother Robert, "I hope Nathaniel has given up the thoughts of going to see for some years at least, he has not written to me yet."[2] Whether or not he seriously considered "going to see" (as his father and a few uncles had done), even broaching that possibility subverted Manning control. Though they did their best for him, and his Uncle Robert's horticultural experiments and his Uncle Sam's horse-buying trips demonstrated how varied a businessman's life might be, Hawthorne wanted no part of their life.

There was frustration on both sides. Robert did "not know what to do with him," Mary Manning told his mother in February; but she reported that a Salem lawyer thought well of "his talents &c. and is solicitous to have him go to Colleg." Robert would try to "defray the expences" and she would also help, because "the prospect of his makeing a worthy & usefull man is better in that way than any other."[3] Hawthorne soon began "to fit for College under Benjm L. Oliver, Lawyer," warning his mother that she was "in great danger of having one learned man in your family"; but beyond a vague plan to "come down and learn Ebe. Latin and Greek," he had no idea of what he might do with his learning. "Shall you want me to be a Minister, Doctor, or Lawyer?" he asked his mother, naming the three most "worthy & usefull" professions open to those who "got through college." But he immediately eliminated the first, firmly declaring, "A Minister I will not be" (117).

Though he had not decided what he would be, he wanted the right to choose. "I am 16 years old," he wrote his mother on 16 July 1820. "In five years I shall belong to myself" (124). Meanwhile, the dollar a week he earned for bookkeeping in the Manning stagecoach office enabled him to buy and rent books: "I have read all most all the Books which have been published for the last hundred Years," he told Elizabeth (134). He was also writing poems, a facetious family newspaper, and letters to Raymond. But tutorials and office work stifled his imagination. "I have almost given up writing Poetry," he told Elizabeth in October. "No Man can be Poet & a Book-Keeper at the same time." College would only mean "living upon Uncle Robert for 4 years longer"; and he declared, "How happy I should feel, to be able to say, 'I am Lord of myself' " (132).

Only the prospect of vacations in Raymond reconciled him to throwing away "four years of the best part of my Life" at Bowdoin, he told his mother. He was going along with the Mannings' plan to make him a useful citizen, partly because he thought they were right. But however cryptically, he let his mother know why he had already rejected all the paths to success that college could open. "A Minister is of course out of the Question," he said, expanding on his earlier flat rejection: the life was dull, and he "was not born to vegetate forever in one place." He flatly ruled out the law on mock-pragmatic grounds: there were so many lawyers that at least half were "in a state of actual starvation." His rejection of medicine was only slightly more straightforward: he did not want "to live by the diseases and Infirmities of my fellow Creatures," and the death of a patient would trouble his conscience. Only one sentence carries complete conviction—the exclamation, "Oh that I was rich enough to live without a profession." But his real project emerges for the first time, couched as an afterthought and punctuated by joking self-denigration:

> What do you think of my becoming an Author, and relying for support
> upon my pen. Indeed I think the illegibility of my handwriting is very
> authorlike.

We can only guess at his mother's response; but beneath the joking lay the
hope of winning recognition as a writer:

> How proud you would feel to see my works praised by the reviewers, as
> equal to proudest productions of the scribbling sons of John Bull.
> (138–39)

If he was not entirely committed to the impracticalities of "becoming an
Author," he could not imagine becoming anything else, and an author he
would become.

Marking time at Bowdoin College until he was of age meant
following well-defined paths, but Hawthorne cut a few capers and took a
few bypaths. He completed the traditional curriculum, adding an elective
course in anatomy and physiology in his senior year (which explains why
his degree is recorded "A.B.; Med. Sch. 1825"), though he amassed fines
for cutting chapel, "neglecting" declamation, playing cards, and drinking.
By joining the Athenean Society, one of the college's two literary clubs, he
gained access to a library of six hundred books which included "many of
the best English Authors" (159). He also continued to be a "scribbler," and
his friend Horatio Bridge "foretold his success if he should choose literature
as a profession."[4]

But even though his classmate Longfellow predicted in his com-
mencement address that "palms are to be won by our native writers" and
urged "a noble self-devotion to the cause of literature," the anomalousness
of that choice is evident from the careers of their other classmates.[5] Five of
the thirty-eight became ministers, eighteen became lawyers, and six
became doctors (proving Hawthorne had been right about the options for
college graduates and the preponderance of lawyers). Of the remainder,
four went into business (one as a bookseller), and the other four became
teachers — including Longfellow, the only college professor. Most pursued
more than one career, Longfellow and Hawthorne among them, though
only Hawthorne put writing first.[6] Alumni of the 1820s eventually
produced nearly 150 books, but only Longfellow and Hawthorne produced works of literature.[7]

Hawthorne returned to Salem in September 1825 to try his hand at
the profession of literature, though with no great hope of winning
"palms": he did not expect to "make a distinguished figure in the world,"
he told Elizabeth, but only "to plod along with the multitude" (194). Now
that he was legally Lord of Myself, he became "a scribbler by profession"
(270), willing to take on editing or other "sorts of drudgery, such as
children's books &c" (252) to supplement what his stories brought in. But

his income was minimal; and until 1837, when his name appeared on the cover of *Twice-told Tales*, he won no public recognition.

It is easy to understand why Hawthorne accepted an appointment as Measurer in the Boston Custom House in January 1839, though also why he soon resigned. Throughout his year in office, he thought of himself as a writer who was temporarily engaged in another occupation. "As a literary man, my new occupations entirely break me up," he told Longfellow (310); and to his fiancee Sophia, he complained of turning into a machine because his work did not engage his intellect, heart, or soul (330). It was an aggravated case of an earlier malady: he could not function simultaneously as poet and bookkeeper, and he felt wholly alive only as a writer.

Yet he did not consider writing his "true" vocation or "calling" in the tradition of his Calvinist forefathers — that work which God had placed him on earth to perform. He did not believe in that kind of divine absolute: his was a secular concern. He became a professional writer not out of compulsion but because he had to choose something, and only in writing did his abilities and his inclinations join. In his self-deprecating letter to Longfellow in June 1837, acknowledging his praise of *Twice-told Tales*, Hawthorne reported, "having nothing else to be ambitious of, I have felt considerably interested in literature" (252). He was dramatizing his anxieties about leading a passive and useless existence, and also the strong element of resignation in his commitment. Seven years later, in a sketch entitled "The Intelligence Office," he could ironically distance himself from "the man out of his right place" who enters the employment office. "I want my own place! — my own place! — my true place in the world! — my proper sphere! — my thing to do, which nature intended me to perform," that man insists. Hawthorne's spokesman is the Man of Intelligence, who wryly says that most people are "more or less, in the same predicament," but adds that a request for "something specific" might be negotiated "on your compliance with the conditions."[8]

In 1846 Hawthorne negotiated a job at the Salem Custom House and, in his judgment, fully complied with the conditions of his appointment. This he explained three years later in "The Custom-House." Seething about his ouster, he could nonetheless appreciate the paradox of being forced to resume the career he had initially chosen, the career he had always preferred. At the beginning of "The Custom-House," resuming his temporarily relinquished role as author and adopting the genial tone of his introduction to *Mosses from an Old Manse*, Hawthorne announced that he intended to tell "the few who will understand" about his years in office, decorously veiling his "inmost Me." Attentive readers might take the references to the "few" and the "veil" as in invitation to decode. Next, adopting a mask rather than a veil, Hawthorne said the "true" purpose of his essay was to declare his "true position" as "editor, or very little more" of his long narrative, providing proofs of its "authenticity."[9] Astute readers would take that statement as a conventional stratagem for legitimizing a work of the imagination; but the few who really understood would try to discriminate whatever was authentic in the autobiographic essay and the fiction to follow.

Hawthorne's next involuted self-presentation was through an act of ventriloquism, condemning himself as an idler through the mouths of his "stern and black-browed" Puritan ancestors: "A writer of story-books! What kind of business in life, — what mode of glorifying God, or being serviceable to mankind in his day and generation, — may that be?" (10). As he had often done before, Hawthorne was trying to preempt attack by disarming potential critics and using their weapons on himself. Yet this time he took pains to cancel his self-indictment. As "chief executive officer of the Custom-House," he had been superior to the other functionaries; in fact, he had been "as good a Surveyor as need be." Yet he had been more of an idler as an officeholder than as a storyteller, and the "wearisome old souls" who served under him were idler still. As a Surveyor, he had to use "faculties of his nature" that he did not need at Brook Farm or the Old Manse, but he denigrated those faculties. Any "man of thought, fancy, and sensibility" could become "a man of affairs, if he will only choose to give himself the trouble," but no one could simply choose to become a man of letters. Despite the ambivalence that made him conjure up his ancestors in the first place, Hawthorne was affirming that it was harder (and more important) to be a writer than a man of affairs (12–26).

At stake here is a measure of self-fulfillment. Hawthorne believed it was "the best definition of happiness to live throughout the whole range of [our] faculties and sensibilities," from the animal self at the bottom to the spiritual self at the top (40). But because we all differ in our capacities and gifts, what is natural for one person is unnatural for another. Hawthorne's account of discovering the scarlet letter is a paradigm of self-recovery, at once the most fictitious and most self-revealing section of his introduction. His Custom House duties made no demands on his "thought, fancy, and sensibility," he said, but encountering the germ of the story of Hester Prynne brought his mind back "in some degree, to its old track," and the Surveyor who exhorted him to tell that story was himself (31–33). Just as bookkeeping had hindered the would-be poet, surveying had disabled the mature writer of fiction, dulling his imagination and draining him of intellectual energy — the problem that frames the "neutral territory" passage. Hawthorne said nothing about the financial security his job had brought nor about his efforts for reinstatement. Yet he was not being duplicitous in saying he had felt reduced to "an unnatural state" while in office, "withholding myself from toil that would, at least, have stilled an unquiet impulse in me." The silver lining of his dismissal was his return to his natural state, performing the toil his "inmost Me" required and using all his faculties, his imagination in particular. As a Surveyor, he was first rendered torpid and then killed off; but as a writer, he returned to life.

One of Hawthorne's self-vindicating stratagems was to co-opt the rhetoric of the expedient politicians who had him removed from office (and of popular novels like Susan Warner's *Wide, Wide World*) by claiming that he had always done his best to perform the tasks imposed on him. He varied that stratagem to explain his deeper commitment, invoking Surveyor Pue to impose upon him the task of writing *The Scarlet Letter*. His scripted response itself demands attention. Earlier, he had vivified his affectionate sketch of a famous old general who was ending his days as a Custom House collector by quoting a phrase which merited "heraldic honor": "On the very verge of a desperate and heroic enterprise," the stalwart soldier had said, "I'll try, Sir!"; and Hawthorne, even more firmly committing himself to his own heroic enterprise, "said to the ghost of Mr. Surveyor Pue, – 'I will!' " (23, 34).

The same inventive energy that conjured up the eighteenth-century Surveyor Pue to counsel him had gone into invoking his seventeenth-century ancestors to judge him. As their heir and their victim, assimilating them in order to exorcise them, he was empowered to create a book about what he once called the "Judgment Letter."[10] Although Hawthorne could not help being the topmost bough of his family tree, as he could not reverse his ouster from office, he could create and destroy with his pen, with each stroke resuscitating and passing judgment on the Puritan past. He took vengeance on real and imagined antagonists while exonerating himself. He even casually settled his accounts with the seamen and merchants in his own family by relegating the "sea-flushed ship-master" and the "smart young clerk" to Salem's passing parade (6). His birthplace kept its hold on him, and he had needed his Custom House income, especially when his mother and sisters were part of his household. But his mother died, his sisters went off on their own, and his detestation of everyone who had anything to do with his ouster made him eager to leave town. By declaring himself "a citizen of somewhere else" (44), he rhetorically severed all ties to his birthplace.

The Custom House officials who had taken shelter "under the wing of the federal eagle" (5) endure in Hawthorne's introductory pages as contemptible specimens of reduced human capacity. He wrote them off as mere shadows, as images which his "fancy used to sport with, and has now flung aside for ever" (44). With special vindictiveness, he presented "a certain permanent Inspector" as little more than an animal, and later announced his death (16–20, 44). The "martyred" and "decapitated" surveyor emerges as a literary prestidigitator who can perform executions of his own. Taking Pangloss's position that "every thing was for the best," Hawthorne wryly announced his return to his real vocation in marketplace terminology: "The real human being" had made "an investment in ink, paper, and steel-pens, had opened his long-disused writing desk, and was again a literary man" (43).

Hawthorne's assumptions about a real human being's faculties and gifts, natural state and habitual tracks, form an integral part of *The Scarlet Letter*, underlying his contempt for ensconced men of affairs who condemn individuals of imagination and sensibility. The entire novel draws on his original problem of deciding what to do with his life and reaffirms his original choice. Through Bellingham, Dimmesdale, and Chillingworth, Hawthorne explained why he had refused to become a lawyer, a minister, or a doctor. Unlike them all, he was committed to work that was entirely private and independent. As respected and authoritative figures in the community, the governor, the minister, and the doctor were committed to observe its proprieties (or at least appear to do so), while the writer was free to be marginal and insubordinate. Yet in some measure, he resembled each of these men; and he was closer still to his heroine—the proud, intelligent, passionate, and creative individual who stood condemned by the self-righteous multitude though evidently superior to them.

Through Governor Bellingham, who had been "bred a lawyer" but served his country as "a soldier, as well as a statesman and ruler" (106), Hawthorne explained why he had not taken that broad path. Bellingham represents established law and its control over people's lives; he is an authoritarian fundamentalist, certain of his own righteousness. As when he advises Hester to surrender her three-year-old daughter to be "disciplined strictly, and instructed in the truths of heaven and earth" (110), he advocates submission to religious and social law and condemns any deviations, any eruptions of inner drives. He is cut from the same cloth as the earnest progenitors Hawthorne invoked in "The Custom-House," each "a soldier, legislator, judge" who incarnated "all the Puritanic traits, both good and evil." Such a "rigid and severe" man could never understand a woman like Hester.

The sympathetic open-minded author and the stern governor seem wholly at odds. Yet Hawthorne had confessed that "strong traits" of his ancestors entwined with his own; and to the extent that his narrative criticizes Hester and her wayward child, he identified with Bellingham. It can even be argued that he admired the magistrate as a trained lawyer who subordinated private interest to public service, as many of his Bowdoin classmates had done. The Governor's pumpkins, cabbages, and apple trees recall the environs of the edenic Old Manse. Moreover, although Hawthorne could never be a staunch proponent of any law or any creed, and had resisted marketplace values, he had nevertheless assumed positions of secular authority in Boston and Salem, and he would do so again in Liverpool. His pleasure in exercising his imagination and his fascination with human mysteries had led him to become a writer. But through Bellingham, he projected his own internalized conformity—as he had done whenever he praised his Puritan forbears, mocked himself as an idler, or accepted Manning authority.

As the story begins, Dimmesdale appears to be a model minister, his black garments signifying his sober commitment to a narrow ecclesiastical calling — perhaps what the teen-aged Hawthorne had in mind when he refused to become a minister because he "was not born to vegetate in one place." A minister's public responsibilities would have been intolerable to him. "In declamation he was literally *nowhere*," Bridge declared, recalling their college days;[11] and whether from desk or podium, Hawthorne could never be the spokesman for any creed. Perhaps one reason for making the minister a hypocrite was that if Hawthorne had become a minister, he would necessarily have been a hypocrite.

In assigning Dimmesdale the vocation he had himself most firmly rejected, Hawthorne nonetheless identified with him. Dimmesdale's sermons employ the strategies Hawthorne had employed from the time of his schoolboy letters to his family: self-display conjoins with self-concealment, assertion with denial. Certainly no one could ever have called Hawthorne a "godly youth," as the Reverend Wilson calls Dimmesdale when we first meet him, nor describe him as eloquent. Yet anyone could say (as the narrator does of Dimmesdale) that he had "a very striking aspect," that he demonstrated "high native gifts and scholar-like attainments," and that he enjoyed trodding "the shadowy by-paths" of life (65–66).

Even more important, Hawthorne expressed some of his literary ambitions through the minister. Dimmesdale's ability to express and communicate emotion was so great that even when hypocritical self-concern twisted his sermons, his audience felt "one accord of sympathy" (67). Although (like his creator) he never admitted them into his "inmost Me," he gave sympathy and evoked sympathy, in the end affirming and exemplifying the importance of being true to oneself. Dimmesdale had what Hawthorne wanted: his community's admiration and approbation for doing "worthy and usefull" work. In the forest scene, when Hester urges him to leave the scene of his torment, she tells him to "Preach! Write! Act!" (198). We can imagine Hawthorne similarly exhorting himself as he sat down to write his book.

Through Chillingworth, Hawthorne expanded on his early antipathy to the career of a doctor. In his youth, he had rejected medicine as a parasitic and morally threatening profession. Chillingworth is a horrible example of someone who profits from the diseases of others. As a leech, he sustains his life on Dimmesdale's illness, feeding on and increasing his patient's anguish. Hawthorne had worried about inadvertently sending a patient "to the realms below," but that is precisely what Chillingworth schemes to do. His conscience is not at all troubled. Worse still, he denies moral responsibility, thinking of himself as merely an agent of the "dark necessity" ensuing from the well-intentioned error of his marriage. He is welcomed into the Puritan community as a physician, and his ministrations to the infant Pearl prove he can perform "worthy and usefull" service. But he remains morally detestable.

Yet Hawthorne, who at Bowdoin had elected medical school courses in anatomy and physiology, identified with the scholar-physician, and not only because of his scientific training. Both were men of penetrating intelligence who knew that emotional distress can cause physical illness. Less happily, Hawthorne could identify with Chillingworth as a man who probed the mysteries of someone else's inner life for selfish reasons. By indicting Chillingworth as a pryer and a manipulator, a man destroyed by cold alienation from the human community, Hawthorne indicted and warned himself. To the extent that Chillingworth mirrored the psychological romancer, he was a cautionary figure.

Hawthorne's sympathetic identification with his heroine has suggested to many readers that her "Judgment Letter" might well signify *Artist* or even *Author*. Behind the woman on the scaffold stands the decapitated surveyor. Both are martyrs, victims of secular authority, and both make terms with their humiliation. Coming back to life as "a literary man," Hawthorne turned shame into vindication in "The Custom-House" and the romance it introduced. Hester, his avatar, acts as if by her own free will from the moment we first see her led from jail, thereafter choosing her own paths as a single parent who "possessed an art. . . . and imaginative skill" (81) and becoming a sister of mercy and a counsellor. Both are open-minded, passionate, self-assertive, and creative individuals, separated from their hostile communities, yet managing to support themselves and (however indirectly) to manifest their deepest concerns and commitments.

In representing his fascination with "the old scarlet letter" in "The Custom-House," and his certainty of its "deep meaning," Hawthorne was performing as author, protagonist, reader, and ideally sympathetic critic all in one (31). As Hester did in elaborating her letter, so Hawthorne in contriving his romance. Because Hester was thrown on her own, she discovered the power of her artistry, expending "imaginative skill" and "fantastic ingenuity" in embroidering and in attiring her child, doing other needlework for "emolument," but suppressing her pleasure in her own "exquisite productions" in the penance of "making coarse garments for the poor" (83). Each sent a message "most worthy of interpretation" that communicated to the sensibilities, evading the mind's analysis; but that problem suggests its own solution. As an author, a public figure, and a private man, Hawthorne was asserting the importance of paying attention to our rich if inarticulate innermost experience. In writing from that inner reservoir and trying to address the sensibilities of his readers, he was acting on the moral of his own book: "Be true!" (260).

The entire book can be approached as a network of statements about vocations chosen, evaded, and changed; and the action in that sense can be seen as the consequences of willful self-assertion, self-fulfillment, self-discovery, self-evasion, and self-repression as conjoined with the pragmatics of survival. Because the scholarly Chillingworth had mastered alchemy in Europe and herbal medicine during his Indian captivity, and because he was ransomed into a community that needed a physician, and because he could exact vengeance in that role, he presented himself as a leech. Circumstances affect individual development and deployment of faculties, sensibilities, and talents, Hawthorne was saying, but choice also effects change. Only Dimmesdale remains firmly committed to his vocation despite the anguish it increasingly entails and the self-repression it increasingly requires; and only his is a vocation in the traditional sense — his one "thing to do." But all the protagonists are held responsible for their choices. Hawthorne was using his characters to express problems of his own. Only writing fulfilled him; but as a writer, he was an inadequate breadwinner. As a Surveyor, he had abandoned that role; but after three years in office, because of circumstance but also by choice, he was trying to survive by putting "his ability to good purpose" as a writer.[12]

Even before *The Scarlet Letter* was published in March 1850, many of Hawthorne's purposes had been accomplished. The most eminent Boston publisher had enthusiastically praised the manuscript and prophesied success, and his wife had been overwhelmed by its power. He had also taken the revenge he had announced to Longfellow the previous June. He would "surely immolate one or two" of those who ousted him from the custom house, letting "one little drop of venom" make his victim writhe before the grin of the multitude" — not for personal reasons, Hawthorne claimed, but because he had violated "the sanctity of the priesthood to which we both, in our different degrees, belong."[13] Six months later, his aggressiveness barely under control, he responded to Fields's suggestion that *The Scarlet Letter* should be the only story in his new book by saying it would be like loading his gun with only a single bullet.[14] He was on the attack, though for both practical and personal reasons, he feared losing readers who might find his long story too somber.

But his venom was potent and his bullet hit its mark: "The Custom-House" provoked "the greatest uproar that ever happened here since witch-times," he boasted to Bridge[15]; and his daring romance about an admirable seventeenth-century adulteress, her hypocritical pastor, and their rigid community won critical acclaim. He had worked furiously on his "h-ll-fired story," aware of its power though fearing it would never appeal to "the broadest class of sympathies."[16] Yet he soon reached a wider public than ever before: the entire first edition of 2,500 copies sold out in ten days.

Through his plot, his characters, and his imagery, Hawthorne had set forth the assumptions that governed his choice of career, beginning with his conviction that we each have an integral self. Conscious and unconscious experience occurs along a continuum of profundity down to the innermost self, which can never be entirely comprehended or controlled. Character determines action (Hester's he called combative, Pearl's resistant to rules), deploying native gifts or faculties (Chillingworth's intellectual gifts, for example, or Dimmesdale's gift of eloquence, or his own faculty of imagination). A latent faculty can become activated (as with

Chillingworth's malice) and an active faculty might become dormant (as with Hawthorne's imagination during his years in the Custom House), depending on the parts we choose to "perform in the world" (84). As he said through his story, life places us on particular pathways (and within particular "spheres"), but permits us to move onto other tracks and sometimes to retrace our steps. Hawthorne, Hester, Dimmesdale, and Chillingworth all discovered that a freely chosen path may turn into a labyrinth, and that all choices are in part determined by circumstance. But Hawthorne insisted that as individuals and community members, we are responsible for those choices, responsible for expending our gifts while respecting individual integrity. Thus he condemned the malicious Chillingworth and vindicated himself.

Even as a schoolboy, Hawthorne had tried to put his abilities to good use. Before his seventeenth birthday, Hawthorne had asked his mother what she thought of his becoming a professional writer, imagining how proud she would be to see his work praised "as equal to the proudest productions of the scribbling sons of John Bull." Following his own chosen by-paths, he had finally won that distinction. More self-possessed than ever before, he had survived decapitation and was restored to what he wished to become — "a literary man."

Notes

1. Bowdoin College manuscript. This segment appears in *The Letters, 1813–43*, ed. Thomas Woodson et al. (Columbus: Ohio State University Press, 1985), 113. Like Woodson, I preserve manuscript spellings.

2. Bowdoin College manuscript, 25 January 1820. This line appears in Woodson, *Letters*, 118.

3. Bowdoin College manuscript, 29 February 1820. This segment appears in Woodson, *Letters*, 118.

4. *Personal Recollections of Nathaniel Hawthorne* (New York: Harper, 1893), 15, 35–37.

5. Quoted by Lawrance Thompson, *Young Longfellow (1809–1843)* (New York: Macmillan, 1938), 71. Longfellow, like Hawthorne, rejected the ministry, the law, and medicine, and yearned for literary eminence. Aware that most American authors began in one of those professions, he was resigned to study law, but instead accepted an invitation to become Bowdoin's first Professor of Modern Languages. See Samuel Longfellow, *Life of Henry Wadsworth Longfellow*, vol. 1 (Boston: Houghton Mifflin, 1891), 52–66.

6. *General Catalogue of Bowdoin College and the Medical School of Maine: A Biographical Record of Alumni and Officers, 1794–1950* (Brunswick, Maine: Bowdoin College, 1950). Hawthorne is also identified as the Consul to Liverpool, with no mention of any other appointments.

7. For a wider study of the careers of Bowdoin graduates that clarifies Hawthorne's career options and America's dependence on its educated elite, see Wilmot Brookings Mitchell, *A Remarkable Bowdoin Decade, 1820–1830* (Brunswick, Maine: Bowdoin College, 1952), 1–7.

8. *Mosses from an Old Manse*, ed. William Charvat et al. (Columbus: Ohio State University Press, 1974), 323.

9. *The Scarlet Letter*, ed. William Charvat et al. (Columbus: Ohio State University Press, 1962), 3–4, hereafter cited in the text.

10. The phrase occurs in an undated draft of a letter sent to his publisher James T. Fields on 20 January 1850. Woodson, *Letters*, 308.

11. *Personal Recollections*, 33.

12. Woodson, *Letters*, 309f. Bitter and ashamed to accept the purse George Hillard had collected, Hawthorne declared he would shun no drudgery that would "win bread."

13. Woodson, *Letters*, 269f.

14. *Ibid.*, 307.

15. *Ibid.*, 329.

16. *Ibid.*, 311f.

Hawthorne, Upham, and
The Scarlet Letter   Thomas Woodson[*]

Everyone who has read *The Scarlet Letter* knows that Hawthorne wrote this, his first novel, soon after his dismissal from federal employment at the Salem Custom House. He frequently connected his dismissal with this writing, noting that without the free time imposed on him by the government's decision, he could not have started it. But it is not well known that three days before he learned officially of his fate, he wrote to his friend Henry Wadsworth Longfellow about how he planned to respond. Longfellow is the only important writer, American or British (except for Herman Melville), with whom Hawthorne ever established a friendship of any intimacy, and we are lucky to have this letter, since in it Hawthorne reveals his self-image at this crucial time as he would to no person other than his wife. He begins with thanks for Longfellow's sending his new book, the prose tale *Kavanagh*, and then launches into speculation about his own fate:

> It stirs up a little of the devil within me, to find myself hunted by these political bloodhounds. If they succeed in getting me out of office, I will surely immolate one or two of them.

He goes on to describe the victim he would select as not a "common political brawler" but one of those

> who claim a higher position, and ought to know better. I may perhaps select a victim, and let fall one little drop of venom on his heart, that shall make him writhe before the grin of the multitude for a considerable time to come. This I will do, not as an act of individual vengeance, but in your behalf as well as mine, because he will have violated the sanctity of the priesthood to which we both, in our different degrees,

*This essay was written specifically for this volume and is published here for the first time by permission of the author.

belong. I do not claim to be a poet; and yet I cannot but feel that some of the sacredness of that character adheres to me, and ought to be respected in me, unless I step out of its immunities, or make it a plea for violating any of the rules of ordinary life.

In this formulation it is clear that Hawthorne's loyalty is not to the Democratic party but to the priesthood of poets. He intimates here, as in other letters of this time, public and private, that he had "obtained a pitiful little office on no other plea than his pitiful little literature" and "ought not to be left to the mercy of these thick-skulled and no-hearted ruffians" who would remove him. He was, he affirms, "an inoffensive man of letters,"[1] but here to Longfellow he confides his willingness to use the unique, secret and deadly weapons of such men:

> If they will pay no reverence to the imaginative power when it causes herbs of grace and sweet-scented flowers to spring up along their pathway, then they should be taught what it can do in the way of producing nettles, skunk-cabbage, deadly night-shade, wolf's bane, dogwood. If they will not be grateful for its works of beauty and beneficence, then let them dread it as a pervasive and penetrating mischief, that can reach them at their firesides and in their bedchambers, follow them into far countries, and make their very graves refuse to hide them. I have often thought that there must be a good deal of enjoyment in writing personal satire; but, never having felt the slightest ill-will towards any human being, I have hitherto been debarred from this peculiar source of pleasure. I almost hope I shall be turned out, so as to have an opportunity of trying it. I cannot help smiling in anticipation of the astonishment of some of these local magnates here, who suppose themselves quite out of the reach of any retribution on my part.[2]

What should concern us about this letter is the mysterious relation of this passionately diabolic celebration of the "imaginative power" to the conception and composition of *The Scarlet Letter*. Biographers have generally accepted Hawthorne's claim in "The Custom-House" that he was only another "incumbent at the in-coming of a hostile administration" and that in spite of the "irksome" and "disagreeable" qualities of that situation, he "kept his calmness throughout the contest," and that he not only wished publicly to forgive his enemies, but to thank them for helping him to regain what he quaintly called "the realm of quiet" (1:40, 44). In fact, he retained a bitter, vindictive attitude long after *The Scarlet Letter* was published and made him famous — even to the end of his life. The day after he completed the book he wrote to his close friend Horatio Bridge, "I detest this town so much that I hate to go into the streets, or to have the people see me" (16:312–13). Presumably, he had felt so throughout the weeks of intense effort at writing. Two months later, assured that the book was "highly successful," he wrote to Bridge that the Salem people did not deserve his "good-natured" treatment in "The Custom-House," for they had permitted "two separate attacks, or false indictments," against him. In his rage Hawthorne reminded his friend and himself that he was "their most distinguished citizen; for they have no other that was ever heard of beyond the limits of the Congressional district." He followed this sarcasm and hyperbole by identifying the "false witnesses" as men of small fame who had since been elected or reelected to public office: Congressman Daniel P. King, State Senator Charles W. Upham, and Mayor Nathaniel Silsbee, Jr. (16:329–30).

While "The Custom-House" was read in most places as a charming piece of local description, in Salem there was outrage among the Whigs in particular at the author's bald admission that he had discharged two infirm and aged inspectors of that party, the anger being greater for the casual and heartless ridicule of the account. The reviewer for the Salem *Register* seems to have intuited that Hawthorne had displaced his satiric revenge onto these harmless, ridiculous bystanders from the man in the "higher position" he had written to Longfellow he would select. This reviewer makes an interesting connection: "The only thing we can liken it to, in refinement of cruelty, is the fell purpose with which old Roger Chillingworth sets about wreaking his vengeance on Arthur Dimmesdale—but without the visible motive for so much malice, which is palpable in the *avowed* Romance."[3]

The *in*visible motive, the transition that took place in Hawthorne's imagination from the facts of his own humiliating dismissal to the plot and characters of *The Scarlet Letter*, is what I aim to reconstruct. In a curious way the rejected surveyor, the poet deposed from his deserved office, becomes Chillingworth, the elegant artist and diabolical outsider of the story, who almost literally produces the poison of Dimmesdale's self-hatred.[4] Chillingworth, the narrator tells us, converts every wholesome growth into something "deleterious and malignant at his touch." His very corpse will produce from the earth the "hideous luxuriance" of "deadly nightshade, dogwood, henbane, and whatever else of vegetable wickedness the climate could produce" (1:175–76). So the romance repeats the litany of potent flowers of the letter to Longfellow. In another autobiographical hint Hawthorne hangs Dimmesdale's apartment with a tapestry depicting the story of the guilty lovers David and Bathsheba, with Nathan the Prophet, a "woe-denouncing seer," secretly observing them (1:126). Chillingworth is of course this story's Nathan. Hawthorne was acutely sensitive to the literary suggestions of his own biblical first name.[5]

In Longfellow's *Kavanagh*, which Hawthorne read just before his dismissal, and whose power he acknowledged in the letter I have quoted at length, a village minister named Pendexter is described at the moment of his dismissal by his congregation after twenty-five years of service. He composes his farewell sermon far into the night, and is rewarded for his watchfulness by a "silvery shaft of light, like an angelic salutation." The sermon is remarkable, such "as had never been preached, or even heard of before"; it ends by excoriating the townspeople for their "obstinacy and evil propensities."[6] Through Hawthorne's ordeal at the Custom House he must have identified with Pendexter—for he too was being expelled as the town's self-appointed storyteller—but when he wrote *The Scarlet Letter* he transformed the character into Arthur Dimmesdale, who "fancied himself inspired" to compose the Election Sermon, but is only "bedazzled" by a sunbeam when he completes at dawn the writing that will lead to a brilliant public triumph—he will seem to his listeners "an angel" who showers "golden truths upon them" (1:225, 249)—but his fatal confession of personal failing will soon follow. I want to suggest that although as a literary character Dimmesdale far transcends the mean-spirited bickering that led to Hawthorne's dismissal and his efforts to regain his place, the novel's characterization and plot nevertheless show the traces of the writer's impulsive and commanding desire to "immolate" a political victim, "to make him writhe before the grin of the multitude," as he wrote to Longfellow he would.[7]

All the evidence suggests that through Hawthorne's ordeal in the spring and summer of 1849, from his original notice of dismissal through the frantic letter-writing campaign by his Boston Whig friends for his reinstatement, to the final and successful counterattack of the Salem Whigs, his own principal adversary was Charles Wentworth Upham. Upham had been pastor of the First Church of Salem from 1824 to 1845 and at the time of Hawthorne's ouster was a member of the Massachusetts legislature and leader of the Whig party of Essex County. He wrote the "Memorial," the detailed letter to Washington, D.C., that prevented Hawthorne's reinstatement. From the start he was responsible for expressing the false charges about Hawthorne's partisanship, and for other charges that seem on the basis of the documentary record to show clearly that Hawthorne unwisely allowed his Democratic friends in the Custom House to use his office for partisan purposes while he maintained an aloof and condescending indifference to politics.[8] But whatever Hawthorne's failings, it is most clear that Upham took the Democratic claims of his invulnerability as a literary man as a personal challenge, and that he strove mightily and successfully to convince state and national Whig leaders that the dismissal should stand.[9]

The full history of Hawthorne's relationship to Upham has not been told, and it is enlightening. When the minister first came to Salem in 1824 from the Harvard Divinity School, he brought the "large and free and generous" attitudes of Unitarian doctrine to the mainly Calvinist congregation of Salem's First Church with a new and youthful vigor. In a letter Hawthorne wrote while in college he teased his orthodox spinster aunt Mary Manning that she had fallen "deeply in love" with this revolutionary clergyman (15:190). Apparently he approved the more rational and liberal Unitarian ideas, and he became Upham's friend, particularly because the minister was a scholar of considerable energy, with a particular interest in local history and in the traditions of Puritanism in Massachusetts.[10] Upham published his *Lectures on Witchcraft* in 1831, and in 1835 contributed *The Life of Sir Henry Vane* to Sparks's Library of American Biography. Hawthorne was, of course, writing historical tales and sketches on similar subjects throughout the 1830s. In "Alice Doane's Appeal," published in the 1835 *Token*, he refers to a recent "historian" of the Salem "witchcraft delusion" (11:267), certainly Upham,[11] and in "Young Goodman Brown" he makes use of documents and historical judgments apparently provided by Upham.[12] In 1838 Hawthorne wrote to an autograph seeker recommending Upham's life of Vane as a "distinguished" work, and Upham's as indispensable to a collection of American autographs (15:260). At about this time Upham gave Hawthorne an inscribed copy of a memorial pamphlet "intended for private circulation among the friends, benefactors and young companions" of his recently dead eleven-year-old son.[13]

But it was also in 1838, if not earlier, that Upham began to show the attitudes toward the priesthood of poets and "inoffensive men of letters" that led to the controversy with Hawthorne in 1849. When Jones Very, a delicate and sensitive young poet and scholar, suffered fits of insanity at Harvard and was returned to his home in Salem, Upham charged publicly that the mental illness had come from listening to Ralph Waldo Emerson's lectures! He considered the new Transcendentalist ideas to be atheistic nonsense: Elizabeth Peabody, Very's friend and promoter, tried in vain to persuade him to moderate his angry condemnation of both Very and Emerson.[14]

By 1844 Upham had repaired his quarrel with Emerson, who had been with him a member of the Harvard class of 1821, and who had then predicted great accomplishments from him.[15] Emerson invited Upham to dinner in Concord with Hawthorne, during one of Sophia's absences from the Old Manse to visit her family in Boston. Hawthorne did not write to her about the dinner conversation, but later on a visit to Salem he was dismayed to report to her that on returning there Upham "told the most pitiable stories about our poverty and misery; so as almost to make it appear that we were suffering for food. Everybody that speaks to me seems tacitly to take it for granted that we are in a very desperate condition, and that a government office is the only alternative of the almshouse" (16:70–71). When the office did arrive in 1846, after months of impassioned begging of the Polk administration by Hawthorne's friends, he must already have associated Upham's attitude with the frustrations of making a living as a writer. Upham, now a very influential citizen of Salem, was coming to represent the social and political establishment in its most cruel indifference to the claims of literature and of literary men.[16]

Hawthorne's sisters proposed, and it has been accepted by biographers, that the characterization of Judge Pyncheon in *The House of the Seven Gables* is largely based on Upham. At the climax of the narrator's exultant account of the judge's death he condemns him as a "subtle, worldly, selfish, iron-hearted hypocrite" (2:283). The only other character in Hawthorne's fiction after 1849 to receive such a description is Arthur Dimmesdale, who on two occasions is called a "subtle, but remorseful hypocrite" (1:144, 200). The difference is significant: Judge Pyncheon is the gross and unmistakable portrait of Upham, of whom Louisa Hawthorne wrote from Salem in 1850: "The papers are full of his praises, and speak of his public services and private virtues, as if such things were!"[17] The disparity of public and private self-images is also, of course, the keynote of Dimmesdale's situation.

It has been suggested that the Election Sermon is Hawthorne's ironic comment on the contemporary "progressive" faith in a unique American destiny.[18] Dimmesdale's purported "mission to foretell a high and glorious destiny for the newly gathered people of the Lord" (1:249) precedes only by a moment his ignominious confession and death. The Election Sermon is permeated with the New England Whig view of history, the vivid filial attachment to the collective past of the region and the vision of its future greatness through the piety of the descendants of those heroic ancestors. Already a respected Fourth of July orator in Salem, Upham in 1846 was honored to be chosen to address the New England Society of New York. The occasion was the annual celebration of Forefathers's Day, 22 December, the date of the landing at Plymouth Rock. In his address he typically evoked the "prophetic dream" of the Pilgrim fathers, and exhorted the sons of New England to keep the faith.[19] We can presume that Hawthorne heard of or read a summary of this speech. And when in the course of writing *The Scarlet Letter* he came to think of his heroine Hester Prynne in conjunction with the historical figure of Anne Hutchinson, he must have opened Upham's *Life of Sir Henry Vane* to the chapter on the Antinomian Controversy. There he would read that Vane as Anne Hutchinson's adherent had become "one of the earliest advocates of religious liberty," a characteristic "progressive" interpretation. But Upham's view of the woman herself was more unique. He felt that her "deportment" was offensive to the "personal characters of the ministers" and "might easily have been shown to be in the wrong." For "every minister . . . was expected to give evidence in his whole manner of life . . . that he was not of the world . . . but Mrs. Hutchinson's doctrine cut up the whole matter by the roots, destroyed the very foundation upon which reputation had been made to rest, poisoned the fountains of confidence, and in consequence of the personal and satirical design imputed to her, had a direct tendency to make men suspect of hypocrisy all whom they had before been disposed to revere for their piety."[20] The personal note, the ex-minister's concern that he not be seen as the hypocrite he knows he is, must have jumped out at Hawthorne, and may well have richly suggested the psychological pressure both Chillingworth and Hester bring upon Dimmesdale, as well as the idea of witchlike poisoning.

Another suggestion about the story's genesis in Hawthorne's mind comes not from Upham's writing but from Hawthorne's, from the recently rediscovered "Lost Notebook":

> Scene in Mr. Roberts' office — Police Judge Mack proposing to Rev. Mr. Upham to marry a couple who were waiting in his office. The fellow had seduced the girl and gone off — she having a child during his absence. On his return, he was brought before the police, and expressed his willingness to marry the girl; but it was considered dangerous to trust him at large during the time requisite for publication of the banns; — the alternative, therefore, seemed to be, between marriage and committal to jail. Mr. Upham demurred against violating the marriage statute; yet was unwilling not to lend a hand in obtaining justice for the girl and her child — which latter would be, to a certain extent, legitimated. Moreover, he seemed to consider that he should be partly responsible for the illegitimate intercourse which would doubtless continue to be carried on. Much consulting of the revised statutes. Judge Mack declined to marry them himself, because, having once before haltered a couple, the union had turned out so unhappily, that he had resolved never to burthen his conscience with such another act. Mr. Upham seemed to be more hardened in the performance of his awful duty. Finally, the couple were dismissed unmarried — the man giving the girl a note for $400, as security for marrying her. The girl appeared willing to trust to his faith, and thought it would be more decent to wait for publication. Among Mr. Upham's proposals was to give the ceremony the sanctions of religion, if Judge Mack would perform it. I was sorry that the affair did not end in marriage.[21]

This "scene" was written in 1838, at about the time Upham flew into a rage over poor Very, and a few months after Hawthorne presented, in "Endicott and the Red Cross," "a young woman, with no mean share of beauty, whose doom it was to wear the letter A on the breast of her gown, in the eyes of all the world and her own children" (9:435). In the notebook the relations of the actors come to suggest something like the first scaffold scene of *The Scarlet Letter*, but especially the interview in Governor Bellingham's house, "The Elf-Child and the Minister." David Roberts, Hawthorne's lifetime friend and a Salem attorney, becomes the governor; Elisha Mack, judge of the Salem Police Court, becomes the Reverend John Wilson; Charles Upham has the part of Dimmesdale, whose job is to control his parishioners' sexual waywardness, but he is, of course, also the seducer, the disreputable and irresponsible "fellow." Hawthorne, the silent observer, ends the episode with a private expression of tolerant sympathy for the "criminals," observing, like Chillingworth with Dimmesdale, how the case has put Upham to a test of character. What if Mr. Upham could not become "more hardened in the performance of his awful duty," because he was the seducer himself? Such a question would come to Hawthorne upon rereading the notebook after the Custom House episode put Upham's hypocrisy into a new and glaring light.

Some such mental leap must have occurred to enable Hawthorne to connect the young woman wearing the "A" in scarlet cloth on her gown in his story to the young minister. This character now strives to reconcile his involvement with her to his fervent support of a religion, not really so different from Upham's, of "legitimating" behavior and of ministerial "awful duties."

The Scarlet Letter is not only the first American novel to challenge the Whig view of American progress; it is also the first to make a Puritan minister's weakness of character the tragic center of the action. These facts, if recognized at all, are not important to much modern criticism of the novel. But to Hawthorne, and to his Whig critics like Upham, they were paramount. For instance, the *Christian Examiner's* review of *The House of the Seven Gables* included this gratuitous final paragraph: "We may say here, what we should have said at greater length had we noticed *The Scarlet Letter*, that it contains the grossest and foulest falsification of truth in history and personal character, that we have ever encountered, in romance or narrative."[22] If readers were not clear on what that meant, the *Examiner's* reviewer of *The Blithedale Romance* a year later took up the subject again. He found that *The Scarlet Letter*

> involves the gross and slanderous imputation that the colleague pastor of the First Church in Boston, who preached the Election Sermon the year after the death of Governor Winthrop, was a mean and hypocritical adulterer, and went from the pulpit to the pillory to confess to that character in presence of those who had just been hanging reverently upon his lips. How would this outrageous fiction, which is utterly without foundation, deceive a reader who had no exact knowledge of our history! . . . We cannot admit the license of a novelist to go the length of a vile and infamous imputation upon a Boston minister of a spotless character.[23]

These reviewers were Unitarian ministers allied with Upham: the first, Charles Card Smith, later became secretary of the Massachusetts Historical Society; the second, George Edward Ellis, was to be Upham's biographer for that society, and to write of him: "The simple truth, the uncolored facts of history, were good enough for him, in their burdens of romance, heroism, earnestness, and weight of importance. In his judgment, they did not need, and were none the more engaging or impressive when cunningly wrought in with the nightmare and distempered vapors of a morbid imagination."[24] The slighting comparison with Hawthorne is unmistakable, perhaps even recalling the characterization of the dead Judge Pyncheon as a "defunct nightmare" (2:252).

Finally, even Hawthorne's best friend among the Whigs of Boston, the lawyer George Hillard, felt moved eventually to comment about this irregularity in the treatment of Dimmesdale:

> A queer peculiarity about Hawthorne is that while other writers throw the mystic and mysterious into the obscure of history—he brings them boldly into its open light. No historical obscurity rested upon the time or the locality of *The Scarlet Letter*. The history of Boston is open to all who care to read it. The name of every minister who preached any Election Sermon is known to all the readers of such history; but you might as well expect to find Friar Tuck in the history of old England, as to find the Rev. Mr. Dimmesdale in that of New England. In this tendency there is a strange contempt of facts—which only a very singular genius could overcome.[25]

It is in the context of Upham's treachery and his own irreverent ideas about the relation of history to literature that Hawthorne conceived the character of Dimmesdale. Hawthorne finally served the altar of art not by an act of personal vengeance but by transforming Upham into Dimmesdale, thus making the poison of personal and vindictive satire into the ambivalent drama of *The Scarlet Letter*. This masterpiece feeds on the historical and biographical materials of the moment in which it was written, but Hawthorne showed by his development of the story that he well knew the power of literature to not simply reflect experience, but to transform it.

Notes

1. Hawthorne to George Hillard, 5 March 1849, in *The Letters, 1843–1853*, vol. 16 of the Centenary Edition of the *Works of Nathaniel Hawthorne*, ed. William Charvat et al. (Columbus: Ohio State University Press, 1962–), 264. Subsequent references to the Centenary Edition will be in the text by volume and page.

2. Hawthorne to Longfellow, 5 June 1849, in *Letters*, vol. 16 of *Works of Hawthorne*, 269–70.

3. *Salem Register*, 21 March 1850; reprinted in Benjamin Lease, "Salem vs. Hawthorne: An Early Review of *The Scarlet Letter*," *New England Quarterly* 44 (1971):113–17. Lease identifies the reviewer as "almost certainly, John Chapman, editor of the *Register* and an active participant in the Whig conspiracy against Hawthorne."

4. Since Jemshed A. Khan's "Atropine Poisoning in Hawthorne's *The Scarlet Letter*" appeared in the *New England Journal of Medicine*, 9 August 1984, attention has been attracted to conflicting physical and symbolic interpretations of Hawthorne's use of poison. The evidence given here seems to me to support both.

5. See Hawthorne's answer to an autograph seeker who addressed him as Samuel rather than Nathaniel (15:259).

6. Henry W. Longfellow, *Kavanagh: A Tale* (New Haven: College and University Press, 1965), 42–44.

7. Watson Branch has recently argued that Hawthorne first wrote a version of *The Scarlet Letter* as an "allegorical" conflict between a satanic Chillingworth and a sinning Dimmesdale, with Hester keeping no secret from her lover, before he made Chillingworth her

husband, and introduced sexual jealousy as a main theme. Such a first version would be close to the biographical situation I have described. See "From Allegory to Romance: Hawthorne's Transformation of *The Scarlet Letter*," *Modern Philology* 80 (1982):145–60.

8. Winfield S. Nevins, "Nathaniel Hawthorne's Removal from the Salem Custom House," *Essex Institute Historical Collections* 53 (1917):104: "It is undoubtedly true that Nathaniel Hawthorne was not popular while he was connected with the Salem surveyorship. Salem businessmen did not like him overmuch, and he was not especially cordial to the merchants and shipmasters who did business with him. They thought him arrogant, but it was simply a mannerism which Hawthorne himself did not realize, and which he could not well avoid. He was a good deal of a recluse, especially at times, and had few intimates, although those few were truly 'close companions.' " Other historians who share this judgment are Paul Cortissoz, "The Political Life of Nathaniel Hawthorne," Ph.D. dissertation, New York University, 1955; and Stephen Nissenbaum, "The Firing of Nathaniel Hawthorne," *Essex Institute Historical Collections* 114 (1978):57–86. More literary biographers have tended to accept "The Custom-House" at face value.

9. See the portion of the "Memorial" reprinted in 16:294–95, which presents an image of Hawthorne as "the abused instrument" of his political cronies.

10. In his *American Notebooks* in August 1837 Hawthorne recorded the visit from Boston of his relative Eben Hathorne, an amateur antiquarian, who said "there was nobody except Mr. Upham whom he cared about seeing" in Salem (8:74). The context suggests at least that Hawthorne was not surprised at this idea.

11. This identification seems to have been first made by Anne Henry Ehrenpreis, "Elizabeth Gaskell and Nathaniel Hawthorne," *Nathaniel Hawthorne Journal 1973*, 100–1; and, independently, by Charles Swann, " 'Alice Doane's Appeal': or, How to Tell a Story," *Literature and History* 5 (1977):24.

12. Among these are Upham's quotation from Cotton Mather that Martha Carrier had been promised to become Queen of Hell, his statement that among the accused witches was "the wife of the Governor, Sir William Phipps," and his description of the place, the time and the appearance of the devil in meetings at Salem Village. See Charles W. Upham, *Lectures on Witchcraft, Comprising a History of the Delusion in Salem in 1692* (Boston: Carter, Hendee, and Babcock, 1831), 32, 46–47, 81; compare 10:85, 86.

13. See Carroll A. Wilson, *Thirteen Author Collections of the Nineteenth Century*, ed. Jean C. S. Wilson and David A. Randall, vol. 1 (New York: Charles Scribner's Sons, 1950), 154. Hawthorne wrote on the front wrapper that he received the pamphlet from Upham. Edward C. Upham died at the age of eleven.

14. See Edwin Gittleman, *Jones Very: The Effective Years, 1833–1840* (New York: Columbia University Press, 1967), 219; Alfred Rosa, *Salem, Transcendentalism, and Hawthorne* (Rutherford: Fairleigh Dickinson University Press, 1980), 148–53; John Olin Eidson, *Charles Stearns Wheeler: Friend of Emerson* (Athens: University of Georgia Press, 1951), 47; Elizabeth Palmer Peabody, *Letters*, ed. Bruce A. Ronda (Middletown: Wesleyan University Press, 1984), 208–9.

15. Emerson wrote to his aunt Mary Moody Emerson in June 1822: "There are two rising stars in our horizon which we hope shall shed a benign influence from the sources of Religion & Genius—I mean Upham & [George] Bancroft" (*Letters*, ed. Ralph L. Rusk, vol. 1 [New York, Columbia University Press, 1939], 117).

16. There is a strong hint of intellectual separation from Upham in Hawthorne's statement to Evert Duyckinck in October 1845 that he had "often thought" of writing a History of Witchcraft (16:126). By 1851 he flatly told an undistinguished would-be historian: "I think your account of Salem Witchcraft is the most lucid and satisfactory that I have seen" (16:496).

17. Julian Hawthorne, *Nathaniel Hawthorne and His Wife*, vol. 1 (Boston: Houghton Mifflin, 1884), 437.

18. See Michael Davitt Bell, *Hawthorne and the Historical Romance of New England* (Princeton: Princeton University Press, 1971), 141–46, 189–90, 216–20.

19. *The New England Society Orations: Addresses Sermons and Poems Delivered Before the New England Society in the City of New York 1820–1885*, ed. Cephas Brainerd and Eveline Warner Brainerd, vol. 1 (New York: Century, 1901), 419–66. Upham's *Oration Delivered at the Request of the City Authorities of Salem, July 4, 1842*, was published as a pamphlet; see the review by Rev. William Ware in the *Christian Examiner* 33 (September 1842):124–25.

20. Charles Wentworth Upham, *The Life of Sir Henry Vane* (Boston: Hilliard & Gray, 1835), 127, 129–30.

21. *Hawthorne's "Lost Notebook," 1835–1841*, ed. Barbara S. Mouffe (University Park: Pennsylvania State University Press, 1978), 59–60.

22. *Christian Examiner* 50 (May 1851):509.

23. *Christian Examiner* 53 (September 1852):293.

24. "Memoir of Charles Wentworth Upham," *Proceedings of the Massachusetts Historical Society* 15 (December 1876):195. Upham's expanded and revised *Salem Witchcraft*, published in 1867, has recently won considerable praise from historians. It is "the most substantial exploration" of the 1692 Delusion prior to Boyer and Nissenbaum's *Salem Possessed: The Social Origins of Witchcraft* (Cambridge: Harvard University Press, 1974), according to Keith Thomas in the *New York Review of Books*, 8 August 1974, 22. David D. Hall goes further, judging that "*Salem Witchcraft* remains a powerful book, more successful because of its restraint than any successor at interpreting the tumultuous events of 1692"; see *Essex Institute Historical Collections* 114 (1978):47.

25. *Boston Courier*, 5 April 1860, 1: col. 6 (a review of *The Marble Faun*).

Pearl and Hester: A Lacanian Reading

James M. Mellard*

Nathaniel Hawthorne's *The Scarlet Letter* is widely regarded not only as a masterpiece of moral, cultural, and religious, but also of prescient psychoanalytic insight. The classic Freudian psychoanalytic reading of the book is by Frederick C. Crews; there are non-Freudian readings as well, including several recent essays.[1] Because of its history of psychological interpretations, Hawthorne's romance is no longer merely one of any number of works of fiction that have elicited such readings; it has become almost a paradigm for the psychological interpretation of other fiction. Hawthorne's great work may do so in part because literature in general and fiction in particular appear to be our best model of the workings of the psyche. Such is in fact a major premise underlying psychoanalysis, whether initiated by Freud or reinterpreted by Jacques Lacan. Lacan makes the point for Freud and himself: "Indeed, how could we forget that to the end of his days Freud constantly maintained that . . . a training [in

*This essay was written specifically for this volume and is published here for the first time by permission of the author.

literary analysis] was the prime requisite in the formation of analysts, and that he designated the eternal *universitas litterarum* as the ideal place for its institution."[2] But as Lacanian scholar Ellie Ragland-Sullivan points out, "Psychoanalytic meaning is not immanent in a text because it is the medical discourse of a symptom." Rather, "literature operates a magnetic pull on the reader because it is an allegory of the psyche's fundamental structure."[3] Viewed in the light of Lacanian theory, *The Scarlet Letter*, though perhaps not actually more privileged than other texts, does nonetheless provide a particularly insightful model for analysis, not least because its dominant symbol is precisely Lacan's: the letter.

I

In his essay called "The Agency of the Letter in the Unconscious or Reason since Freud," Lacan makes the claim upon which his theory of psychoanalysis is based, namely, that "what the psychoanalytic experience discovers in the unconscious is the whole structure of language."[4] By this statement Lacan does not mean to claim that the unconscious is a language, but only that it is structured like a language and functions in similar ways. These ways are akin to the Freudian concepts of condensation and displacement, whose parallel linguistic concepts are metaphor and metonymy. For Lacan, the letter is the "material support that concrete discourse borrows from language,"[5] the letter itself standing, metonymically (part for whole), for the word or words upon which access to the unconscious depends. As he writes elsewhere, Lacan drew from Freud the understanding that "words . . . are the object through which one seeks for a way to handle the unconscious. Not even the meaning of words, but words in their flesh, in their material aspect." Lacan's summation is very explicit: "words are the only material of the unconscious."[6]

Regarding the unconscious as a linguistic object, Lacan also approaches it through linguistic principles based on the concept of structure, or, more precisely, on the structuralist principles of linguist Ferdinand de Saussure. Saussure revolutionized the study of language by insisting upon the arbitrariness of the relationship between words and things, words and their meanings. His primary formula, taken over by Lacan, is the algorithm showing the relation of a signifier (a word or other sign) to a signified (a thing or meaning). The algorithm looks like a fraction: S/s. It is read, Lacan tells us, as "the signifier over the signified, 'over' corresponding to the bar separating the two stages."[7] For Lacan, the bar represents a primordial barrier separating signifier from signified and demonstrating the "arbitrariness of the sign."[8] Lacan uses Saussure's algorithm largely because it suggests both the topographic structure of the psyche and the functioning of the psychoanalytic subject. The algorithm, that is, provides Lacan a topography of the psyche, because the linguistic (really, the ontological) barrier between signifier and signified can be

equated to the barrier between the conscious and the unconscious topographic "regions" of mentality.

Lacan has formalized his conception of the structure of the psyche in
a series of schemas.[9] The most basic of these, in effect, merely turns the
algorithm into a square whose four corners are connected only through a
mediating pattern that forms a Z. Lacan calls his simplest one Schema L;
it shows the fundamental topographical relation of conscious to unconscious processes, the fields of the two "registers" (the Imaginary and the
Symbolic) to each other, and the pattern of mediation from I (self) to other
(a mirror image) to *moi* (ideal self), and from Other (law, father, ultimate
authority) toward *moi* back toward other and I. Somewhat modified,
Schema L would look like this:

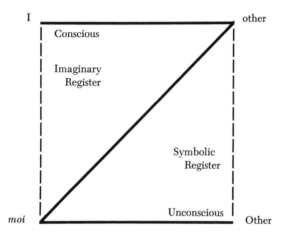

Although this schema in no way represents a "picture" of the psyche, it
does represent the psyche's significant *topoi* of structure and functioning as
Lacan envisions them. In the top triangular half of the square Lacan
locates the field of consciousness and the Imaginary register; these are
associated with the subject — the "I" who speaks or thinks — and with the
projective or introjective relations of the subject consciousness to identificatory others and to the ideal self or ego-ideal reflected in images of the
other or others. This triangle shows that the I and *moi* are mediated
through the figures of the other, and, since they do not connect directly,
that the I can reach no certainty about the *moi*; in this triangulation one
begins to observe the unavoidable slippage, in Lacan's terms, that the
structuralists posit in the relation between the signifier (here located on the
line between the I and the other) and the signified (here located on the line
between the *moi* and the Other). In the square's bottom triangular half,
mirroring the top, Lacan locates the field of the unconscious and the
register of the Symbolic; they are associated with the powerful cultural

and linguistic domain into which the subject consciousness normally is absorbed and by which, beneath the threshold of awareness, it is ruled.

Though Lacan has devised more complex versions of this schema, its two halves suggest clearly the splitting (or, in Freud, the *Spaltung*) of the primal neonate subject that comes with the formation of consciousness and an unconscious in the initiatory passage Lacan calls the mirror stage. The mirror stage (perhaps the most famous of Lacan's concepts) occurs in the life of the infant between about six months and eighteen months. In this developmental period the infant (cf. *infans*, from Latin *infari*: "not speaking") loses its intense symbiotic relation to the mother; the mother then becomes the primal identificatory other for the infant; simultaneously, the infant learns the power of abstract symbolization that informs the language of the culture into which, willy-nilly, in a second birth, it is now borne. Lacan calls this rite of passage the mirror stage because it is best represented in the phenomenon of mirroring or imprinting observed not only in the animal world, but also in the infant's imprinting on the mother. In a secondary imprinting that Lacan calls the mirror stage, the infant actually or symbolically recognizes its own image in a mirror. This mirror recognition initiates the infant's alienation from itself, for, individuated from the mother, it now gets caught up in the quest for identity in an object separate from itself, whether that object is its own specular image in the mirror or its now irremediably separate image of the mother.

To illustrate the separation from the mother and the accession to symbolization (in other words, to the domain of the symbolic represented in language), Lacan refers to a game—the *"Fort! Da!"* memorialized by Freud—in which the child finds a pleasure built on a loss.[10] In this game, the child discovers its ability to symbolize the departure and (hoped for) return of its mother in the willed disappearance and reappearance of a spool tossed away and retrieved by a thread tied to it. The German words, which stand for *there!* and *here!*, suggest the absence of the object (spool = mother) and then its reappearance. But for Lacan the real significance of the game is linguistic and lies in the ability of the contrasting vowel sounds (*oooh* and *aaah*) to suggest meanings in themselves apart from the actual object. The child discovers the principle of symbolization in the substitution of sounds for the object; as the spool had come to stand for mother and the abstract concepts of departure and return, absence and presence, so too will the "words" come to stand for them. On such structural differences, Lacan contends, are constructed not only the human capacity for language (as, say the structuralists, language itself is so constructed), but also the recognition of the mother's otherness and the otherness of the self, now (as a result of the mirror stage) invested in another person or even an object (for example, the child's image in the mirror).

In short, for Lacan the mirror stage and a child's game such as *"Fort! Da!"* represent the infant's identificatory absorption of an alienating self image, but at the same time they represent its recognition of the mediating authority of others and of objects, whether a specular image (as in the face of the mother or the child's reflection in a mirror), or a representative object (a spool, a Teddy Bear, or Linus's blanket), or a symbolic sound (*oooh* and *aaah*, or, more generally, the tones of a voice, or perhaps a nursery tune). Thus, all at once the child assumes an identity perceived in otherness and accedes to the law or principle of difference upon which language is predicated. In one moment, then, the infant is split into pieces, as it were. A previously unperceived unified being is suddenly separated into a subject and an object, and the lost and now desired unity becomes identified with the other, identity forever after to be sought in others or symbolic objects that Lacan calls *"objets petit a."*[11] The subject (thinking, speaking) self, now "split," shall be identified in the (triangular, topographical) register of the Imaginary, while the images of the evanescent objects over time shall be displaced by other images and shall slip into the register of the Symbolic, identified with the unconscious and found in the bottom topographical triangle of Lacan's schema.

Hawthorne's *The Scarlet Letter* is especially helpful in illustrating Lacanian principles because it focuses on four major characters whose experiences exemplify the major psychoanalytic issues as Lacan conceives them. The two I shall consider represent "normal" — as opposed to neurotic or psychotic — subjects. The child, Pearl, graphically illustrates the normal processes of the passage through the mirror stage, and her mother, Hester Prynne, equally well illustrates, in relation to the gaze, the dynamics of the registers of the Imaginary and the Symbolic in the adult subject. Though there is not space here to consider them, one should understand that the other two major characters represent pathological subjects. Arthur Dimmesdale illustrates Lacan's conceptions of neurosis, symptoms, and cure, and Roger Chillingworth illustrates psychosis even as he enfigures the analyst and the Lacanian Other. All four subjects illustrate the slippage of the signified beneath the signifier, as each of them at different moments takes different places in the schematized quadrature Lacan outlines as one inserts different characters in the place of the subject. A result of such analyses is that the four personalities, split into four agonistic parts whose mediations are effected by that most Lacanian agent, the letter *A*, seem finally to represent a total history of the subject.

II

Pearl's story, in Lacanian terms, is the most fundamental of those represented in the subject-consciousness of *The Scarlet Letter*. Pearl's development toward psychological maturity, in fact, is a paradigm case of the passage from infancy (meaning, in Lacan's terms, the *infans* stage of the child without speech) through the steps of the mirror stage. She is at the *infans* stage when she is first seen, on the scaffold of the pillory with

Hester at the novel's beginning; there, her response is directed totally by visual and auditory stimuli. Then she is shown in the early chapters going through the first step of the mirror passage, where she finds images of identification and antagonism. Finally, in the last chapters, she is shown taking the climactic step of the mirror passage; this step takes her through recognition of the loss of the phallic symbol, through acceptance of symbolic castration, and at last through submission to the identity and authority of the father. Each of these moves clearly illustrates Lacanian principles, for Pearl experiences the world in relation to those dominant images of which Lacan so frequently speaks: the mother and images associated with her, objects symbolizing the other, and intimations of the symbolic presence of the Other to be found in the name of the father.

We might say that for Pearl, as in Lacan, the whole of the mirror passage is represented in the child's quest for a father to whose authority, vested in the name of the father, it might cede its life. An adumbration of this quest occurs in the earliest glimpse readers have of the infant Pearl. Even on the scaffold with Hester, the infant breaks her determined passivity in order to respond to the sound of Arthur Dimmesdale's voice. That voice, in retrospect, shall represent the intrusion of biological authority, just as it actually represents the voice of cultural authority speaking from the place of the father. As Lacan would have it, Pearl's response is not to words as such, but to the materiality of the sound itself. In this response she is little different from the crowd in the square. "The young pastor's voice was tremulously sweet, rich, deep, and broken," Hawthorne tells us, as Dimmesdale speaks over Hester's ignominious display on the scaffold. "The feeling that it so evidently manifested, rather than the direct purport of the words, caused it to vibrate within all hearts, and brought the listeners into one accord of sympathy. Even the poor baby, at Hester's bosom, was affected by the same influence: for it directed its hitherto vacant gaze towards Mr. Dimmesdale, and held up its little arms, with a half pleased, half plaintive murmur."[12] Pearl's gesture here fore-shadows in every respect the aim and end of the infant's developmental relation to self, other, and the Otherness represented in the high place from which the minister speaks.

Although the goal (as *telos*, not as conscious aim) of the child's early life, in Lacanian terms, is to enter a proper relation with the authority of the father, the focus of the neonatal and postnatal infant inevitably is on the mother. Because Pearl is isolated not only from her father, but also from the larger community, her early development, besides serving Hawthorne's own aims as a storyteller, is especially representative of Lacanian principles. The first image on which the infant ordinarily fastens is the face of the mother, but, following the law of displacement, this image, by the process of metonymy, normally slides very quickly into other images. One image signifying the symbiosis of infant and mother is usually the maternal breast or bosom. What happens in Pearl's case, however, is that she quickly shifts the identity of the mother not to the image of the breast, but to the object located on Hester's breast — namely, the scarlet letter A. Though such metonymic displacements (according to Lacan) are not particularly unusual, Hawthorne makes an issue of Pearl's attachment to the emblem: "The very first thing which she had noticed, in her life," writes Hawthorne, "was — what? — not the mother's smile, responding to it, as other babies do, by that faint, embryo smile of the little mouth. By no means! But that first object of which Pearl seemed to become aware was — shall we say it? — the scarlet letter on Hester's bosom!" (96). The scarlet letter becomes Pearl's first "little object," the *objet petit a* that stands for the mother herself.

The object, at the outset, indeed stands for the mother. But as the child moves further along the path toward differentiation from the mother (in other words, toward the passage through the phases of the mirror stage), the child develops an ambivalent relation to her and, therefore, to the objects representing her. The ambivalence is illustrated very clearly in Pearl's behavior. Immediately after the revelation that Pearl's first significant object of Imaginary identification is the scarlet letter, Hawthorne also recounts Pearl's aggressive attack on it. "In the afternoon of a certain summer's day, after Pearl grew big enough to run about, she amused herself with gathering handfuls of wild-flowers, and flinging them, one by one, at her mother's bosom; dancing up and down, like a little elf, whenever she hit the scarlet letter" (97). Such ambivalence manifests the mirror process of psychic differentiation, for it acknowledges the child's awareness of the otherness of both self and mother in the other-directed aggressivity (as Lacan points out in an essay on that topic).[13] In Hawthorne's text, the ambivalence is also associated with the child's Oedipal awareness, its indebtedness for creation not to one, but to two (a recognition that Lacan, like Lévi-Strauss,[14] places at the center of human development). Pearl's attention here, Hawthorne shows us, is directed toward the question of paternity in the Real, not in the Symbolic. When Hester tells Pearl that the Heavenly Father had sent the child, Hawthorne writes that it is "with a hesitation that did not escape the acuteness of the child. Whether moved only by her ordinary freakishness, or because an evil spirit prompted her, she put up her small forefinger, and touched the scarlet letter" (98). With her finger on the symbol, Pearl tells her mother that the Heavenly is not her father, at least not her real father. The symbol under her finger suggests to Pearl that her real father lies elsewhere, indeed, lies somewhere behind the scarlet letter. Eventually, she will discover that both her Real and her Symbolic father are signified by the letter.

The other side of the ambivalent behavior that marks the Lacanian register of the Imaginary is Pearl's exaggerated veneration of the "little object." That veneration is evidence that Pearl has begun to identify herself with the letter, to see herself as much as her mother in the letter.

Consequently, in certain moments typical of the ambivalence of the Imaginary identifications with the other or the objects representing the other, her aggressiveness is modulated toward what at root is a self-directed, narcissistic affection. In the chapter called "Hester and Pearl" (15), for example, Pearl injures a tiny bird as she flings pebbles at a flock; with its gray coloring and a brightly contrapuntal breast, the bird by metaphoric similarity, represents Pearl's mother, who dresses in gray, but wears the scarlet letter on her bosom. Thus, Pearl's aggressive rock-throwing is characteristic of the child's puzzling hostility toward Hester. But Hawthorne's text, by the further process of metonymy, clearly identifies the tiny birds with Pearl, too. First, we learn that she gave up her throwing "because it grieved her to have done harm to a little being that was as wild as the sea-breeze, or as wild as Pearl herself." Then, in a passage just further, Hawthorne notes that upon the child's hearing her mother's voice, she flits "along as lightly as one of the little sea-birds" (178). Thus, in the metonymic chain of metaphoric substitutions (bird for mother, and bird for child) the text's attention comes to rest on Pearl's imitation not of the bird, but of the scarlet letter. "As the last touch to her mermaid's garb," which Pearl had made for herself of sea-weed, "Pearl took some eel-grass, and imitated, as best she could, on her own bosom, the decoration with which she was so familiar on her mother's. A letter, — the letter A, — but freshly green, instead of scarlet!" (178). Finally, as if to assure readers of the connections among child, green letter, mother, and scarlet letter, Hawthorne recounts Pearl's pointing once again to the letter on Hester's bosom and inquiring of its signification. Once again, however, the end of this chain of displacements is none other than an invocation not of the maternal, but of the paternal signifier, as Pearl wonders if Hester wears the letter on her breast "for the same reason that the minister keeps his hand over his heart!" (179). Plainly, the letter A stands polysemously not only for mother, *l'autre* or other, but also for *L'Autre* — the law of the Other and the name of the father.

Hester will not answer the child's questions about the letter or the minister's hand over his heart, but it seems clear enough that Pearl's questions will stop only when (through the agency of the letter) she knows her real father and thus can recognize the authority of the Symbolic father and, along with it, the inevitability of the loss of phallic plenitude (associated with the mother and, here, with the scarlet letter) Lacan defines as castration. The scene in which this phase of the Lacanian mirror stage is depicted occurs most visibly in chapter 19, "The Child at the Brook-Side." This phase of the mirror passage is characterized by the overt emergence, in the consciousness of the subject, of the Oedipal triangle. That the Oedipal question has shadowed Pearl's life throughout is evident in her behavior, her almost mystical intimations regarding the identity of her father, and her inquiries regarding the metaphoric linkage between the letter on Hester's bosom and the hand over the minister's heart. The question, moreover, is central to each of the three scaffold scenes. It is broached in the first, nearly finds its answer in the second, where Arthur should have announced his true paternal relation to the child, and is finally answered in the third, which concludes Pearl's passage through the mirror. But the most dramatic evidence of the Oedipal structure (necessary, Lacan contends, if the child is to enter the Symbolic as a normally functioning subject) occurs earlier in the dark forest.

There, the brook that separates Pearl from Hester and Arthur serves as the mediating figure of the mirror. The brook, early on, is identified in the text both as mirror and as child. It is enfigured, for example, as an object that could "mirror its revelations on the smooth surface of a pool," but also as one whose babble is "kind, quiet, soothing, but melancholy, like the voice of a young child that was spending its infancy without playfulness" (186). Later, and most significantly, the brook forms the mirror in which, in remarkable Lacanian terms, Pearl herself is projected. On the one hand, as Lacan argues concerning the other in the mirror, this projection is idealized by the text, if not the subject: "it reflected a perfect image of her little figure, with all the brilliant picturesqueness of her beauty, in its adornment of flowers and wreathed foliage, but more refined and spiritualized than the reality" (208). On the other hand, the subject absorbs something of its own identity back from the mirror's reflection: "This image, so nearly identical with the living Pearl, seemed to communicate somewhat of its own shadowy and intangible quality to the child herself" (208). Most important of all, however, is the onset of alienation (but, Lacan would say, also of subjectivity and symbolization) that occurs in this reflection in the mirror. "In the brook beneath," Hawthorne writes, "stood another child, — another and the same." The alienation is observed by the mother as much as by the child. "Hester felt herself, in some indistinct and tantalizing manner, estranged from Pearl; as if the child, in her lonely ramble through the forest, had strayed out of the sphere in which she and her mother dwelt together, and was now vainly seeking to return to it" (208). Pearl — as Hester perceives — now belongs to a world of differences, of otherness even in the same, of identity found only in others or the other. Such is the fall from grace in Lacanian terms.

That which will prevent Pearl from returning to the sphere of union with the mother is the symbol of the other — that is, the father. "In the Oedipal complex phase," writes Eugen Bär, "the law imposes itself in the symbol of the father on the infant, separating the latter from the mother."[15] The contour of the Oedipal structure is plain in the forest scene, though Hawthorne ascribes Pearl's estrangement not to some inevitable passage of the child, but to an act of the mother. After the child has wandered from her mother's side there in the forest, "another inmate had been admitted within the circle of the mother's feelings, and so modified the aspect of them all, that Pearl, the returning wanderer, could not find her wonted place, and hardly knew where she was" (208). Her shock could not have been greater had she found Hester and Arthur copulating. The potent intruder, Hawthorne notes, points out "that this brook is the boundary between two worlds, and that thou canst never meet thy Pearl again" (208). But, for her part, Pearl does not yet know or acknowledge the minister as her father and certainly not as the signifier of paternity or authority awaiting her beyond the mirror. Instead, she directs her attention to the scarlet letter once more, for, again, the letter is the symbol of the child as a little thing that fulfills the desire of the mother, just as it is a symbol of the unity of being the child has identified with the body of her mother. Clearly, the letter has phallic significance for Pearl. When Hester, in a moment of abandon with Dimmesdale, takes the emblem from her breast and tosses it toward the brook, the gesture must represent her recognition of her own castration. Seeing the object symbolizing herself and her mother now separated from her mother, Pearl feels the panic of the child suddenly become aware of castration—its own and its mother's. Her demand, therefore, is for Hester to put it back on, Pearl (like the child in the *"Fort! Da!"* game) perhaps hoping its return will close the gap and restore the plentitude lost with the symbolic phallus. But now the letter will not and cannot fill or restore anything. Nor will the Oedipal kiss— proffered by Arthur—until it comes (in the third scaffold scene) with the acknowledgement (Pearl's *and* Arthur's) of actual fatherhood. Then, however, what the father's kiss will accomplish is not restoration of plentitude, but the impress of gender and the lesson of the law, the phallus, and castration.

The final step in Pearl's journey through the mirror, since it matches Dimmesdale's assumption of the Law of the Father, too, occurs in chapter 23, "The Revelation of the Scarlet Letter." The scene in the forest is, as it were, merely a reflection of the mirror stage: the appropriate Oedipal structure is present, but the immediate results are not conclusive for Pearl. By her imperious demands she forces Hester to don the letter again, and, by her hostility toward the minister, she drives him away from the mirroring, dividing brook. Thus, in the chapter leading up to the minister's revelation, Pearl displays the same intemperate, essentially lawless behavior that has always marked her. Not yet under the rule of law and the phallic authority, Pearl manifests pure, prepotent desire: "Whenever Pearl saw any thing to excite her ever active and wandering curiosity, she flew thitherward, and, as we might say, seized upon that man or thing as her own property, so far as she desired it; but without yielding the minutest degree of control over her emotions in requital" (244). So long as Pearl maintains such a relation to others and the world, she will remain caught in the illusory web of the Imaginary. For her psychic (and cultural) maturation to occur, she must move into the register of the Symbolic. The Imaginary gives any subject 1) a self and 2) an other, but the Symbolic gives a third, necessary agency: a concept of mediation, one represented in the father. "The child," writes Bär, "has to learn to receive his value, that is, what it desires to be, the phallus, from others, from the father, from the sociocultural system. In this process, he is divided into the roles, designed by others, which he has to assume, and the impulse of his own absolute desires, which he has to repress."[16] What Pearl gains when she is recognized publicly (and recognizes herself) as Dimmesdale's child is the obverse of what she loses: she gains identity under the law of the father, but she loses the absolute narcissistic freedom of her natural ("premirror") condition. She gains the phallus as a signifier in the register of the Symbolic, but she loses illusory plenitude in the register of the Imaginary. She loses her identity as a child, finally, but she gains the capability of mature womanhood. No description of the passage through the mirror stage could be better than Hawthorne's account of Pearl's acceptance of her father: "Pearl kissed his lips. A spell was broken. The great scene of grief, in which the wild infant bore a part, had developed all her sympathies; and as her tears fell upon her father's cheek, they were the pledge that she would grow up amid human joy and sorrow, nor for ever do battle with the world, but be a woman in it" (256).

III

The second of the two "normal" subjects of consciousness in *The Scarlet Letter* is Pearl's mother, Hester Prynne. The dynamics of Hester's first appearance manifest several Lacanian concepts, for the power of the cultural gaze to which she is subjected will activate the dialectic of the Imaginary and the Symbolic that develops in the mirror stage seen operating in Pearl. Forced to emerge from a dark jail into the bright noontime sun, then to stand exposed on the scaffold of the pillory of Boston, Hester is made to wear the letter in which her crime insists, but that is also the scopic object focusing her punishment under the communal gaze. Hester's crime—in Lacanian terms—is an expression of her psychic involvement in the Imaginary, her punishment an expression of the dominating authority of the cultural Symbolic. Thus, Hester's ambivalent relationship to the scarlet letter she wears becomes an expression of the general psychic ambivalence manifested in her apparent submission to communal law at the same time she finds a way to deny it. On the one hand, the letter is placed on her by the town fathers so that the gaze— being seen—is the only form of punishment to which she will be subjected; on the other, she herself has transformed the stigma into such a compelling work of visual art that she and the letter she wears can hardly fail to attract the punitive gaze. The psychic split is evident in Hawthorne's first description of Hester's encounter with the audience for which her emblem is intended: "wisely judging that one token of her shame would but poorly serve to hide another, she took the baby on her arm, and, with a burning blush, and yet a haughty smile, and a glance that would not be ashamed, looked around at her townspeople and neighbours. On the breast of her gown, in fine red cloth, surrounded with an elaborate embroidery and fantastic flourishes of gold thread, appeared the letter A. It was so artistically done, and with so much fertility and gorgeous luxuriance of fancy, that it had all the effect of a last and fitting decoration to the apparel which she wore" (52–53). All Hester's problems as a subject caught between the Imaginary and the Symbolic are represented here, and it is these problems that Hester, accepting normality, will resolve by the narrative's end.

Hester is trapped at this initial moment — and will remain trapped for virtually the entire account — in the Imaginary. The Imaginary, according to Ragland-Sullivan, "is the domain of the *imago* and relationship interaction."[17] Whereas the register of the Symbolic operates "by a differential logic which names, codifies, and legalizes," the Imaginary operates by an "identificatory, fusional logic."[18] The crucial fact of the Imaginary, where Hester is concerned, is that without adequate recourse to the Symbolic she will be incapable of consistent self-reflection or self-awareness. Caught in the identifications of this register, she simply cannot understand or appreciate the drives operating on or within her. In effect, she must deny her unconscious. But, from an analytic perspective, it is clearly possible to make those unconscious drives or forces manifest. They will be evident in the images or figures of speech Hawthorne uses to represent her relation to others within her social environment. The most obvious others, of course, are Pearl, Dimmesdale, and Chillingworth. Hester's psychoanalytic profile can be drawn from her relations to these, for those relations will suggest the images that, within the topography of her psyche, fill the place of the other and provide glimpses of the personal *moi* and the cultural Other.

In the Imaginary, all identificatory others (persons, things, sensory impressions) become objects of desire in the field of the subject consciousness — that is, in the subject who relates through desire to those others. Hester — as desiring subject — relates to those identificatory others primarily through the function of sight — what Lacan calls the scopic field. Thus, for Hester, the Lacanian *objets petit a* (the objects that focus her identifications) will be visual, and, more than that, will be artistically shaped. The principal example of this scopic identification with an object representing desire is Hester's relation to the infant Pearl, on the one hand, and the scarlet letter, on the other. But under the gaze, these *objets petit a* are ambiguous. From the first moment of their appearance, the letter A and the infant are joined as tokens signifying Hester's phallic desire, but also her shame. Thus either may substitute, metaphorically, for her sexual desire and for her relation to the dominant, symbolic Other — the community and its punitive agent, the gaze. As signifiers, child and letter (as in the algorithm S/s) stand for the hidden signified that the community desires to see and that Hester determines to keep hidden: the name of the father. The index of Pearl's ambiguous objectivity to Hester as a subject lies in the contrapuntal aims of the two. It is the name of the father that Hester will not divulge; it is the father's name that Pearl shall demand. Similarly, the letter Hester wears denies the father's name, but at the same time it, metonymically (part for whole, A for Arthur), reveals it. In this respect, since the community and its gaze represent the Symbolic Other, Pearl and the letter as *objets petit a* mediate a relation for Hester to the unconscious. Thus, not only are Pearl and the letter A links to the name of the father; they also forge links between Hester's conscious and unconscious, Imaginary and Symbolic registers.

Pearl's identity, for Hester, is almost immediately absorbed into that *objet a* represented by the letter. Apparently unconsciously, Hester turns the child into a replica of the scarlet emblem, whereas at the outset the child and the letter were linked only by contiguity on Hester's bosom. It is the nature of identifications in the Imaginary that they function by similarity or contrast, sympathy or conflict. Both principles operate in the identificatory relation between Hester and Pearl. The contrast occurs in the drab attire of the mother compared to the bright finery of the child. The relation represented here in the difference is the same as that between the field (gray — or, as Hester's heraldic epitaph has it, sable) on which the letter stands and the letter (scarlet — or the heraldic gules) itself as opposed to the bright finery of Pearl and the field of drab Puritan fashion against which she stands. Of the relation between the exotically embroidered letter A and the communal standard, Hawthorne says that it "was of a splendor in accordance with the taste of the age, but greatly beyond what was allowed by the sumptuary regulations of the colony" (53). Of the contrast between Hester's attire, generally, and Pearl's, Hawthorne writes: "Her own dress was of the coarsest materials and the most sombre hue; with only that one ornament, — the scarlet letter, — which it was her doom to wear. The child's attire, on the other hand, was distinguished by a fanciful, or, we might rather say, a fantastic ingenuity, which served, indeed, to heighten the airy charm that early began to develop itself in the little girl, but which appeared to have also a deeper meaning" (83).

The deeper meaning of Pearl as an identificatory other (or *objet a*) lies in Hester's use of her as a two-sided medium channeling her relation to the community. Pearl (like the scarlet letter) is one side of the artistic expression that Hester permits herself; the other is the "good work," "the exquisite productions of her needle" (83), that she performs for the Puritan community. In effect, Pearl becomes Hester's living letter to the Puritan world. Here the principle of similarity or affinity found in the Imaginary can be seen in operation. Hester mimics through Pearl the luxurious beauty of the scarlet letter so that there can be no doubt of the similarity (and, thus, symbolic identity) of the one object and the other, the child and the letter. Dressed by Hester all in crimson velvet tunics, "of a peculiar cut, abundantly embroidered with fantasies and flourishes of gold thread" (102), Pearl mirrors the emblem on her mother's breast. The child's garb "irresistibly and inevitably reminded the beholder of the token which Hester Prynne was doomed to wear upon her bosom. It was the scarlet letter in another form; the scarlet letter endowed with life" (102). Thus, for Hester, Pearl is both "the object of her affection and the emblem of her guilt and torture. . . [;] only in consequence of that identity had Hester contrived so perfectly to represent the scarlet letter in her appearance" (102).

The identificatory association of Pearl and the letter, while representing the contrasting values of affection and punishment, are no more ambivalently expressive of Hester's relation to the community than her other works — the "finer productions of her handiwork" (82) that provide mother and child a livelihood. As the child and the letter both focus and symbolize the punitive gaze of Hester's social structure, so the works of her hands focus and symbolize the submissive relation Hester exhibits to the representatives of authority there. Whereas Pearl and the gorgeous emblem on Hester's bosom flout that authority, her other artisanal creations unconsciously recognize its power. The market she discovers for her products involves major domains of the social Symbolic: birth, death, and "public ceremonies, such as ordinations, the installation of magistrates, and all that could give majesty to the forms in which a new government manifested itself to the people" (82). Although Hester, as a symbol of repressed female desire, is never permitted "to embroider the white veil which was to cover the pure blushes of a bride," she is given access through her good work to all the most potent symbols of the law, up to and including the law of mortality: "Her needle work was seen on the ruff of the Governor; military men wore it on their scarfs, and the minister on his band; it decked the baby's little cap; it was shut up, to be mildewed and moulder away, in the coffins of the dead" (83). As Hawthorne points out, the exception made of the bridal veil indicates "the ever relentless vigor with which society frowned upon her sin" (83), but at the same time the various permissions give evidence (in the symbolic difference) of the agency and the potency of the law.

One of the impressions given by Hester's involvement in the plot of *The Scarlet Letter* is that her psychic conflict as a subject is ended once she steps out into the sunlight flooding the scaffold of the pillory. But awareness of the ambiguity of her relation to Pearl and the letter, on one side, and to the authority of public law, on the other, suggests that indeed there is a conflict that must be resolved. She must finally accept the law, its symbols of authority, and through them the rule of the register of the Symbolic. The signifiers of that register constantly appear in aspects of what Lacan calls the gaze, along with the metonymical imagery associated with it such as the eye, the look, and the stare. Together, these represent one of the most important motifs in the narrative. The gaze, as

Lacan might say, cuts in many directions, as it links the subject to the object and by that linkage turns each into the other whenever one reverses (by a shift in point of view) the scopic field. For Hester, in her conscious life, the gaze dominates as a double for the community — the public law to and under whose scrutiny (her "doom") she has been sentenced. Thus, for her, the gaze is even more important as an image of the Imaginary other than her lover, Arthur Dimmesdale, who in the ordinary love story might normally be regarded as the dominant figure of her Imaginary register.[19] But the public's gaze and its symbols also connect Hester's unconscious with the more powerful source of law, authority, and the name(s) of the father in the Symbolic register. Says Lacan, "The gaze is presented to us only in the form of a strange contingency, symbolic of what we find on the horizon, as the thrust of our experience, namely, the lack that constitutes castration anxiety."[20] The gaze cuts like a knife, and what it excises — in the passage from the Imaginary to the Symbolic — is the phallus.

Dimmesdale — like most readers — assumes that Hester has escaped psychic torment simply because her sin has been made public. But the power of the gaze and the agency of the eye work their effects into Hester's life just as rigorously as the minister's self-scrutiny into his. The insistence of the law of the Other that must finally be observed comes to Hester in her punishment. The scarlet letter she wears, for example, is held "up to the public gaze" (55), and she feels the "heavy weight of a thousand unrelenting eyes" (57). Hester can escape the gaze, the eyes, of neither friends nor strangers, nor friends who are strangers, as in the case of Roger Chillingworth, who is really *Prynne* and Hester's husband, lost and presumed dead at the tale's start. Roger is "the stranger" in the opening scene who "had bent his eyes on Hester Prynne" (61), and it is he who looks into her eyes with "a gaze that made her heart shrink and shudder" (72). But actual strangers and familiar faces trouble her, too. "Another peculiar torture was felt in the gaze of a new eye" (85), we are told, yet the "accustomed stare," in its "cool . . . familiarity" (86), is no pleasure for Hester either. Even Pearl — the one closest to Hester — is a constant reminder of the virtually absolute power of the gaze of the Other. "Weeks . . . would sometimes elapse," we are told, "during which Pearl's gaze might never once be fixed" on Hester's emblem of sin, "but then . . . it would come . . . like the stroke of sudden death" (96–97). The only gaze not so painful is Arthur Dimmesdale's, but that is because Hester and Arthur share the same pain, as perhaps they wear the same letter on their breasts: "Here," in the forest tableau, "seen only by his eyes, the scarlet letter need not burn into the bosom of the fallen woman" (195–96). For her part, what Hester has endured for the seven long years has been, simply, "the world's ignominious stare" (251). That stare is nothing less than the Other of law, authority, and the place of the father Lacan associates with the register of the Symbolic.

Hester will move from the debilitating entrapment of the Imaginary into the ambivalent freedom of the Symbolic, but there is a suspenseful moment in the tale's plot that suggests she might fail. That moment, in which it appears that Hester will throw away not only the scarlet letter, but also seven years of development toward the Symbolic, occurs in the forest scene when she tries to persuade Arthur to escape Boston and the gaze of the Puritan law under which they both are condemned. The escape she plans would take them away from those eyes that seem always to penetrate her. Above all, the escape she plans would take the both of them away from Roger (Prynne) Chillingworth; "Thy heart," Hester tells Arthur, "must be no longer under his evil eye" (196). While there is never a doubt in the book that Roger is Hawthorne's agent of evil, the devil, the Black Man, he is also more importantly the ambiguous agent of the symbolic Other, the law of the father. Moreover, Roger's gaze is no less symbolic of the communal law under which they suffer and the more universal Oedipal law they had breached together. As Hester's husband under the law, he should have stood in the place of the father in relation to Hester's child. There is, as Hester discovers, no escaping Roger, just as there is no escaping the Black Man, who, we are assured, "hath a way of ordering matters so that the mark [of sin] shall be disclosed in open daylight to the eyes of the world" (242). It is because Roger stands for the Other that Hester (with Pearl and Arthur) cannot give him the slip and depart on a ship bound for the "lawless" sea.

One cannot know for certain that Hester would have experienced the same sense of acceptance of the law of the Other had Roger not foiled her escape and Arthur not chosen to make his public revelation of his own share of her sin. But, psychologically, her acceptance — or capitulation — seems inevitable. Moreover, we do see one instance of that acceptance. Although it comes at a moment when she believes they all will indeed escape Roger together, "after sustaining the gaze of the multitudes through seven miserable years as a necessity," Hawthorne writes, "she now . . . encountered it freely and voluntarily" (227). But should one deny the importance of her acceptance here, one ought to consider her return to Boston later in life and to the very site of her public ignominy after she had for awhile sojourned in the Old World with the mature Pearl. Her return is precisely an acceptance of her life under the burden of the law, the rule of the Symbolic Other. That acceptance, finally, is most vividly symbolized in terms inevitably associated with the most potent reminder of our human submission to the Other. Death is the most emphatic expression of the human limitation represented in the Symbolic by the law of castration. In Hester's tale, the symbol of her final acceptance is the token, the tombstone, erected over her grave, bearing words authored by her and given authority by her submission to the Other: "On a field, sable, the letter A, gules" (264). That escutcheon is the ultimate expression of Hester's existence (*l'être*) under the letter and the law of the Lacanian *Autre*.

IV

As a way of concluding this discussion of Pearl and Hester in *The Scarlet Letter*, one might suggest the advantages that Lacanian analysis offers to literary criticism. There are two major ones. First, regardless of the close historical relation between the development of Freud's concepts and his literary examples, Lacanian analysis is immediately more "literary" than Freudian analysis, for Lacan insists upon the absolute primacy of language and tropes or figures of speech in psychoanalysis. One does not need to search out traumatic events, actual happenings, in order to locate the psychological cruxes of character or personality. By focusing on language, on the mechanisms of language, Lacan brings his analysis immediately into the domain of literary analysis (or vice versa, Lacan might say), and whatever the consequences for psychoanalysis, that congruence between psycho- and literary analysis makes the work of the critic much more familiar and compatible to ordinary habits of work. The second major advantage of Lacanian over Freudian analysis is its ability to deal with the "normal" subject, and I have dealt with Hawthorne's Pearl and Hester in order to illustrate that feature. Although Freudian literary analysis is not limited to the neurotic and the psychotic, it appears that it is so limited in the critical praxis, despite the excellent analysis of the nonpathological that Freud himself performs in his essay on Jensen's *Gradiva*.[21] This limitation in the praxis, if not in the actual theory, can be observed in Frederick Crews's classic Freudian interpretation of *The Scarlet Letter*. Crews seems solely interested — perhaps only capable of interest — in one character: Arthur Dimmesdale. Crews occasionally refers to Hester and Chillingworth as potential subjects in his interpretation, but never to Pearl. Despite his insight that Chillingworth is "the psychoanalyst *manqué*,"[22] virtually all his attention is devoted to Dimmesdale as the pathological subject in whom is manifest the combination of guilt and repression Crews's Freudianism must assess. While Crews's essay will remain a landmark in psychoanalytic interpretation of fiction, it may well remain as a representation of the blindness of Freudian analysis as well.[23] One may hope that the rereading of Freud found in Lacanian analysis, as well as the Lacanian rereading of *The Scarlet Letter* through its two normal subjects, may illustrate the critical openness of the philosophy of psychoanalysis found in Jacques Lacan.

Notes

1. For Frederick C. Crews's Freudian analysis, see *The Sins of the Fathers: Hawthorne's Psychological Themes* (New York: Oxford University Press, 1966). See also Michael Vannoy Adams, "Pathography, Hawthorne, and the History of Psychological Ideas," *ESQ* 29 (1983):113–26; John Dolis, "Hawthorne's Letter," *Notebooks in Cultural Analysis* 1 (1984):103–23 and "Hawthorne's Morphology of Alienation: The Psychosomatic Phenomenon," *American Imago* 41 (Spring 1984):47–62; Thomas L. Hilgers, "The Psychology of

Conflict Resolution in *The Scarlet Letter*: A Non-Freudian Approach," *American Transcendental Quarterly* 43 (Summer 1979):211–24; John Irwin, *American Hieroglyphics: The Symbol of the Egyptian Hieroglyphics in the American Renaissance* (New Haven: Yale University Press, 1980), 239–84; and Michael Ragussis, "Family Discourse and Fiction in *The Scarlet Letter*," *ELH* 49 (Winter 1982):863–88. For criticism considered structuralist, poststructuralist, or postmodernist, see also Millicent Bell, "The Obliquity of Signs in *The Scarlet Letter*," *Massachusetts Review* 23 (Spring 1982):9–26; *New Essays on "The Scarlet Letter*," ed. Michael J. Colacurcio (Cambridge: Cambridge University Press, 1985); *Nathaniel Hawthorne: New Critical Essays*, ed. A. Robert Lee (Totowa, NJ: Barnes and Noble, 1982); John Carlos Rowe, "The Internal Conflict of Romantic Narrative: Hegel's Phenomenology and Hawthorne's *The Scarlet Letter*," *MLN* 95 (1980):1203–31; and Marianna Torgovnick, *Closure in the Novel* (Princeton: Princeton University Press, 1981), 80–100.

2. *Écrits: A Selection*, trans. Alan Sheridan (New York: Norton, 1977), 147.

3. "The Magnetism between Reader and Text: Prolegomena to a Lacanian Poetics," *Poetics* 13 (1984):381.

4. Sheridan, *Écrits: A Selection*, 147.

5. *Ibid.*

6. "Of Structure as an Inmixing of an Otherness Prerequisite to Any Subject Whatever," in *The Language of Criticism and the Sciences of Man: The Structuralist Controversy*, ed. Richard Macksey and Eugenio Donato (Baltimore: Johns Hopkins University Press, 1970), 187.

7. Sheridan, *Écrits: A Selection*, 149.

8. *Ibid.*

9. Lacan's different schemas L, R, and I appear in Sheridan, *Écrits: A Selection*, 193, 197, 212; Jacques-Alain Miller comments on them, 332–35.

10. Freud's discussion of the *"Fort! Da!"* game occurs in *Beyond the Pleasure Principle*, in *The Standard Edition of the Complete Psychological Works of Sigmund Freud*, vol. 18 (New York: Macmillan, 1964–), 4–17. Lacan discusses the consequences of the *"Fort! Da!"* game in the formation of the register of the Symbolic in the essay in *Écrits* called "Function and Field of Speech and Language in Psychoanalysis," 30–113; esp. 103–4.

11. Lacan's use of the term *objet a* (which sometimes appears as *objet petit a*, as *objet* only, or as *a* only) occurs throughout his work. In a "Translator's Note" to Lacan's *Four Fundamental Concepts of Psycho-Analysis* (New York: Norton, 1978), Alan Sheridan explains the *objet petit a* this way: "The '*a*' in question stands for '*autre*' (other), the concept having been developed out of the Freudian 'object' and Lacan's own exploitation of 'otherness.' The *'petit a'* (small 'a') differentiates the object from (while relating it to) the '*Autre*' or '*grand Autre*' (the capitalized 'Other'). Lacan refuses to comment on either term here, however, leaving the reader to develop an appreciation of the concepts in the course of their use. Furthermore, Lacan insists that '*objet petit a*' should remain untranslated, thus acquiring, as it were, the status of an algebraic sign" (282).

12. Nathaniel Hawthorne, *The Scarlet Letter, The Centenary Edition of the Works of Nathaniel Hawthorne*, vol. I (Columbus: Ohio State University Press, 1962), 67. Further references to this text will be included parenthetically and without abbreviation within the text.

13. See "Aggressivity in Psychoanalysis," in Sheridan, *Écrits: A Selection*, 8–29. It is very important to understand that the *imago* found in the mirror images may be both positive and negative for the subject, and thus treated quite ambivalently.

14. Claude Lévi-Strauss exerted an important influence on Lacan, not only because the anthropologist was one of the fathers of Structuralism, but also because he shared Lacan's conviction regarding the centrality of language to human development, whether cultural or psychological. Like Lacan, Lévi-Strauss stressed the dominance of signs and the primacy in

culture of Laws regarding incest; from the apparent universal human concern with incest comes the preponderance of myths (such as those Lévi-Strauss examines in *Mythologiques* I, II, III, *The Elementary Structures of Kinship*, and *The Savage Mind*, for example) regarding birth-from-one or birth-from-two. Lévi-Strauss also shares Lacan's emphasis (taken from Ferdinand de Saussure and Roman Jakobson) on metaphor and metonymy — that is, principles (or tropes) in language of substitution and displacement.

15. Eugen Bär, "Understanding Lacan," in *Psychoanalysis and Contemporary Science*, vol. 3, ed. Leo Goldberger and Victor H. Rosen (New York: International Universities Press, 1974), 513.

16. *Ibid.*, 515.

17. Ragland-Sullivan, *Jacques Lacan and the Philosophy of Psychoanalysis* (Urbana: University of Illinois Press, 1985), 130–31. This book has become the standard exposition and interpretation in English of Lacanian thought.

18. Ragland-Sullivan, *Lacan*, 131.

19. See Ernest Sandeen, "*The Scarlet Letter* as a Love Story," *PMLA* 77 (1962):425–35, for a discussion in which Hester and Arthur would, perforce, remain as objects to each other in Lacan's quadrant (in Schema L) of the "other."

20. Lacan, *Four Fundamental Concepts of Psycho-Analysis*, 72–73.

21. See Sigmund Freud, *The Standard Edition of the Complete Psychological Works of Sigmund Freud*, vol. 9, trans. James Strachey (London: The Hogarth Press, 1959), 7–95.

22. Crews, *Sins of the Fathers*, 141.

23. In fairness to Crews, one must point out that he later rejects Freudian literary analysis: see *Out of My System* (New York: Oxford University Press, 1975).

"Take Shame" and "Be True": Hawthorne and His Characters in *The Scarlet Letter*

Richard D. Rust*

> I know not whether these ancestors of mine bethought themselves to repent, and ask pardon of Heaven for their cruelties; or whether they are now groaning under the heavy consequences of them, in another state of being. At all events, I, the present writer, as their representative, hereby take shame upon myself for their sakes, and pray that any curse incurred by them — as I have heard, and as the dreary and unprosperous condition of the race, for many a long year back, would argue to exist — may be now and henceforth removed.[1]

> Be true! Be true! Be true! Show freely to the world, if not your worst, yet some trait whereby the worst may be inferred! (1:260)

When Hawthorne in "The Custom-House" essay says he takes shame upon himself for ancestral guilt, he "hereby" does so not simply by stating

*This essay was written specifically for this volume and is published here for the first time by permission of the author.

his shame, but through writing a novel in which being put to shame is the greatest form of humiliation and taking shame the crux of personal redemption. An echoing of Hawthorne's response to an imputed curse upon the family line helps establish a link between Hawthorne's purposes in writing *The Scarlet Letter* and the climactic actions of his two main characters. Dimmesdale's only hope for repentance is freely to step forth "to take my shame upon me" (1:254); for Hester, it is to return to Boston "of her own free will" and take up "her long-forsaken shame" (1:263, 262). With taking shame an act of being true, there is a necessary connection between Hawthorne's writing *The Scarlet Letter* as an expiation of guilt and his moral about showing freely to the world (1:260). Just as Dimmesdale finally was being true by taking his shame upon himself, so Hawthorne shows the truth about a stern Puritan society (the world of Hawthorne's prominent ancestors) which forces Hester Prynne to display her shame, but which conceals its own evil.

In *The Scarlet Letter* Hawthorne uses the word "shame" in multiple ways. Most obviously, Hester's "badge of shame" signifies sexual impurity. (Shakespeare uses the word in this sense when Isabella in *Measure for Measure* refuses to "yield / My body up to shame" [2.4.103–4].) "Shame" can mean "the consciousness of something dishonouring, ridiculous, or indecorous in one's own conduct or circumstances (or in those of others whose honour or disgrace one regards as one's own), or of being in a situation which offends one's sense of modesty or decency" (*Oxford English Dictionary*). (Self-righteously feeling this dishonor, the most pitiless of Hester's self-constituted judges cries out: "This woman has brought shame upon us all, and ought to die" [1:51].) Hester is "set up to public shame" (1:61) — in other words, is covered with contempt and disgrace. (In this sense, the word is similar to the usage in Heb. 6:6: "They crucify to themselves the Son of God afresh, and put him to an open shame.") The word also denotes a painful emotion caused by consciousness of guilt or impropriety, as when Hawthorne says regarding the pillory that there is no more flagrant outrage against our common nature than "to forbid the culprit to hide his face for shame" (1:55).

According to editors of the *OED*, "shame" may well come from the pre-Teutonic "skem" — meaning cover, with "covering oneself" being the natural expression of shame. (In this connection one thinks of Prov. 12:26: "[B]ut a prudent man covereth shame.") With his hand — or with both hands — Dimmesdale does involuntarily cover this badge of shame, his scarlet letter. And given Dimmesdale's intense desire to cover up his shame, his distress on learning of the identity of Chillingworth is understandable: "O Hester Prynne, thou little, little knowest all the horror of this thing! And the shame! — the indelicacy! — the horrible ugliness of this exposure of a sick and guilty heart to the very eye that would gloat over it!" (1:194). Yet there is truth in Chillingworth's earlier argument to Dimmesdale regarding guilty men who bury their secrets: "They fear to take up the shame that rightfully belongs to them. . . . Wouldst thou have me to believe, O wise and pious friend, that a false show can be better — can be more for God's glory, or man's welfare — than God's own truth? Trust me, such men deceive themselves!" (1:133).

There is thus a tension in *The Scarlet Letter* between concealing and revealing shame, between being put to shame and taking shame. While the impulse to hide one's shame is very strong, the free-willed taking of shame is a most difficult yet necessary showing forth of truth. A forced exposure of shame, though, is a "horrible ugliness" and an outrage against our common nature. We are made to sympathize with Dimmesdale's argument that it is "wronging the very nature of woman to force her to lay open her heart's secrets in such broad daylight, and in presence of so great a multitude" (1:65). Set against this, however, is the need to reveal and confess, to accept blame or disgrace as merited, to acknowledge that one is at fault.

For what was Hawthorne taking shame? Most obviously in "The Custom-House" introductory, it was for William Hathorne's cruelty toward the Quakers and John Hathorne's toward accused witches. Regarding the former, in "Main-Street" the showman exhibits Ann Coleman whipped through Salem "to fulfill the injunction of Major Hawthorne's warrant. . . . The crimson trail goes wavering along the Main-street; but Heaven grant, that, as the rain of so many years has wept upon it, time after time, and washed it all away, so there may have been a dew of mercy, to cleanse this cruel bloodstain out of the record of the persecutor's life!" (11:70). His son was notorious as a magistrate in the Salem witchcraft delusion. Unlike Samuel Sewall, John Hathorne did not accept "the Guilt contracted upon the opening of the late Commission of Oyer and Terminer at Salem," nor did he plead, as did Sewall, "to take the Blame and shame of it, asking pardon of men" and praying that God would "not Visit the sin of him, or of any other, upon himself or any of his."[2] It remained for his third greatgrandson to take that shame.

Nevertheless, Hawthorne was ambivalent in his feelings toward his ancestors.[3] As Arlin Turner points out, while John Hathorne was "a stern, relentless prosecutor," his descendant the novelist "might see him as a man who could be respected, dignified and business-like."[4] Turner further states that while William Hathorne's cruelty toward the Quakers was a matter of record, Hawthorne also took pride in William's prominent role in asserting a degree of independence from Great Britain. This first ancestor held both a Bible and a sword; "he had all the Puritanic traits, both good and evil" (1:9). On the one hand, Hawthorne seems to admire the "respectability" of "these two earnest and energetic men" (1:10); on the other, he condemns their persecuting spirit. In "Main-Street," written shortly before *The Scarlet Letter*, he acknowledges the "far-seeing worldly sagacity" of the first settlers of Salem, yet recognizes their severity and intolerance and defines the rigidity and hypocrisy of the second-generation Puritans (one of which was John Hathorne). His ambivalent declaration is tinged with both humor and relief: "Let us thank God for having given us such ancestors; and let each successive generation thank him, not less fervently, for being one step further from them in the march of ages" (11:68).[5]

If Hawthorne had in mind both ancestors while writing *The Scarlet Letter*, we might well look for the common element in William Hathorne's persecution of Quakerism and John Hathorne's persecution of "witches." A critical point Hawthorne illustrates so well in "The Gentle Boy" is that condemnatory Puritans were just as guilty as those they accused. The excesses of the Quakers were more than matched by the bigotries and cruelties of the Puritans who self-righteously persecuted them. In like manner, what was considered witchcraft was based on unfounded accusations, harsh local animosities, and so forth. The besetting sin of Hawthorne's Puritan ancestors, then, was their hypocrisy and self-righteousness.

Taking that sin as a dominant theme, Hawthorne in *The Scarlet Letter* exposes hypocrisy with multiple ironies. Chillingworth, the respected physician, is shown to be fiendlike in his relentless persecution of the minister. In Arthur Dimmesdale we have the apparently sanctified but secretly adulterous Puritan.[6] Adultery is especially appropriate to illustrate self-righteousness and hypocrisy because it is a sin that can expose one party (the woman, if she has a child by the affair) but not the other (unless the woman identifies him). Hawthorne emphasizes that while Hester, the outcast, and Arthur Dimmesdale, the beloved clerical leader, seem poles apart, they actually are in the same situation: "The sainted minister in the church! The woman of the scarlet letter in the market-place! What imagination would have been irreverent enough to surmise that the same scorching stigma was on them both?" (1:247). Likewise implicit in Hawthorne's statements in "The Custom-House," taken in context with pieces such as "The Gentle Boy," "The Maypole of Merry-Mount," and "Main-Street," is denial of moral distance between persons like his illustrious ancestors and the people they persecuted.

As with Quakers or "witches," Hester Prynne is set apart — yet others are no better than she. This is clarified forcefully in the narrator's telling how Hester "felt or fancied . . . that the scarlet letter had endowed her with a new sense. She shuddered to believe, yet could not help believing, that it gave her a sympathetic knowledge of the hidden sin in other hearts." She has intimations that "if truth were everywhere to be shown, a scarlet letter would blaze forth on many a bosom besides Hester Prynne's" (1:86). Yet Hester Prynne "struggled to believe that no fellow-mortal was guilty like herself" (1:87).

This is one of Hawthorne's main points in *The Scarlet Letter*: we all are guilty to some extent or another, hardly a condition from which to judge others. Indeed, the greatest hypocrisy is condemning others while concealing the truth about one's own sins. As Hawthorne affirms in "The

New Adam and Eve": A heavenly court "may set judge, jury, and prisoner at its bar all in a row, and perhaps find one no less guilty than another. . . . Feeling its symptoms [of "the plague of sin"] within the breast, men concealed it with fear and shame, and were only the more cruel to those unfortunates whose pestiferous sores were flagrant to the common eye" (10:254).

The very texture of *The Scarlet Letter* has to do with establishing the truth and removing hypocrisy. Hawthorne's story deals with hidden identities, secrets, variations between appearances and reality, public tableaux and private interviews, concealments and discoveries, attempts at confession, and confessions — ending when all concealments are revealed. It is confession of the riddle of his true identity that saves Dimmesdale, it is this that finally satisfies the truth-seeking Pearl, and it is this that eventually thwarts the vengeful Chillingworth.

Each adult character has a special challenge relating to truth-telling and acknowledgment of wrongdoing. (A token of her mother's shame like the scarlet letter with which she is identified, the child Pearl has nothing to conceal and is appropriately called "truth's reflector.") For Hester, the one deviation from truth is keeping the secret of Chillingworth's identity. "In permitting this," she acknowledges to Chillingworth, "I have surely acted a false part by the only man to whom the power was left me to be true!" (1:171). While she rectifies this in the forest meeting with Dimmesdale, it is not until much later that she returns to Boston and takes up "her long-forsaken shame" of her own free will (1:262). As Hester recognized her limitations as part of the "reality" brought about through being true, her scarlet letter "ceased to be a stigma which attracted the world's scorn and bitterness, and became a type of something to be sorrowed over, and looked upon with awe, yet with reverence too" (1:263), suggesting that through her endurance to the end, Hester eventually worked out her repentance. ("Here had been her sin; here, her sorrow; and here was yet to be her penitence" [1:263].)

Our first view of Dimmesdale hints at the source of his downfall and prepares us for exploring his inner conflict. The very fact that the terms "godly," "good," "angel," "heaven-ordained apostle," and "miracle of holiness," are used to apply to him at various times, suggest to the alert reader that like "honest" Iago, this man probably has a feigned degree of sanctity. Hawthorne's progressive revelation of the depths of Dimmesdale's hypocrisy is climaxed in this theme found in the center of the novel: "To the untrue man, the whole universe is false, — it is impalpable, — it shrinks to nothing within his grasp. And he himself, in so far as he shows himself in a false light, becomes a shadow, or, indeed, ceases to exist" (1:145–46). After wandering in a moral "maze," Dimmesdale begins to cast off his hypocrisy, starting with his destruction of the insincerely written Election Sermon. His victory is achieved after the emotional revelation of the secret in the delivered Election Sermon and the physical revelation on the scaffold where he asserts a true position with man, nature, God, and his own better self. With support from Hester, he makes "haste to take my shame upon me" and confess the truth in "triumphant ignominy" (1:254, 257).

The complete hypocrisy of Chillingworth is seen in his professing to be a healer, but being in actuality a destroyer. He was "exemplary, as regarded at least the outward forms of a religious life" (1:120), but secretly he was giving himself over to the devil. By his prying out secrets of the human heart, his malicious lack of pity and intellectualized hatred, his betraying the confidences of his close companion, and his full knowledge of his deceit with absolutely no accompanying desire to "show the worst," he justifies Dimmesdale's assertion that Chillingworth's "revenge has been blacker than my sin" (1:195).

Most of the symbols associated with these characters relate as well to the theme of sincerity / hypocrisy: The *scarlet letter*, we are told, serves to discipline Hester to the truth. When Dimmesdale has completed writing the Election Sermon, the *sunlight* falling across his eyes symbolizes his new vision, his willingness to be true, and his new dawning or reawakening. *Mirrors* (such as Dimmesdale's mirror or the stream in the forest) momentarily reflect the truth. *Clothes* show the disparity between appearance and reality. (For example, Dimmesdale's tearing off the ministerial band symbolizes his tearing away all impeding hypocrisy.) And for Dimmesdale the *scaffold* becomes the best vantage point from which redemptively he can show his worst to the world.

The enigmatic heraldic device with which Hawthorne relieves his "somber" tale indicates the final working out of the vestiges of hypocrisy so that the truth is no longer concealed but rather etched on a lasting monument, a place where the "curious investigator may still discern" its legend. In a similar manner, Hawthorne's *The Scarlet Letter* is another lasting monument, showing forth the truth about the world of his ancestors.

Besides feeling shame through being the representative of his sinful, albeit illustrious, Hathorne ancestors, Hawthorne might well also have had in mind the public shaming of two incestuous sisters in his Manning line.[7] More certainly, Hawthorne was distressed by his humiliating dismissal from the Custom House and may have seen an identification between the vindictive spirit of ancient Puritans and that of modern Whigs who had a tendency "to grow cruel, merely because they possessed the power of inflicting harm" (1:41). Other factors contributing to what Hawthorne in "The Custom-House" essay speaks of as the "seething turmoil" in which *The Scarlet Letter* was written may well have been the recent death of his mother and his ambivalence regarding his vocation as a writer. In respect to the latter, Hawthorne imagines that his ancestors scorn him for being an idler, a mere "writer of story-books" (1:10).

Perhaps all these fuse in Hawthorne's shame-taking through writing

The Scarlet Letter. Hawthorne's characters finally come to terms with truth, human frailty, and sinfulness, symbolized by the scarlet letter; so does he. The novel becomes an oblique confession of family and regional sins and hypocrisies. Further, it may well involve Hawthorne's transmutation of grief in the portrayal of Hester Prynne's strength of character as well as her tragedies. Exposing the diabolizing effects of revenge as found in a Roger Chillingworth, Hawthorne abstains from revenge against those who wrongfully cast him out of the Custom House. Finally, his writing *The Scarlet Letter* is designed to remove the curse on the Hawthorne line.

As recounted in the introductory essay, that curse is considered to have caused the race to decline — to be unprosperous, but especially to be unnoteworthy. Rather than accept being *put* to shame — by a birthplace infamous for persecution of "witches," by unrepentant ancestors, by ignominious dismissal from office — Hawthorne forthrightly *takes* shame in showing forth the truth about all of these. Despite habitual self-deprecation and earlier self-reproach "for having been so long a writer of idle stories" (10:4), he must have anticipated making the Hawthorne name noteworthy again through recognition of the work at hand which his genius surely told him would ultimately bring fame. Hawthorne's "hereby tak[ing] shame" through his writing is like Arthur Dimmesdale's Election Sermon — a convincing outpouring of the heart; it is like Hester's transmutation of the meaning of her "A" into something positive and good.[8]

Hawthorne's writing *The Scarlet Letter* is expiation through art, the memorable telling "the truth of the human heart" but telling it "slant." In Melville's phrase, truth is revealed to this master "of the great Art of Telling the Truth" only "covertly, and by snatches."[9] Hawthorne's injunction to "be true" is not a Sunday-school lesson, as at least one critic avers,[10] but rather a powerful statement of Hawthorne's artistic and moral position. He has dreamed "strange things," and through the "authenticity of the outline" has made them look like truth (1:36, 33).

Thus in writing *The Scarlet Letter*, Hawthorne reveals the good and bad traits of the Puritans (long a topic which preoccupied him) exemplified by his ancestors; works through — and rids himself of — his feelings of revenge toward those who expelled him from office; asserts his self-identity and his identity as a creative artist of value; and reaffirms thematically the value of sincerity and the necessary exposure of hypocrisy. This "taking shame" before the world is a redemptive purification which frees him from joyless ties to Salem and the past. He can now be "in the realm of quiet" (1:44).

Notes

1. Nathaniel Hawthorne, *The Scarlet Letter*, vol. I of *The Centenary Edition of the Works of Nathaniel Hawthorne*, ed. William Charvat et al. (Columbus: Ohio State University Press, 1962–), 9–10. Subsequent references to Hawthorne's works will be to the Centenary Edition and will appear in parentheses in the text.

2. Quoted by Ola Elizabeth Winslow in *Samuel Sewall of Boston* (New York: Macmillan Co., 1964), 136.

3. In *Hawthorne's Ambivalence Toward Puritanism* (Logan: Utah State University Press, 1965), 4, J. Golden Taylor says, "[W]hile he could recognize and affirm certain real virtues of the early Puritans such as their intense moral earnestness and an incipient democratic spirit opposed to the royal aristocratic English autocracy, he could not condone their stultifying theological pessimism, their deadening spiritual pride, nor their repressive harshness."

4. Arlin Turner, *Nathaniel Hawthorne: A Biography* (New York: Oxford University Press, 1980), 64.

5. Hawthorne's mixed condemnation and extenuation of the Puritans is echoed by his sister Elizabeth, who is quoted by Julian Hawthorne in *Nathaniel Hawthorne and His Wife: A Biography*, vol. 1 (Boston: James R. Osgood and Co., 1885), 6, as saying: "The witch's curse is not our only inheritance from our ancestors; we have also an unblemished name, and the best brains in the world." She further asserted to Una, "Your father told me that he believed there were not many of the English nobility better born than ourselves."

6. In his hypocrisy, Dimmesdale reminds one of the second-generation Puritans described in "Main-street." Michael Davitt Bell, *Hawthorne and the Historical Romance of New England* (Princeton: Princeton University Press, 1971), 138, may well be right in arguing that Arthur Dimmesdale is a second-generation New England Puritan—at least by age and subordinate position if not by actual birth.

7. See Gloria C. Erlich, *Family Themes and Hawthorne's Fiction: The Tenacious Web* (New Brunswick: Rutgers University Press, 1984). Philip Young, *Hawthorne's Secret: An Un-Told Tale* (Boston: David R. Godine, 1984), elaborates upon incest in the Manning family and posits Hawthorne's own guilt for that sin.

8. Several critics have found connections between Hawthorne and Hester and between Hawthorne and Dimmesdale. James R. Mellow, *Nathaniel Hawthorne in His Times* (Boston: Houghton Mifflin Co., 1980), 306, comments on an analogy between Hawthorne's own art and Hester's craft—a luxury "in a land that afforded comparatively little scope for its exercise." Too, he sees an analogy between Hester's ordeal on the scaffold and Hawthorne's recent public humiliation (307). Michael Davitt Bell, 140, finds a connection between Hawthorne and Dimmesdale in their both being distinguished for intellectual ability.

9. *The Portable Melville*, ed. Jay Leyda (New York: Viking Press, 1952), 408.

10. Frederick C. Crews, *The Sins of the Fathers: Hawthorne's Psychological Themes* (New York: Oxford University Press, 1966), 153.

INDEX